PS 3571 .P4 Z55 2013
Batchelor, Bob.
John Updike

WITHDRAWN

DATE DUE

PRINTED IN U.S.A.

Parkland College Library
2400 West Bradley Avenue
Champaign, IL 61821

JOHN UPDIKE

JOHN UPDIKE

A CRITICAL BIOGRAPHY

BOB BATCHELOR

Parkland College Library
2400 West Bradley Avenue
Champaign, IL 61821

PRAEGER

AN IMPRINT OF ABC-CLIO, LLC
Santa Barbara, California • Denver, Colorado • Oxford, England

Copyright 2013 by Bob Batchelor

All rights reserved. No part of this publication may be reproduced, stored in a retrieval system, or transmitted, in any form or by any means, electronic, mechanical, photocopying, recording, or otherwise, except for the inclusion of brief quotations in a review, without prior permission in writing from the publisher.

Library of Congress Cataloging-in-Publication Data

Batchelor, Bob.
  John Updike : a critical biography / Bob Batchelor.
    pages cm
  Includes bibliographical references and index.
  ISBN 978-0-313-38403-5 (hardcopy : acid-free paper) —
ISBN 978-0-313-38404-2 (ebook) 1. Updike, John. 2. Authors, American—20th century—Biography. I. Title.
  PS3571.P4Z55 2013
  813'.54—dc23
  [B]   2012047894

ISBN: 978-0-313-38403-5
EISBN: 978-0-313-38404-2

17 16 15 14 13   1 2 3 4 5

This book is also available on the World Wide Web as an eBook.
Visit www.abc-clio.com for details.

Praeger
An Imprint of ABC-CLIO, LLC

ABC-CLIO, LLC
130 Cremona Drive, P.O. Box 1911
Santa Barbara, California 93116-1911

This book is printed on acid-free paper ∞

Manufactured in the United States of America

To Phillip Sipiora, a wonderful scholar, mentor, and friend whose encouragement and thoughtful guidance made this book possible; and to Kathy and Kassie, who occupy every part of my heart and soul.

Contents

Preface	ix
Acknowledgments	xv
1 John Updike: An American Writer and His Times	1
2 Why Write: Updike as Craftsman, Professional, and Celebrity	19
3 Pennsylvania as American Ideal	37
4 Updike's Poetry	53
5 *Rabbit, Run* and American Culture	63
6 Chronicler of American Sexuality	79
7 Rabbit Lives and Dies	93
8 Between Writer and Reader: Updike as Critic	107
9 Master Storyteller	119
10 Radical Departures: Updike as Experimental Novelist	133
11 Updike's Audience	147
12 Racing toward the Apocalypse: Updike's New America	173
13 Evolution of a Literary Lion	197
Conclusion	211
Bibliography	219
Index	225

Preface

> For my susceptible heroes, no acquaintance, where the opposite sex is concerned, can be too glancing to strike a spark and kindle some excitement. Love makes the world go around, and its licks can be feathery but keenly felt.
> —John Updike, Foreword to the Easton Press limited edition of *Licks of Love*

First, a confession: outside of a lifelong commitment to basketball and an undying love for my wife and daughter, nothing is as close to my heart as John Updike. To me, he is the über American of the American century. In a life that spanned from the Great Depression of the 1930s to the Great Recession of the late 2000s, Updike chronicled the bounds of this era by probing what it means to be a citizen of this confounding world. What I find so unparalleled about his work is that he shined this light, in his words, on "the inner lives of hidden men," with the deft skills of a social historian and the lyrical grace of a fabled poet.

Second, an assertion: though Updike excelled at fiction exploring the American middle-class, suburban life, and the coupling and decoupling of those who populate these enclaves, critics and readers who suppose that this is where Updike's work begins and ends are woefully ill-informed. Examining Updike's opus, however, one cannot ignore the enduring value of the Rabbit tetralogy, the four books featuring the life and death of Harry "Rabbit" Angstrom. Yet, my belief is that one should not use the critical popularity and canonization of the Rabbit books as a reason for condemning his later work.

As a matter of fact, I think that one could make the argument that Updike was an experimental writer who also wrote realistic fiction, a notion that boldly challenges the common misperception about his work. This avowal is based on the range and scope of Updike's fiction, particularly when one considers the magical realism, invented lands, and mythology contained throughout his catalog. This belief is why I have spent so much of my time in this book focusing on Updike's novel *Terrorist* and other work that came out more recently. What I believe I have demonstrated (perhaps even as bold as declaring *revealed*) is that there is something in that specific novel and his other material that perfectly captures our post-9/11 society within the broader landscape of the contemporary United States.

Third, a goal: the primary objective of this book is to provide readers new to Updike additional context and nuance about his work. An additional aspiration is to add to the scholarly conversation about Updike and his role in contemporary America. As a result, this book draws heavily on my background as a cultural historian to place the author within his times. Given Updike's inclusion of the world around him in so much of his fiction, placing him within the grander scale of his times is necessary and beneficial.

The subtitle of this book is "A Critical Biography," which is appropriate because I am not focusing just on Updike's body of work or his life in the minute-by-minute style of many biographers. Instead, focus is directed at ideas regarding the authorial life and its consequences on the writer's evolving worldview. The reader should also note that the biography aspect of this book is not an attempt to produce a scandalous or salacious portrait of Updike. By biography, I specifically mean the aspects of his life that influenced, guided, or pushed his work in one direction or another.

The subtitle demonstrates that Updike's life and his work were so intricately intertwined that one could not be comprehended without the other. Like all people—perhaps even to a greater extent given his fame and celebrity—Updike lived within, symbolized, and embodied his times. Based on the vast number of scholars, critics, and writers who have written about Updike over these many decades, it is appropriate to emphasize the life-and-times perspective that takes the reader beyond his work and into the broader culture.

Next, I provide what I believe is a fuller portrait of Updike as an author, celebrity, artist, and product in our consumer society. I feel that this perspective is an important piece missing from many detailed studies of writer's lives and work. Thankfully, with Updike, there is a long lifetime of nonfiction essays, interviews, Q&As, television programs, documentaries, speeches, and other sources that provide the researcher with multiple methods for exploring this intersection.

***

After working in the corporate world for many years, speaking with friends who write popular books, and studying the nation's celebrity obsession, I realized that few writers find success without a team of agents, editors, designers, and marketers. Even Updike, who eschewed much of the glitz surrounding prominent novelists, could not thrive without taking part in the modern consumer society. In essence, writers are cultural products themselves, whether they like it or not. In some cases, an author becomes more famous than her or his work, just as some actors and artists become famous for being famous.

This is not the case with Updike, but certainly his status as one of the United States' literary lions played a significant role in his ongoing success, as did the ways he presented and manipulated his public persona. An anonymous commentator who knew Updike well both personally and professionally told me that the author actively contemplated this public/private dichotomy. He knew that public perception had to be managed. Later, we will deal with this idea in greater detail, including drawing heavily from Updike's writing on the subject.

I spent a great deal of time considering Updike's role as an artist, professional writer, and celebrity to draw out a sense of his life across the twentieth century and into the twenty-first. Employing Updike as a case study and placing him within his cultural epoch propels the present analysis to include his changing role as a literary writer who also had major best sellers, as well as his standing as a celebrity and public intellectual. In addition, I contrast Updike's dance with celebrity in relation to other literary greats of the age, most notably Norman Mailer, who stood at the opposite end of the spectrum regarding these issues, thus providing a striking contrast. Rather than dismiss these cultural influences, I explore how they intersect with audiences, readers, and critics.

For example, it seems naïve to believe that Updike's status as a public figure did not influence how critics and scholars assessed his work. A rising star among journalistic critics could gain a reputation for toughness by attacking an author of Updike's prominence. Likewise, anyone looking into the publishing industry aspect of being an author (appearances, marketing, etc.) would be remiss in not assessing Updike's role in building up and/or creating his specific public persona. Piecing together his commentary regarding fame and celebrity creates a model of the public Updike that scholars can examine, particularly as his archives open at Harvard and allow for a view into areas historically shut off from scholars.

***

My primary task centers on a close examination of Updike's writing and providing contextual analysis of how his nonwriterly life influenced his work. It is significant in looking at a stylist like Updike to tackle the themes he addressed, as well as the literary techniques he employed to disseminate those ideas. From this textual analysis, Updike's vision of the United States and the world emerges, not only in the late stages of the twentieth century, but also in the new millennium.

Writers provide us with guideposts that help one understand what it is to navigate life's uncertainties. Without literature, our quest for self-fulfillment or the American Dream not only is lonelier, but also contains greater ambiguity. Like no other writer before him or since, Updike provides signs for interpreting the world we inhabit—both for its beauty and unpredictable nature and for its ambiguity and chaos.

Reading Updike, we never lose sight of the sense of wonder that seems to be the essence of being. Some might link this vibe to the author's often quavering, but heartfelt spirituality. Others might read in his hopeful characters the willingness to persevere, despite the knowledge that age and entropy are just around the corner. Rabbit Angstrom, Updike's most infamous character, longed for meaning and perfection, which in his limited understanding simply called *it*. The quest for *it*, whether derived from love, sex, religion, or the perfect drive on the perfect day at a perfectly manicured golf course, propels Updike's characters to persevere and prevail. This theme ricochets around the author's books, short stories, and nonfiction, providing a central tenet that may help in explaining his enduring significance. The search for the powerful, yet mysterious, *it* serves as a kind of natural yearning for people in contemporary America.

This book advocates for a far-reaching examination of Updike, encompassing large chucks of his catalog, and in contrast to some critics and scholars who zero in on one novel or group of novels and use those works to pigeonhole Updike and his significance. For those who undertake this challenge with me, I believe that you will find in Updike an author who is vast, deep, and broad in his examination of the United States and the larger world. Furthermore, while Updike himself deferred to his colleagues who did more overtly political or topical writing, often drawing on or even participating in the day's major events, what one finds in his work is a forceful critique of the United States and the world.

The list of societal ills and events Updike directly addressed in his work encompasses the full scope of life in modern society. In Updike's books, the reader encounters racism, xenophobia, sexism, religion, adultery, warfare, the ravages of the capitalist consumer economy, crooked authority figures, the pitfalls of popular culture, and much more. Taken as a whole, one must conclude that Updike—while certainly earning scholar William H. Pritchard's title as "America's Man of Letters"—must be also be considered either the World's or Humanity's Man of Letters. This is Updike full steam ahead.

One of the stunning stylistic features of the Rabbit novels is the way Updike ended each book. So, mimicking his style, we can sum up Updike a simple Updikean phrase: Yes: matters. Matters.

Acknowledgments

Mentally, emotionally, and physically, writing a book whips one's soul, yet this work is never done completely in isolation. Dozens of people are involved in the effort, some close at hand, while others are half a world away. As a result, this intense solo effort is anything but lonely, despite the agitation the writing life sparks.

Just as it does for so many of its members, The John Updike Society (JUS) nourishes my soul. I would like to thank Jim Plath, founding president, and the other scholars who created the organization in early 2009. Its appearance has rewarded Updike aficionados from all over the world with two wonderful conferences and a journal devoted to Updike's work. While there are too many members to list in full, I would like to mention Don Greiner, Jim Schiff, Quentin Miller, Bernie Rodgers, Jack De Bellis, and Bob Luscher for serving as academic role models and friends. Thanks to fellow member Charles Michaud, who provided a sales document that illuminated Updike's sales from the beginning of his career through *In the Beauty of the Lilies*. In addition, JUS purchased Updike's boyhood home in Reading, Pennsylvania, which now stands as The John Updike Childhood Home museum. I would like to thank Jim Plath and the JUS Board of Directors for appointing me the director of Marketing & Media for the museum, which might cause Updike to chuckle if he were alive, but is important in carrying on his legacy.

The Praeger team is fantastic. My friend and former senior editor Dan Harmon and I formulated the book. I appreciate Dan's help and am grateful for his encouragement. A big thank-you, as well, to James Sherman, ABC-CLIO editorial manager, who later took over the project and provided wonderful counsel and support. In addition, I would like to thank the outside reviewers, as well as Praeger's design, marketing, and production teams for their efforts.

Others offered encouragement along the way, including Chris Burtch, Larry Leslie, Kelli Burns, Thomas Heinrich, Josef Benson, Gary Hoppenstand, Larry Mazzeno, and Tom and Kristine Brown. I have been lucky to have many fantastic mentors, whom I would like to thank, including Lawrence S. Kaplan, James A. Kehl, Sydney Snyder, Richard Immerman, Peter Magnani, and Anne Beirne. A special thanks to Ray B. Browne (1922–2009). He served as a wonderful spiritual guide and continues to be an inspiration for me. Thanks to my popular culture scholarly teammates: Brendan Riley, Brian Cogan, and Leigh Edwards! This book is dedicated to Phillip Sipiora, a wonderful scholar, mentor, and friend. He has been an inspiration and role model. Thank you.

In addition, I would like to thank my colleagues at Kent State University for their support and encouragement. The friendship of colleagues Bill Sledzik, Tim Smith, Jeff Fruit, George Cheney, and Gene Sasso is priceless.

On a personal note, nothing I do is possible without the support of my family. Thanks to my parents, Jon and Linda Bowen, for everything they do to make our lives infinitely better. My wife Kathy and daughter Kassie bring immeasurable joy into my life on a moment-by-moment basis. Kassie possibly knows more about Updike than any elementary school student should, but her good cheer and constant smile make my heart swell. I cherish every instant we all spend together—thank you.

CHAPTER 1

John Updike: An American Writer and His Times

> Well I don't know all this about theology, but I'll tell you, I *do* feel, I guess, that somewhere behind all this . . . there's something that wants me to find it.
>
> —Harry "Rabbit" Angstrom to Reverend Eccles, *Rabbit, Run*

John Updike's death in early 2009 launched shock waves around the world. Few people knew the famed writer battled cancer, so the announcement took most by surprise. As one would imagine, the reaction set off an outpouring of accolades that probably would have embarrassed Updike, had he been around to witness such an outburst. Surely, the keenest observer could not have guessed at the author's condition given the prodigious output near the end of his life, including *Due Considerations* (2007), a 736-page collection of essays and criticism, and *The Widows of Eastwick* (2008), his last published novel.

Shortly after Updike passed away, three new works appeared: *Endpoint and Other Poems* (2009) and two short story collections—*The Maples Stories* (2009) and *My Father's Tears and Other Stories* (2009). Both received widespread acclaim. Subsequent years witnessed the publication of additional posthumous books, including another collection of nonfiction and essays, *Higher Gossip* (2011), and *Hub Fans Bid Kid Adieu* (2011), a publication of his famous short story by the Modern Library.

Given the phenomenal success Updike enjoyed in one of the most stellar literary careers in history, it would seem that his reputation is set in stone, as if a place on literature's Mount Rushmore is predestined. Yet, surveying the state of reading and the place of literary fiction in contemporary American culture, the long-term viability of any writer may be up for grabs. While some surveys reveal that people might actually be reading as much as in the past due to the "hot" status of various e-readers, such as the iPad and Kindle, most observers agree that "literature" and "classics" are read less frequently. As a matter of fact, based on the changes in K-12 education, there is less reliance on canonical novels in today's curriculum. As a result, a writer like Updike, who at one time might have had his novels serve as required reading, is now less likely to achieve this kind of widespread adoption.

A century from now, the question may not be if Updike is still read (a preoccupation of scholars interested in the writer and his work); rather one might wonder if any literature is read or if people even read anything that does not fit on a single computer screen. If this statement seems to touch one as alarming, then so be it. The situation is dire now and looks even more ominous for the future. Many more scenarios exist that reveal a society without books than ones that focus on some kind of rebirth in the United States' literary tastes or reading habits.

For this study, however, maybe the concern regarding whether Updike will be read in the future is immaterial. This book argues that Updike and what he wrote is important, both as a chronicle of the modern United States (arguably at the zenith of its global power and prestige) and in defining his standing as a towering figure in literary history. In the first instance, Updike prevails as the nation's foremost literary social historian, offering readers penetrating analyses of what it meant to be an American from the mid-twentieth century through the first decade of the new millennium.

Following closely on the heels of Updike's role as a national storyteller is his position within literary history. From this perspective, the author is one of the last of his kind—a writer's writer, tackling the written word in all its forms. Examining Updike's vast output as a literary critic, for example, reveals a single facet of his specific writing career that would have accounted for the entire oeuvre of another writer. The same idea could be expressed when viewing his work as a poet or essayist, and perhaps even art historian. As this study demonstrates, Updike is a craftsman, artist, and professional. These three strands were woven into his DNA as a writer and influenced what he wrote.

From a cultural perspective, Updike's significance takes on a multifaceted perspective. On one hand, the public tackles Updike as artist—an individual whose writing draws countless readers, whether in magazine form or in novels. Additionally, in modern society, celebrity often follows closely on the back of achievement. Taken together, these influences coalesce to create the modern writer, which at different times encompasses varying hues of talent, luck, fame, buzz, marketing, entertainment, and other characteristics that on paper are far afield from the act of writing.

Perhaps what I am advocating here is that for many writers in today's literary world, the examination of their work must stretch into cultural avenues outside (and perhaps simply beyond) writing. Writers are part of a larger culture industry that at various times usurps their individual work. For the handful of writers at the upper echelon—a mix of talent, sales, and fame—the demands are exhaustive. The vicious cycle is that more success necessitates greater exposure, which actually draws one away from the thing that made the writer famous. Updike, a person raised in the long shadow of the Great Depression, viewed himself as a freelance hired hand and felt that he always needed to make additional money. From the perspective of being a writer, spending countless hours alone at a desk researching, reading, and composing, capitalizing on one's celebrity might be a drag, but remained vital. On more than one occasion, Updike spoke about the fear of the money running out and equated that with the words running out.

The celebrity world these literary stars enter, according to scholar Joe Moran, "is not simply an adjunct of mainstream celebrity, but an elaborate system of representations in its own right, produced and circulated across a wide variety of media" (4). Certainly, Updike epitomizes these writerly and nonwriterly components. As one of the world's most celebrated and famous writers, it is as if he serves as the sun in a galaxy of necessary (but often competing) forces of editors, publishers, journalists, critics, academics, and readers. Simply stated, Updike means something beyond the written word, a kind of symbol of an age and day that might have disappeared with his death.

Also interesting in this Updikean cosmos is that the parameters of his celebrity underwent a striking change over the course of his career. What it meant to be a celebrity in the late 1950s and early 1960s would be barely recognizable in the first two decades of the twenty-first century. Yet, simultaneously, Updike also seems to embody the role of a celebrity author, though he often criticized his own place in that pantheon. Others thrust the celebrity mantle on him, from the editors of *Time* magazine, who twice placed him on the cover, to those awarding literary prizes. Yet, Updike also fueled the fire by simply doing the things writers must do remain successful—promote, be interviewed, submit to feature stories in newspapers and magazines, appear on television and radio, use the Web as a sales tool, and generally market themselves as products as much as their work.

Due to this consideration, an attempt to completely extract Updike the writer from Updike the celebrity/symbol is virtually impossible. One representation feeds off the other and, in Updike's case, transforms his career into one shared by perhaps less than a dozen others in American literary history.

Who Is John Updike?

Some readers might pick up this *critical biography* with little previous knowledge of Updike (1932–2009), so let us briefly put the great writer in context. Updike, first and foremost, experienced family life in the hills and valleys of Southeastern Pennsylvania in a way that might seem foreign to contemporary readers. His early experiences living with both his maternal grandparents and his parents clued him into adult challenges, like financial difficulties wrought by the Great Depression and other mature stresses at a young age. While he often recalled his grandparents fondly in his later work, it is clear that he often held conflicted ideas about his parents—portraying his mother Linda at times as not only overbearing and overprotective, but yet also demonstrating her intense love and devotion to him at others. His father Wesley seemed alternatively stuck in small-town Pennsylvania and to exult in that life where his position as a high school teacher and coach put him at the center of attention. The older Updike is drawn by his son as a George Bailey-like figure, but more at ease than the fictional character with his truncated dreams.

Updike himself seemed destined for greatness, particularly with Linda's wind at his back. A sensitive, yet fun-loving boy, he overcame a stutter to become a town favorite, quick with a joke and certain charm among females. He knew how to talk with adults, who found him engaging and charismatic. Like a true American success story, Updike left Reading and its rural communities behind and headed to Harvard. He would never again live in his home state, yet these experiences later served as his primary material for much of his career, particularly in the early years when Updike established himself as one of the nation's rising literary stars. Pennsylvania, for example, functioned as the central location of his most famous works (*Rabbit, Run*; *Rabbit Redux*; *Rabbit Is Rich*; and *Rabbit at Rest*), the chronicle of everyman Harry "Rabbit" Angstrom published in roughly 10-year intervals between 1960 and 1990.

Updike excelled at Harvard, graduating in the class of 1954. After a nearly yearlong stint on a fellowship at Oxford, Updike returned to the United States and landed a job at the revered magazine *The New Yorker*.

Updike wrote for the magazine, but more importantly, its editors continued to buy his fiction and poems. His first short story ("Friends from Philadelphia") appeared in the magazine on October 30, 1954. His success as a budding writer enabled him to quit the magazine in 1957 and move his growing family to the village of Ipswich, Massachusetts, where he churned out numerous works across genres, from the poetry collection *The Carpentered Hen and Other Tame Creatures* (1958) to his first novel *The Poorhouse Fair* (1959) and short story collection *The Same Door* (1959).

Based on the success of these early works and his short fiction in *The New Yorker*, Updike gained recognition as one of America's literary stars. Based on his prodigious output—usually publishing a book of fiction or prose each year, while also writing for a variety of magazines—Updike's fame grew exponentially, which placed him among the highest pantheon of American writers of the era, such as Saul Bellow, Norman Mailer, Philip Roth, and Toni Morrison. Updike embodied the idea that talent, dedication, and hard work could enable one to achieve the American Dream.

A blow-by-blow examination of Updike's career, however, is outside the scope of this book. Instead, readers interested in learning about Updike's biography in greater detail should turn to the many biographical sketches contained in the books and articles listed in the Bibliography. Also one might just begin reading Updike's short stories and novels, which contain a great deal of biographical information and provide a rich examination of his life. He also authored many nonfiction pieces drawn from his life and wrote a memoir, *Self-Consciousness* (1989). Certainly, as more archival materials become open to researchers, there will be additional books written that analyze Updike's life and work from an outsider's perspective.

Updike and American Literary History

One primary goal of this book is to convince the reader that Updike matters, neither by trumpeting his armful of national and international literary awards nor by the millions of published words that poured from him over his long career nor even the best-seller status many of his novels achieved. Instead, I plan to show the reader through deep textual analysis of his work that his extraordinary career not only was one of a kind, but also will probably never be replicated.

This work wrangles with a supposition that will occupy Updike scholars and critics into the foreseeable future: Is there an Updike beyond the Rabbit novels, and is there an Updike beyond suburban nostalgia? Of course, there is not an easy way to quantify this answer or come up with a scientific equation to solve the riddle. What becomes clear, though, is that Updike certainly did not limit himself in this way. Looking across his career at both his fiction and nonfiction, one finds a writer, critic, and essayist with deep interest in writers and works far afield from the suburban United States. I argue that this self-education expanded Updike's worldview, compelling him to write novels that tackled global issues and concerns.

Not surprisingly, Updike understood that much of his long-term legacy would be in the hands of academic scholars who would write about him and assign his work in college classes. Consequently, he lectured at different universities across the nation, always exuding grace and humility. For him, pressing academic flesh was not entirely a calculated move in hopes that scholarly critics would be kind, since Updike's public appearances also helped pay the bills, but one wonders how much of this was out-and-out agenda-setting or reputation-building.

For an example of how Updike managed his celebrity with an eye on his long-term reputation, one should see the thin volume titled *Updike in Cincinnati* (2007), essentially a written documentary of two days the author spent visiting the midwestern city. Throughout the text, edited by James Schiff, Updike playfully interacts with the leading scholars of his oeuvre. At the conclusion of a panel examining his short fiction, Updike says, "I'm appreciative of both these learned men (William H. Pritchard and Donald Greiner) taking the trouble to meditate upon my work, which is composed really in a rather desperate fashion, which doesn't anticipate academic study . . . [producing] a few objects that will somehow be worth examining and treasuring, as in archaeology, later" (61). More telling, however, than Updike's famous graciousness, is his willingness to work with academic critics in producing these kinds of texts. He not only helped edit his recorded remarks with Schiff, but also provided introductory remarks for the book, certainly increasing the odds that it would find a publisher and broader sales.

Using Updike as a kind of case study, this work also examines issues central to being a writer in the twentieth and twenty-first centuries. From basic questions about why one would choose to be a professional writer to the roles marketing and popular culture play in selling books, Updike's career is pivotal. He is one of a handful of writers who personified the post-World War II era and, arguably, made the smoothest transition from a print world to one dominated by television, then the Internet. What separates Updike from his peers, though, is his longevity and commitment to writing, which enabled him to publish at least one book annually for more than 50 years, whether a novel, collection of short stories, poetry, or essays.

Throughout this transition, in a period marked by major popular culture upheavals, Updike played a key role in creating the Updike image for his audience, editorial and publishing staffs that he worked with, and the ever-changing mass media. Through Updike, one gains a better understanding of the intersection of writing, the writing life, celebrity, and fame in his era.

Here, Updike's long career and standing as an exceptional writer of both fiction and nonfiction make him unique—perhaps the nation's most lauded freelance writer. There are few aspects of Updike's life that he did not explore himself or find interrogated at the hands of journalists and scholars. By contrast, one can only imagine what a joy it would be to have this level of introspection and retrospection from Hemingway, Fitzgerald, and other American writers who self-destructed in their own time. Unlike the literary forefathers that he emulated at the early stages of his career, Updike remained viable and productive, thereby providing more material about his life, perhaps, than any writer who ever lived. Few writers in American history have talked more about themselves in interviews, appearances, and mass media channels than Updike.

Across his long career, he understood the link between celebrity and his professional life. Rather than gruffly rejecting fame or feeling inhibited by its calling, Updike sheepishly embraced the idea that he needed to project another image of himself publicly, which would benefit him as a writer. In this cat-and-mouse game, the big-name famous author uses his status to get more work, thereby filling the word-lust of the professional freelancer.

Interestingly, Updike purposely chose not to take the route into academe that so many of his contemporaries did in the post-World War II era. Given his early fame, this path may have been the easiest way of capitalizing on his youthful celebrity. As a result, Updike resides outside (or at best, tangential to) scholar Mark McGurl's "Program Era," the post-World War II time frame in which he asserts "the rise of the creative writing program stands as the most important event in postwar American literary history" (*Program Era* ix).

Ironically, Updike foreshadowed McGurl in a 1974 lecture delivered in Australia, explaining that, "The writer as hero . . . has been replaced in America by the writer as educationist." Further, echoing many of the doomsday scenarios that still exist in the publishing industry, he notes:

> Most writers teach, a great many teach writing; writing is furiously taught in the colleges even as the death knell of the book and the written word is monotonously tolled; any writer, it is assumed, can give a lecture, and the purer products of his academic mind, the

"writings" themselves, are sifted and, if found of sufficient quality, installed in their place on the assembly belt of study, as objects of educational contemplation. (*Picked-Up Pieces* 47)

Still, Updike obviously benefits in a society in which serious writers and serious readers are created—they purchase his books for entertainment and study, attend his lectures, and pay his appearance fees—but he did not teach writing or major in writing while in college. As such, Updike is yet again a case study as one of a dying breed of American authors that we may never encounter again.

If drawn from nothing more than his work as a magazine freelancer and novelist, one must conclude that Updike stood keenly aware of audience. On one hand, he prepped his entire adolescence to become a writer for *The New Yorker*. He understood the magazine's idealized reader as if that person stood next to him.

Despite widespread praise and standing as an undisputed literary giant, many scholars have largely ignored Updike's work outside the Rabbit tetralogy. This claim might seem odd if one simply reviews a bibliographical list of books and articles about Updike. On the surface, there seems no dearth of scholarship, yet under closer scrutiny, one sees little of Updike in the broader swath of academic literature. Much of the important work on Updike has been produced by a couple handfuls of dedicated scholars who understand the writer's widespread consequence. The lack of examination seems particularly odd given the texts and themes addressed in Updike's more recent work, particularly in the new millennium, when his vision of the United States and the world in the twenty-first century emerges. As a result, specific emphasis is placed on Updike's post-9/11 fiction in this book. These works have been hailed for providing deep insight into the American condition since that tragic day.

By reassessing Updike's evolution as a writer, both in subject matter and in literary devices, one realizes how his work reflects an increasing preoccupation with global issues, from American imperialism to terrorism. This study broadens the general conceptualization critics and scholars hold regarding Updike's work by exploring the themes and literary techniques he used to portray the broader world.

Updike and Critics

While Updike achieved great heights in terms of both critical acclaim and sales, he did not escape reproach from literary critics or other writers.

The initial wave of negative commentators early in his career disapproved of his writing style or voice, which they believed emphasized facility with language over substance. This criticism—embodied by the harsh attacks on his work by editors and writers for *Commentary* magazine—stuck the longest. The style over substance declaration haunted Updike's work for the rest of his career and continues to serve as a means of discussing his place in literary history.

Scholar Donald J. Greiner exposes the level of pointed critical attack in *John Updike's Novels*. He demonstrates how Norman Podhoretz, an editor of *Commentary*, lumped censure of Updike with the seemingly elitist status of *The New Yorker* (4–5). Greiner systematically reveals how Podhoretz slammed Updike from the start of his career and kept up the condemnation. The critic called Updike's first novel, *The Poorhouse Fair*, for example, an "utter failure" and asserts that Updike has a long way to go before becoming even a "good novelist" (quoted in Greiner, *Novels* 5). This venom resulted despite the broader general acclaim the novel received.

Other critics later turned on Updike over his stance related to the Vietnam War and protests and activists at home. The idea took hold that Updike blindly supported President Lyndon B. Johnson and an idyllic vision of the United States' righteousness, which created a rift. According to scholar William H. Pritchard, commentators pained the author as a Vietnam supporter, explaining, "Updike, in the eyes of more than one critic, has said Yes . . . to American phenomena on which they would prefer to cast a much colder eye" (6). Critics viewed Updike as overtly conservative and an apologist for Vietnam, which in turn gave them an opening for attack. The crack in his armor over Vietnam opened an avenue for others to jump on the style argument.

Other commentators took a different tact. Their scorn centered on Updike's decision to focus much of his work on the lives of everyday people and situations. We will explore this notion in much greater depth in this book, examining Updike's standing as an experimental novelist who addressed a broad range of topics away from the American middle (see Chapter 10).

Given the length of Updike's career, another line of criticism developed, a kind of two-headed monster that reared up to clamp onto his professional reputation with violent, poisonous fangs. One avenue of this censure contended that his current work, regardless of quality, could not live up to the standards he set earlier. The second, related critique—aired by the likes of David Foster Wallace and Tom Wolfe—basically threw their hands up in disgust, tossed Updike into the outdated bin, and publicly wished for him to go away, retire, or simply be put out to pasture.

Unlike many novelists and writers who claim to either not read their critics or ignore reviews, it is clear that Updike engaged with his detractors. He could be biting, yet playful about it, such as mimicking *Commentary* in the series of novels and short stories featuring the fictional Jewish writer Henry Bech. Updike made the notoriously blocked writer the magazine's poster child. Updike could also show a bit of anger (though often tinged with humor), like during a 2006 interview held in front of a large audience at the New York Public Library when he discussed his relationship with famed *New York Times* book reviewer Michiko Kakutani:

> I've been on tour with this book [*Terrorist*] for two weeks and met a lot of people and faced some audiences and mostly what I get is flattery and "how nice" and "loved your stuff" and all this so you begin to think that you're a pretty swell fellow . . . and Michiko Kakutani brings you back to reality in a very healthy way. ("Bartos Forum")

Obviously, the remark about Kakutani drew widespread laughter because the kind of people who would attend such a lecture in NYC would enjoy the launch of a good literary skirmish. Updike often took such self-deprecating positions when addressing things his critics said or claimed, yet all of us who also engage in these positions recognize how much real anger is masked in the exchange.

Updike as Symbolic Interactionist

Sociology offers literary critics and scholars an approach both for interrogating texts and for gaining certain insight into the author's mind-set. In the case of the former, the use of theories drawn from the work of sociologists enables new potential avenues into the text. In the latter, these methods of inquiry help literary critics contextualize the work of individual authors and movements by providing a glimpse into provocative questions, such as why write, the choice of subject matter, and what influences contribute to the creation of a text.

For a writer as prolific as Updike and as forthcoming about mixing his own life into his fictional worlds, symbolic interactionism provides an additional tool for comprehending him as a writer and part of the broader culture. My hope is that by applying certain sociological theories, this book uncovers innovative ways of looking at Updike across his many guises: freelance writer, novelist, celebrity, public intellectual, critic, and perhaps even simply a man as he ages in the youth-obsessed United States.

Much of the sociologist's goal—studying organized life and society—intersects with the novelist's task in creating stories and narratives, in other words, imaginary worlds for characters and actions to take place. The link between sociology and literary studies seems clear when examining a book as its own isolated or linked world invented by the writer. The formation of creative worlds necessitates that the author act as sociologist in some respects, though the critic occupies a more direct role when studying the creation.

The potential pitfall of using sociological theory in assessing what a writer is thinking as she creates a work is that one cannot truly know or fully understand the person's creative process, even in cases in which the author has spoken at length about these topics. Updike not only explains the consequences of attempting such interpretation, but also hints at the beauty in doing so, saying: "The writer of fiction, a professional liar, is paradoxically obsessed with what is true—what feels true, what rings true in the fabrication being assembled on his desk" (*Due* 72). The challenge is how much to believe when writers talk about themselves, since their inclination for storytelling can become part of their public persona or attempts to shield one's inner self from public consumption. An ostensibly willing subject, such as Updike, then, confounds and enlightens simultaneously.

Symbolic interactionism is the sociological approach that serves as an underlying tool for this discussion, a theory that grew out of the late nineteenth- and early twentieth-century studies by William James, John Dewey, Charles Horton Cooley, and George H. Mead. Scholar Norman K. Denzin explains that interactionist thinkers are "cultural romantics . . . [who] believe in the contingency of self and society and conceive of social reality from the vantage point of change and transformations" (2). Growing out of pragmatism, symbolic interactionism explores how people create meaning for themselves and the broader society through a system of constant negotiation, modification, and reassemblage as they interact with others. In other words, people actively create meanings of themselves and society through dealings with others.

Reality is an ever-changing terrain based on new criteria and experiences bombarding the individual through additional interaction. According to C. Wright Mills:

> The first rule for understanding the human condition is that men live in a second-hand world. The consciousness of men does not

determine their existence; nor does their existence determine their consciousness. Between the human consciousness and material existence stand communications and designs, patterns and values which influence decisively such consciousness as they have. (375)

For scholar Joel M. Charon, then, interactionism provides a worldview of a human being as an active individual, thinking, creating, self-directing, and defining oneself internally and through exchanges with other people and episodes that take place. Thus, it is essential for symbolic interactionism to include perspective on both how people interrelate and how an individual creates her own reality (26–34).

From a literary studies perspective, the value of thinking about an author and her work using a symbolic interactionism perspective is that communication (language and words) lies at the heart of the theory. According to scholar David R. Maines, "Through communication processes, people transform themselves and their environments and then respond to those transformations" (235). Charon is even more explicit, calling the symbol, "the central concept of the whole perspective." Furthermore, he explains, "Words are symbols. They stand for something; they are meaningful; they are intentionally used by actors to represent physical objects, feelings, ideas, values. They are used for communication. Their meaning is social" (43, 50). As a result, everything that one sees or thinks is derived from words, which give things meaning. Our only meaning—what we think, observe, and imagine—is garnered from the words we use to describe those impulses. "We act," says Charon, "not toward a world out there but rather toward a world defined by others through symbolic communications. . . . Meaning does not come from objects. Instead, we label objects with symbols" (61). Consequently, for the writer who employs words as the outward manifestation of a particular worldview, symbols provide meaning both for him and for potential readers who interact with the text.

Another area where literature and symbolic interactionism intersect is in the narrative function of what Denzin labels "the epiphanic moment" (83). He indicates that four such epiphanies mark a person's life: major upheaval, the cumulative consequence, illuminative instances, and the relived moment. Each deals with a real-life crisis situation, yet are not these also common story angles for novelists?

In *Terrorist,* for example, Updike repeatedly employs the major upheaval theme: Ahmad's father deserting the family, the terrorist attacks on the United States, and Ahmad's conversion to Islam. Although Updike uses each epiphanic moment in the novel, major upheaval is a deliberate attempt to connect to the reader's sense of those events, whether derived from one's own experience or through cultural examples that become part of one's internal viewpoint.

Although not directly using the language of sociologists and social psychologists when discussing his notions about writing, Updike sounds similar to a symbolic interactionist in an interview with scholar James Schiff, explaining: "Any piece of writing is an act of communication, an act of social interaction even, so that you are leading the reader on. You are teasing the reader, you are trying to startle the reader, you are trying to give the reader a reason to keep reading" (*Updike in Cincinnati* 87). Updike's narratives appeal to readers because they relate to his sense of the personal and storytelling.

Infusing these features into his writing draws the reader into the narrative and may account for the particular Updikean style, widely heralded by critics as a central facet of Updike's storytelling ability. For Denzin, it is symbolic interaction applied to cultural studies that enables content/words to "connect and join people" (85). In this instance, Updike's facility with language must combine with content to create a specific experience for readers that is uniquely his. At the same time, the author is commodifying his personal stories (regardless of how autobiographical or biographical) to sell books, magazines, and other publications. Furthermore, in Updike's case, he is also offering himself as part of the package in his stance as *celebrity author*.

Writers hold a unique space in the symbolic interaction swirl of identity, selfhood, and one's place within the larger society. They are literally and figuratively selling pieces of themselves as producers of words and public figures. As such, the plea one often hears from writers regarding their lives as their material and the need to hold that close makes sense. The potentially finite number of good stories that translates into great work really may be a well that can dry up. However, the cultural machine feeds on content, forcing authors to become commodities, in fact, rewarding them for becoming *names*, as well as celebrities.

Also at the heart of the symbolic interactionist perspective pertinent to writers is the idea of self and identity. Professional writers, by the very definition of what they do, assume many guises as they go about their jobs. Interestingly, despite similarities between symbolic interactionism and postmodernism, it is on the subject of self that the two split. According to scholar Peter L. Callero:

> Symbolic interactionism's commitment to Enlightenment values that privilege reason and rationality are in stark contrast to the

postmodern break with the discourse of science. In fact, much of the postmodern scholarship assumes a radical anti-essentialism that rejects on philosophical grounds the very concept of self. (116)

However, the value of symbolic interactionism, Callero explains, is that the "self is first and foremost a reflexive process of social interaction . . . [with] the uniquely human capacity to become an object to one's self, to be both subject and object" (119). As such, he claims, this reflexivity is derived from social experience. For authors, the notion of self as outlined earlier enables agency and creative action through the use of signs—similar to a stoplight that permits and holds back thought, deed, and movement. They employ strategies to construct self-meanings, including storytelling, faith, ideology, and cultural narratives, among others.

Callero explains that people deploy these strategies "in social settings to accomplish social objectives . . . particularly evident in the case of storytelling and cultural narratives" (123). In other words, a writer uses these devices to create an internal identity, but at the same time is constructing worlds via the written language that exist outside the self. In contrast to nonwriters, an author's creation of internal identity may well find its way into work meant for public consumption. Although a lifelong stutterer, for example, Updike discusses his ability to overcome the malady in front on large audiences, which reveals him using storytelling as a means of masking the true person underneath. He says: "Reading words I have written, giving my own impromptu answers, I have no fear of any basic misapprehension; the audience has voluntarily assembled to view and audit a persona within which I am comfortable" (*Self-Consciousness* 84). Thus, there is a real possibility for public display of the private self that occurs with writers, which may not be as apparent as in other professions.

The writer unfolds her identity for public consumption. In Updike's long career, this unwrapping of himself took place via interviews across multiple platforms, appearances, in published analysis and criticism, and through scholarly interpretations. The constant interaction that occurs, as a matter of fact, is a necessary part of a writer's development. Callero says:

> The self that is socially constructed may congeal around a relatively stable set of cultural meanings, but these meanings can never be permanent or unchanging. Similarly, the self that is socially constructed may appear centered, unified, and singular, but this

symbolic structure will be as multidimensional and diverse as the social relationships that surround it. (127)

However, this seems to be a necessary aspect of being a professional writer, particularly if one aspires to Updike's level of fame.

As mentioned previously, writers may possess a privileged place in the symbolic interaction worldview, since they not only apply interaction to their own lives, but also add on the additional weight of doing the same thing for readers. From this perspective, writers become guides and acquire influence. As Charon deduces: "The symbolic interactionists . . . conceptualize society in the dynamic sense: as individuals in interaction with one another, defining and altering the direction of one another's acts" (158). Thus, the writer, who provides symbols that society uses to assess, define, and alter itself, plays an important role in the process. In this sense, the writer as a facet of mass media disseminates symbols that others use as stimuli for creating their own worldviews.

An application of symbolic interactionist thought may also help account for the critic's and reading public's widely held perception of Updike as little more than a highly skilled, lyrical chronicler of suburban maladies, while he viewed himself as much more. Many readers, professional critics, and scholars defined Updike based on what they decided stood as his best (or, perhaps, least appealing) novels. As a result, the Updikean symbols they use to classify him as an author are neither correct nor incorrect but instead based on limitations. The most famous example of this is Nicholson Baker's 1991 memoir/homage *U and I,* in which he admits that he looks to Updike as a model, yet has actually read little of his work. Baker admits, "I have been reading Updike very intermittently, but thinking about him constantly, comparing myself with him" (29). At the time, he read "most or all" of only eight of thirty Updike volumes published at the time Baker wrote his book.

Ironically, the assessment of Updike is most likely tainted by his voluminous output. In other words, few readers (whether paid to review or for their own leisure) could keep up with his output, thereby creating an opinion of his books derived from his handful (or perhaps just one or two) best-known or best-selling works. Getting literary critics to admit similar statistics would be impossible, yet one cannot overlook that option when surveying Updike's reviews for *Terrorist* and other novels. I submit that the easiest method of evaluating Updike, if one is going to compare and contrast his early fiction with later novels, is by using Rabbit Angstrom as a kind of fill-in for the author and his ideas.

From Updike's perspective, his catalog of fiction and nonfiction may exist merely as one long collective body of work, which necessitates a fundamentally different outlook regarding who he is as an author. Symbolic interaction asks that the critic or scholar attempt to examine the multiple influences (internally and externally) that lead to this moment's transformations, which may help one understand an author's motivations over the course of a career or lifetime. As a result, there is a constant loop in an individual as an actor in social processes that shapes the person, society, and additional external social interaction. In Updike's case, his role as both writer and writer/citizen combined to create a need to work on global topics as his career evolved, most likely due to the forces reshaping his worldview. Additionally, for Updike himself, an interactionist outlook negates the kind of labels that others would place on his work.

I contend that Updike's dual roles of novelist and critic/journalist melded somewhat in the mid- to late 1960s, resulting in his worldview becoming strikingly more global. Updike's stance on the war in Vietnam and his State Department-sponsored lecture tours in the early 1970s (including stops in Ghana, Nigeria, Tanzania, Kenya, and Ethiopia) played a significant role in this change.

Updike's concurrent career as a professional reviewer and essayist also played a part in his broadening viewpoint. Given his standing as a young, celebrated American novelist in the 1960s, his editors at *The New Yorker* assigned him books most often outside North America, probably to allay criticisms of careerism if Updike reviewed his peers (as he would do later as his celebrity grew). In typical Updike lyricism, he explains how this came to be, saying, "The esoteric fiction of Europe, however, was an ocean removed from envy's blight, and my practitioner's technical side was glad to investigate imported gadgetry. . . . Evidently I can read anything in English and muster up an opinion about it" (*Picked-Up Pieces* 13–14). The outside stimuli of deeply reading and reviewing global literature, combined with the travels he took as a representative of the United States, coalesced, leading Updike to produce works that differed from what outsiders would consider his norm.

***

If we return, momentarily, to the epigraph that begins this chapter, I believe that over the course of his long career, stretching from the early 1950s to the posthumous publications of 2011 and beyond, one must conclude that Updike did indeed find "it." His "it," however, was not uncovered in the rush toward postmodernism, an obsession with political correctness, post-colonialism, or any of the other fads that occupied American literary history during his lifetime.

Rather, Updike—part social historian and part detective—situated "it" in the gritty lives of so-called *ordinary* people who found themselves also on the prowl for that elusive something that would make them complete. Updike understood that the quest could sometimes turn dirty, tragic, and cruel, perhaps even ripping people apart emotionally, but even in their darkest moments, individuals learned to rise again and continue fighting. What else could they do?

Greiner asserts that Updike is one of the few modern writers who produced so much varied and "gifted" work that they essentially cannot be theorized (*Novels* ix). While one could argue that the difficulty (maybe inability) to fit Updike into a theoretical lens, so common among scholars in English literature departments today, will hurt his reputation over the long run, one could argue that Updike's prowess actually forces an investigator to return to the heart of criticism—close reading and analysis.

So while some critics find fault with Updike's focus on everyday Americans and even see his beautiful prose as a sinister way of hiding that he has nothing to say, I counter that what we find in his work is a way of making sense of life that is wholly unique in literary history.

Updike takes us from birth to death, across socioeconomic status, beyond gender, through disparate cultures, and traversing generations to portray a nation and its people on an epic quest. This is the life we lead, the people we face, the situations we encounter, and the love we search for all rolled up at the heart of what it is to be an American. Moreover, these same ideas transpire globally. By extension, then, Updike's focus on *the people* addresses humanity in a way that is profound and valuable for non-American audiences as well.

CHAPTER 2

Why Write: Updike as Craftsman, Professional, and Celebrity

> [W]hat a writer wants, as every aspiring writer can tell you, is to *get into print*. To transform the changing shadows of one's dimly and fitfully lived life into print . . . to lift through the doubled magic of language and mechanical reproduction our own impressions and dreams and playful constructions into another realm of existence . . . into a space far wider than that which we occupy, into a time theoretically eternal: *that* is the siren song that holds us to our desks, our dismal revisions, our insomnia panics, our dictionaries and encyclopedias, our lonely and, the odds long are, superfluous labor.
> —From a 1974 speech by John Updike,
> reprinted in *Picked-Up Pieces* (52)

The generation of writers exemplified by John Updike, Philip Roth, Joyce Carol Oates, Toni Morrison, Don DeLillo, and Norman Mailer provide us with a bounty of content, not only based on their voluminous output, but also in terms of a deluge of popular culture objects, ranging from television and print interviews to magazine profiles and newspaper reviews. Unfortunately, for future researchers interested in studying popular writers, this avalanche may drop to a trickle based on the transformation from print to electronic communications. Obviously, the Web offers greater access to author-specific resources, but I cannot imagine that today's literary stars are saving print copies of their e-mails, texts, tweets, and other easily vaporized communications.

In response to this mountain of information, this chapter examines John Updike from a perspective that he might have found unnerving—as a craftsman, professional writer, and celebrity. By looking at him in this manner, I think that we get an interesting look at how a famous person feels about notoriety, celebrity, and its consequences. In addition, this perspective is outside the boundaries of most contemporary literary criticism, thus an interesting way to approach Updike. My own thinking about popular culture and society is inextricably linked to capitalism and its evil mistress, marketing, so we cannot divorce an author from the realities of his existence as both a producer and a product of goods made for sale. The contrast between author as an artist and author as a salesperson is an interesting and necessary aspect of the literary industry.

Unlike many of his contemporaries, Updike made frank statements about the links between his life and fiction. In *Self-Conscious,* his 1989 memoir, for example, Updike describes many scenes from his life and then provides the reader with a footnote quoting the incident as it worked itself into one of his stories. While the scholar is typically left to assess how much of a particular writer's fiction is derived from real life, Updike often provides the answer. The larger question, perhaps, then becomes why he gives the reader this information, when other authors choose to keep it secret or at least make some effort toward masking it. Is this Updike participating in his own mythmaking?

There are interesting little tidbits about Updike that reveal a great deal. For example, unlike many other well-known authors, Updike participated in every aspect of book design and production, including the details about font to the selection of the author photo that adorns the jacket. One senses that as Updike's fame grew, that familiar wry smile in the author photo struck some reviewers as inauthentic, that his humble, self-effacing attitude served as part of the act—a marketing gimmick, no more sincere than any other advertising copy.

In the end, though, Updike is a writer. Process is important to him, as is dedication to the craft. From his public comments about the non-creative aspects of being a celebrated author, such as book signings and interviews, one finds a professional less sure, yet willing to disclose and divulge, despite a lingering notion that sharing too much will somehow unduly draw from his personal (and possibly finite) fountain of creativity. Studying Updike the person and Updike the writer—a distinction he sometimes used himself in analyzing his career—the researcher uncovers a professional dedicated to the craft of writing, mirrored by a deep commitment to writing as a livelihood.

Writing and the American Dream

The American Dream offers a unifying national concept, yet at the same time is highly individualized. For many people, it is a concrete notion based on singular achievement or acquisition, like getting into medical school or owning a new home. Others create a mental image of the American Dream as a golden ladder leading to destination that culminates in a well-lived or prosperous life. Over time, the idea developed into a central tenet of what it means to be an American, thus establishing its place in the collective popular culture as both a thing to be achieved and a model for living one's life.

What seems nearly universal when considering the American Dream is that the pursuit is about freedom—the belief that individuals have the right to chase after it, particularly if the primary obstacles are based on gender, race, religious views, or other cultural differences. Yet, in modern society, it seems that some dreams are privileged above others, especially if the result vaults the pursuer into the realm of celebrity. As such, young people are applauded for spending hundreds or thousands of hours playing basketball, kicking around on the soccer field, or working out physically in hopes of achieving a one-in-a-million chance at athletic stardom.

Although the ladder to success for actors is less defined, the idea of leaving family and small town behind and heading to Hollywood or Broadway is a well-recognized path for would-be film and television stars. The television series *Glee* is one recent example, perhaps spawned in the karaoke dreams of *American Idol*, a global franchise that demonstrates the public's enchantment with celebrity. People view the chance to become the next big thing, whether it is Michael Jordan or Brad Pitt, as alluring and worth the risk. Later, if one overcomes the odds and achieves stardom, the struggle reinforces the idea that this kind of American Dream is possible. In this respect, the American Dream is a fantasy built on fame and the wealth that accompanies such a life. Moreover, it is a version of the dream that millions of people buy into, perhaps thinking that with the right guidance, their son or daughter can become the next Tiger Woods or Natalie Coughlin.

There is an interesting duality, however, when a person's dream is to become a writer. Although a small percentage of writers achieve fame and wealth, most parents are not urging their children to put down the athletic equipment to huddle feverishly over their keyboards each day. The slim odds are certainly a deterrent, but perhaps are actually no thinner than making it into professional sports.

Despite the difficulty of getting published and the painstaking work required to write a manuscript, however, the overwhelming majority of people consider writing a book something that they should (or could) do. A 2002 national survey conducted by Jenkins Group, a Michigan-based publisher, revealed that 81 percent of Americans believed that they "had a book in them" (quoted in Tharoor). Reacting to this news, writer Joseph Epstein explains, "There is something very American in the notion that almost everyone has a book in him or her . . . Certainly, it is a democratic notion, suggesting that everybody is as good as everybody else—and, by extension, one person's story or wisdom is as interesting as the next's" (*Think*). Jenkins also estimated that about 6 million Americans wrote manuscripts that year, with only about 80,000 books eventually achieving publication (Tharoor). Epstein correctly emphasizes the democratic nature of writing and the ease with which one can enter the profession, by contrast, for example, the average person being able to hit a 95-mile an hour fastball or possessing other skills that would allow a career in pro sports.

The irony of becoming a writer is that most people do not grow up wanting to be writers the same way youngsters yearn and train to become athletes. On the other hand, by adulthood, most people think they could write a book or have a story compelling enough for publication. Untold millions actually write manuscripts, yet relatively few get published. Colleges and universities play a role in this transition, somehow enabling many students to see writing as a viable occupation. Furthermore, the avenues for getting words into print have expanded, which changes the way people view publishing.

Technology plays a vital role in this phenomena—the advent of Web-based communications enables anyone to create their own blog or Twitter feed, which gives off a hint of publication without the messy details, like gaining approval from an editor or working through grammatical and style issues. Compounding the issue, though, is that some professional bloggers achieve a level of fame that they would never realize in the print world. Indeed, many arts and culture websites attain readership figures that would make print magazines like *The New Yorker* and *The Atlantic* drool.

What then, does it mean to be a writer in the modern United States? The answer is fraught with complexity and compounded when investigating the career of a writer like Updike. The challenge of searching for an answer, though, is imperative, particularly if one agrees that the author under consideration and his colleagues atop the Mount Olympus of American letters are a dying breed that will most likely not be replaced as our ever-changing culture and mass media leaves little or no space for future "literary lions." Future generations of the literary elite will actually be far removed from the post-World War II cohort, certainly more technologically savvy and social media-friendly.

The transition from a culture that values writers to one in which everyone thinks that they could or should be a writer is important. Lawrence Grobel recalls Norman Mailer once telling him that writers "may be an endangered species" (293). Another Updike contemporary, Saul Bellow, told Grobel, "The country has changed so that what I do no longer signifies anything, as it did when I was young. There was such a thing as a literary life in this country and there were people who lived as writers. All that changed in my lifetime" (xi). As a young boy, Updike identified his literary heroes (dubbing them "The Professional Writer"), such as Ernest Hemingway, John Steinbeck, Thornton Wilder, Sinclair Lewis, and Pearl Buck, and set out to join the elite fraternity of "tweedy exemplars" (*Due* xviii). Updike, then, serves as a case study for probing the writer's life over his long career spanning from the early 1950s through his death in January 2009.

Actually, Updike's longevity is critical in understanding his career. Unlike many of his colleagues in the top echelon of American writers, he took an active role in unraveling what it meant to be a writer over the course of six decades. His early fame and participation in the burgeoning celebrity industry led to countless written and televised interviews, appearances, speeches, readings, and opportunities to draw out some bit about Updike the writer, not to mention the collection of nonfiction books, each thick with insight into the topic.

Some critics and reviewers took Updike to task, playing off the prevailing notion that every real event that happened in his personal life eventually turned into a piece of fiction. In a derisive 1997 essay, for example, writer David Foster Wallace chided Updike indirectly by placing the question in the mouths of unseen under-40 female readers who ask "Has the son of a bitch ever had one unpublished thought?" Though the preceding quote sounds a lot like a certain then-under-40 male essayist, Wallace goes on to label Updike and his literary colleagues—the "Great Male Narcissists"—"phallocrats," too "incorrigibly narcissistic, philandering, self-contemptuous, self-pitying . . . and deeply alone" to appeal to those readers and writers raised in the 1990s ("John Updike").

Wallace's animosity toward Updike and other writers of his generation captured the attention of the national media and in many respects exemplified the changing role of the writer as the twentieth century came to a close. Updike and his peers undoubtedly participated in their own marketing and fame-building, but did not necessarily need to do it by taking down their predecessors. Wallace's essay paraded the aggressiveness of the subsequent generation, essentially fighting for media space in a cluttered, information-overloaded society.

Given Updike's penchant for divulging his motivations, it would be irresponsible to not follow the clues, searching for hints of what one uncovers to develop a deeper analysis of Updike as professional writer. Clearly, his American Dream centered on the printed word. As a result, the choices he made as a writer, including what topics to explore, are essential in grasping a fuller picture of his work. The questions dig at the heart of who Updike was as a writer. For example, why did Updike deviate from the popular novels examining suburban life, when fans, editors, and critics identified that as a niche he basically owned?

Studying Updike the person and Updike the writer—a distinction he sometimes used himself in analyzing his career—the researcher uncovers a professional dedicated to the craft of writing, mirrored by a deep commitment to writing as a livelihood. One sees this in an article he penned concerning his status as a short story writer: "More closely than my novels, more circumstantially than my poems, these efforts of a few thousand words each hold my life's incidents, predicaments, crises, joys. Further, they made my life possible, for I depended when young upon their sale to supply my livelihood" (*More Matter* 762). In Updike, craft and trade are inseparable.

The Craftsman

Updike is the fictional god of many created worlds, most often centering on the experiences of modest, white-collar male protagonists. The tumultuous universe of Harry "Rabbit" Angstrom, the über Middle American, is the most famous Updikean universe for general readers. Other connected or loosely linked worlds revolve around characters such as Richard Maple, Henry Bech, and David Kern. Some observers see these figures as mere stand-ins for Updike or at least different aspects of Updike's personality.

In this instance, then, one might consider Henry Bech (a writer) as more or less just a Jewish version of his creator, which granted Updike a vehicle for creating a humorous account of a novelist skidding out of control and taking shots at the critics, interviewers, and detractors that the (*real-life*) Updike cannot. Scholar William H. Pritchard labels the Bech character "an opportunity for aggressive self-definition" (152). But one cannot take these similarities too far, even when the links between the author and his creations seem so snug. In a 1999 faux interview between Bech and Updike, the creator explains about his creation, "You are the person I, once a woeful country boy, wanted to be: a New York writer, up to his ears in toxic fumes" (*Due Considerations* 650). Updike cautions against reading too literal a resemblance between himself and his characters.

A unifying feature across these fictional landscapes is Updike's voice, or what Pritchard labels "the writer's sensibility and treatment" (3). It is writing as an art that is the center of Updike's work, his "sentences unsurpassed in their witty, rhythmic, intelligently turned and tuned performance" (12). How his sentences *perform* is crucial in understanding how proponents and critics have assessed Updike's writing over his long career. Supporters relish in the poetic nature of his fiction, the way the words tie together in fresh sentences, regardless of the topic. Many detractors, however, view his style as a smoke screen blurring the reader's vision and covering up a lack of actually saying anything.

Before others can pass judgment on an author's creative work, however, the writer must create a worldview that drives the process. Otherwise, the long lonely hours would never pay off, regardless of accompanying wealth and fame. In *Self-Consciousness*, Updike outlines his writing agenda and its link to his religious faith:

> I have felt free to describe life as accurately as I could, with especial attention to human erosions and betrayals. What small faith I have has given me what artistic courage I have. My theory was that God already knows everything and cannot be shocked. Any only truth is useful. Only truth can be built upon . . . The fabricated truth of poetry and fiction makes a shelter in which I feel safe, sheltered within interlaced plausibilities in the image of a real world for which I am not to blame. Such writing is in essence pure. Out of soiled and restless life, I have refined my books. (243)

Yet in contrast to the spiritual aspect of what writing means to him, Updike acknowledges that fiction and life are both "dirty business[es]," offending family members and friends used as models in stories for either being "reflected all too accurately and yet not accurately enough" (*Self-Consciousness* 244). As a result, there is a price one pays for writing fiction, particularly if the output mirrors the writer's own life.

As a matter of fact, an initial question many readers ask themselves when picking up a novel is: how much of this is *real*, in the sense that it is merely scenes derived from the author's life. Often, this seemingly simple question offers no easy answers, particularly for casual audiences. For many readers, the idea of getting caught up in an imaginary world is the great allure of fiction. Cracking a book, one is suddenly transformed into mystery, suspense, murder, adultery, and heroics, while resting assured that the author will deliver one safely at the end of the journey.

This familiarity is certainly what drives sales for the handful of most successful mass-market fiction writers, such as James Patterson, Nicholas Sparks, Nora Roberts, Danielle Steele, and Stephen King. While many critics write off the huge sales as some indication that readers want easy, formulaic novels that do not put much strain on their intellect, certainly there is something of value in how best-selling authors craft stories that gain widespread appeal repeatedly over time. Or, conversely, does it make a statement about the reading public's unwillingness to engage in literary fiction?

Updike's preoccupation is with truth as he sees it in the beauty and vulgarity of the world around him. In the mid-1990s, Updike discussed the early models he used for putting together short stories, as well as his desire to publish in *The New Yorker,* as a means of both supporting his family and gaining acceptance in the literary world. Reading a John Cheever story, "O Youth and Beauty," a piece examining suburban angst and one man's depression, Updike said to himself, "There must be more to American life than this." Updike's often-anthologized short story "Friends from Philadelphia" resulted from this mind-set, which Updike called an "upbeat little story, with an epiphanic benefaction at the end" (*More Matter* 764). What the author reveals, which dates back to his first fiction sale, is a keen understanding of the literature of the day and where his work fit into the mix.

What one finds shocking is Updike's ability to turn just about any daily occurrence into a piece of sellable fiction. Updike explains: "We shopped at the Atlantic and Pacific supermarket, and so I cooked up a story called 'A & P.' I drove my daughter to her music lesson, and out came 'The Music School.' A car accident at our corner, and thus 'The Corner.'" (*More Matter* 764). The author mined his life for a way to make sense of the world around him. Therefore, we return to his boyhood over and over again: the sandstone farmhouse; the jittery father; the overbearing, misunderstood mother; the aging, humbled grandparents; and the young, precocious boy who knew he was loved, at the center of these adults' worlds, and always fearful of death.

Although Updike addressed the direct influence of daily events on his fiction, he also carefully retreats from the notion that any fiction writer's work is merely a diary of such episodes. Assessing the role of literary biography as a genre of work, he assesses "the nature of artistic creation," saying, "The life of the writer, which spins outside of itself a secondary life, offers an opportunity to study mind and body, or inside and outside, together, as one" (*Due* 12). The key to successful literary biography, in Updike's mind, then, is when details of an author's life and experiences "enhances our access to literature" or, in other words, returns the reader back to the writer's words on the page (*Due* 13).

Getting at truth, Updike says, requires combining the impulse to draw from one's life and then adding fictional components. The result is a stronger piece. In a 1988 interview, Updike explains: "I would say that all of my novels have been somewhat *un*autobiographical. In every case, there was something that kind of stretched me . . . for a novel there has to be something out of the autobiographical to excite the author, and one hopes to excite, then, the reader" (quoted in Plath 209). The challenge is to continue living or imagining experiences that the writer can build on to present some area of the American experience to the reader.

A Professional Writer

If a single line could encompass Updike's thoughts about being a professional writer, it may be the opening of his last nonfiction book collection *Due Considerations* (2007): "Bills come due; dues must be paid" (xvii). In pure Updikean form, the sentence is both direct and mystical. Yes, bills always "come due," but what "dues" is the author paying? One suspects that the dues are to the profession and the "certain salable artifacts" that Updike says makes up his simplistic view of the writer's life at the beginning of his career (xviii). Despite its brevity, the sentence speaks volumes about Updike's commitment to writing as a profession.

An additional reason Updike serves as an interesting case study for a dying breed of writers that will likely never again exist in the United States is that unlike so many of his colleagues, such as Toni Morrison and Joyce Carol Oates, who taught at universities while also writing, Updike derived his income solely working as a freelancer, his only livelihood, outside a short two-year stint at *The New Yorker* in the mid-1950s.

Consistently, in interviews and articles that address his place in the literary world, Updike takes great care in outlining what it is in his mind to be a professional writer. Around the turn of the twentieth century, perhaps a little giddy at the coming millennium, Updike wrote about his youthful aspirations in the anthology *More Matter*. "I set out to be a magazine writer, a wordsmith as the profession was understood in the industrial first half of the century," he explains. "I like seeing my name in what they used to call 'hard type'" (xxi). This romantic notion of seeing one's name in print, which still excites Updike decades later after millions of his words appeared, might meet jaded eyes in the twenty-first century. Getting into print ensures that bills and dues are paid.

Today's era is built around the idea of the blockbuster—a marketing plan and shot at instant wealth and fame—whether used to launch a new film, CD, or book. The release itself is carefully plotted among huddled media executives, yearning for some way to reach a mass audience. Even among best-selling novelists, the primary goal is to debut at number one. Yet Updike, from the rarified air among the United States' greatest modern writers, returned to his foundational notion of what it is to be a professional. "An invitation into print, from however suspect a source" he says, "is an opportunity to make something beautiful, to discover within oneself a treasure that would otherwise have remained buried" (*More Matter* xxi).

It is clear that Updike understood the connection between his status as a professional writer and his participation in the mass media industry, necessarily marketing himself, as well as what he wrote. For example, discussing the lack of attention given to *The Witches of Eastwick* prior to the movie version being released, Updike told scholar James Plath, "Well, what is attention? Now there are so many other claims on our attention, I guess an author is lucky to get any attention. And many quite good ones don't get any in the landslide of books, all of them aimed at what seems to be a narrowing sector of the average bourgeois's energy dispersal" (266). Even though Updike was perhaps the United States' most famous and published freelance writer, he never seemed to forget that he was a hired literary gun. (See Table 2.1 for Updike sales figures.)

At one point in the late 1960s, Updike joked with an interviewer, saying, "I would write ads for deodorants or labels for catsup bottles if I had to" (*Picked-Up Pieces* 497). One can only imagine how those mythical descriptions would have read. His tongue-in-cheek remark, though, has more than a sliver of meaning regarding the state of literature as it evolved over his career. Jump forward another 20 years and Updike discussed the difficulty of establishing oneself as a writer, saying, "it's harder now to take writing seriously. The Gutenbergian age is in its twilight: [today's writer must ask] why should I be doing this for an American audience which basically doesn't read anymore, just flicks on the tube or whatever else it does—goes out and has a beer" (quoted in Plath 199). One is impressed with Updike's prescient foreshadowing, particularly since the Internet Age stood a decade away when he made that claim.

What seems observable is that what constituted the notion of a professional writer for more than a century no longer existed at Updike's

Table 2.1 Sales of Selected Updike's Novels and Short Story Collections—Hardcover and Paperback

Title	Hardcover	Paperback
The Poorhouse Fair	3,335	318,133
Rabbit, Run	37,560	1,931,121
The Centaur	35,487	895,461
Of the Farm	22,876	371,614
Couples	4,239,773	158,252
Rabbit Redux	59,580	1,063,089
A Month of Sundays	32,836	675,538
Marry Me	39,303	694,281
The Coup	61,180	1,172,828
Rabbit Is Rich	87,164	1,192,004
The Witches of Eastwick	80,154	578,585
Roger's Version	57,561	123,647
S.	41,042	73,624
Rabbit at Rest	93,224	204,887
Memories of the Ford Administration	33,079	32,200
Brazil	43,774	136,800
The Afterlife	39,482	NA
The Best American Short Stories of the Century	150,000+	
Terrorist	105,000	
The Widows of Eastwick	101,000	

Sales figures through 1996 for *The Poorhouse Fair* through *The Afterlife*, Knopf. "In the Beauty of the Lilies: Marketing Plan." Winter 1996; additional sales numbers (estimate) from various *Publishers Weekly* articles, see the Bibliography for full citation.

death, at least certainly not as he personified the image. Discussion in the current environment regarding the death of print magazines and newspapers and the subsequent failure of those mass media channels over the last decade might make an Updikean career nearly impossible today. Consequently, the next generation of literary greats faces an entirely different world than Updike did at the start of his career in the 1950s.

Celebrity in a Celebrity-Obsessed Age

As mentioned previously, many aspects of an individual's quest to fulfill the American Dream are private and will never be exposed, unless a person chooses to reveal them. In Updike's time, these explanations were reserved primarily for celebrities (e.g., ghostwritten autobiographies and tell-all memoirs), although confession is much more common today, in an age where Internet-fueled self-exposure trumps discretion on every cyber corner. Even now, though, a person's motivations are often secret and deeply personal. Celebrities, however, live by a different equation. In that case, the admission and explanation of their hopes and dreams seem part of the trade-off for fame.

Updike protests—sometimes too loudly—at his place in the marketing machine, but still relents. Updike explained his position to an interviewer at the height of his national fame in 1968:

> My life is, in a sense, trash; my life is only that of which the residue is my writing. The person who appears on the cover of *Time* or whose monologue will be printed in *The Paris Review* is neither the me who exists physically and socially or the me who signs the fiction and poetry. That is, everything is infinitely fine, and any opinion is somehow coarser than the texture of the real thing. (Plath 31)

The reader senses Updike's conflict regarding the split between true self and professional self, yet he delivered this clarification in the midst of conducting an interview.

Given his voluminous outpouring of nonfiction and countless interviews, it is possible that no other writer in history has written or discussed himself more than Updike. *Updike in Cincinnati: A Literary Performance* (2007), for example, locks together his merged identity as writer and celebrity. The literary performance aspect of the book centers on Updike's short stay in the midwestern city and the star power attached to his appearance. It provides a behind-the-scenes glimpse of how a famous contemporary writer intermingles with the public, fans, scholars, and the academic community.

For further proof of Updike's ubiquity, look no further than his appearance (in cartoon form) on *The Simpsons,* or as the central character in the highly publicized novel *U and I* by Nicholson Baker. As a scholar and fan, James Schiff saw Updike appear in public on many occasions and describes them as "so effortless and graceful that one assumes that this is the very thing he was meant to do his entire life" (xvii). This outwardly natural ability to perform contrasts with Updike's sense of discomfort with his own skin (psoriasis) and voice (stammer) as outlined in his memoir. For example, Schiff explains, "Updike appears to enjoy being on stage, yet doesn't get worked up or worried about it, and seemingly does little advance preparation" (xvii). The duality between his confessed internal discomfort and ease in front of large audiences either reveals the depths of his writer versus person *mask* or exposes an individual highly skilled in image-building and marketing.

Looking for clues that indicate how Updike approached his fame, the investigator realizes that he must have found something in talking through his work and life that made sense to him, because he carried on the task for more than 50 years. Universally described as gracious in public appearances whether in front of large crowds or in smaller settings, Updike must have realized the relationship between the industry aspects of publishing and how playing his part in interviews and campaigns enabled him to write more. For example, in 2006, Knopf launched a national marketing campaign to promote *Terrorist*. Despite five decades of past interviews and talking about himself, Updike (then at 74 years old) actively participated in the process by embarking on a national tour, doing public readings, and also across print, Web, television, and radio. At the same time, National Public Radio host Terry Gross once admitted her fear of interviewing the author, claiming, "I think of all the people I've met, you have the strongest anti-interview feelings" (quoted in Plath xi). This admission comes from a journalist famous for interviewing living literary greats.

One of the methods Updike used to validate his dual life as an individual and also a celebrity meant that he would view "Updike, Writer" as a kind of character or mask outside his *real* self that enabled him to maintain a semblance of privacy while engaging with a growing public. An additional factor, which makes the author unique, is the way the publishing industry transformed as the United States of the 1950s morphed into the technology age over the next five decades. The Updike who experienced early fame in the mid-1950s coped with an entirely different world as his career progressed. In the mid-1990s, Updike penned an essay titled "Updike and I." The piece focuses on the relationship between Updike as a man and the writer/celebrity that the "real" Updike "created . . . out of the sticks and mud of my Pennsylvania boyhood" (*More Matter* 757).

The unnamed "I" in the short piece sees Updike as a "monster" and is horrified at facing "the rooms that Updike has filled with his books, his papers, his trophies, his projects." Yet the two are fused into a "sacred reality" that makes it impossible for one to act without the other (*More Matter* 758). Despite the strident tone at the opening of the essay, the narrator fears Updike abandoning him, a tinge of doubt at the core of many successful people who wonder—am I really that good or did I just get lucky?

Clearly, the continued growth of the nation's celebrity obsession, facilitated by successive technological innovations, has immense consequences for members of its creative class. Writers of Updike's generation, born in an era when radio and film dominated mass media, certainly felt the acute transition as television, cable, and the Internet came to dominate popular culture. With this change, a culture emerged that extolled confession. No scab remains unpicked and no question seems outside the bounds of good taste.

While Updike enacted a plan of self-revelation through his work, such as the 1989 memoir *Self-Consciousness* and personified a gracious manner in interviews and readings that would deflate difficult examiners, some of his contemporaries addressed the change more aggressively. For example, in an interview with Lawrence Grobel, Norman Mailer took offense at being asked repeated questions about his marriages and other personal topics. Rather than smash Grobel in the face, as he might have done at an earlier stage in his career, Mailer explained his rationale, saying, "You want to discuss my life. I'm not going to give away my life. My life is my material. I would give you my life no more than I would give you my mate. That belongs to me, not to an interviewer" (309). Updike, Mailer, and many of their contemporaries wanted to differentiate between their work and the information they provided during celebrity moments. Yet they also understood the connection their confession created with audiences.

Updike also tackled the consequences of celebrity status on the writer's work, boldly declaring, "Celebrity is a mask that eats into the face." For Updike, the recognition that comes with fame and the incessant requests to speak largely on any and all topics creates a wall around his "early impressions, taken in before the writer became conscious of himself as a writer." As a result, "the 'successful' writer acquires a film over his eyes. His eyes get fat" (*Self-Consciousness* 266). Once fame sets in, much of the writer's burden is to introduce new experiences that cut through the haze, returning him to a time prior to fame, when eyes saw events clearer.

In a surprisingly confessional mode, Updike linked his celebrity to internal needs for acceptance on a personal level, as the result of a lifetime of dealing with the skin condition psoriasis and a speech impediment. On one hand, he explains, "I need these excursions," yet they "leave me feeling dirty and disturbed, as though I have wasted this time away from my desk, posing as an author instead of being one" (*Self-Consciousness* 250). In this light, one sees a vulnerable side of Updike, attracted to fame and its diversions, but realizing that it carries a price tag.

The two sides continued at war inside Updike. He lumps writing book reviews, public readings, and appearances together, calling them "superfluous," but done "for the money and the easy exposure of it, the showing-off, the quick certification from a world that I fear is not hearing me, is not *understanding* me." Concurrently, according to the author, "My public, marketable self—the self put on display in interviews and slightly 'off' caricatures in provincial book-review sections, the book-autographing, anxious-to-please me—feels like another skin and hurts" (*Self-Consciousness* 250).

This Updike is wholly realistic about his celebrity status—confessing its use to fulfill an internal desire for acceptance and interaction with the outside world, as well as an additional means for drawing income from his work. In the poem, "At the End of the Rainbow," for example, the author questions traveling to yet another (unnamed) university lecture, which ends with him alone in a drab motel room, with nothing but the electronic clock for company. Hardly the pot of gold at the end of the rainbow, despite his brief stint on the celebrity pedestal, Updike contrasts the "thunderous applause/still tingling in your body" with the mundane realities of time on the road, "Hi-tech/alarm clock, digital. The John. The Check" (*Collected Poems* 253–54). Here Updike offers the reader a behind-the-curtains image of the downside of fame—loneliness, another in a series of somber hotel rooms, and the deep-rooted, almost humiliating, realization that all of this is undertaken for nothing more sacrosanct than money.

In comparison, we can contrast Updike's difficult relationship with celebrity to that of his literary contemporary Norman Mailer, who orchestrated a much bolder dance with fame, yet running in a parallel time frame with Updike. As celebrities, Mailer is his total antithesis—pugnacious, confrontational, brash, and unorthodox. Perhaps a writerly way of comparing the two is to say that in their public personas, Mailer is *Playboy* or early *Rolling Stone* (daresay, *Penthouse*, even?), while Updike is utterly *The New Yorker*.

Both Harvard alums, Mailer and Updike achieved early fame, though at 25 years old, Mailer burst onto the scene, while it would take his colleague until he was 27 years old to begin the trek to literary fame. The two are interesting foils in discussing literary celebrity, first, because they are two of the most prolific writers of their eras, and second, since they took such differing approaches to fame.

While both started from the dream of producing the Great American Novel, Mailer used his quest as an exploration of self and celebrity, virtually absorbing, then personifying, the popular culture of the age. Updike took a less adventurous route (although audiences considered his content salacious) by retiring from the limelight of New York City at the tender age of 25. Where Mailer strutted and charged, Updike tiptoed and uncovered. Each man's decision regarding how to deal with early fame appears to have had major ramifications for the subsequent work they produced.

For Mailer, according to literary scholar Morris Dickstein, fame changed his thinking, because he could no longer take part in "ordinary life," instead leading him to "riskier kinds of fiction that pleased fewer readers, but also to personal reportage fired by the kinds of inwardness and depth that could make fiction so powerful." As a result, "He would move far afield from where he began" ("How Mailer" 119). Applying a symbolic interactionism framework to this transformation reveals an individual using the impulses drawn from internal and external forces to emerge as a fully interactionist thinker. Mailer, much more than Updike, seemed a walking embodiment of symbolic interaction, at least from the height of his initial fame in 1948 through the mid-1970s. Interestingly, this time frame also marks the early rise of television celebrity in the United States, which Mailer employed to build his own fame.

Mailer's agonizing decision to move away from traditional fiction also set him in stark contrast to Updike, who remained committed to probing the soft underbelly of the suburban United States, with the frequent wild fling into more global subject matter. In *Advertisements for Myself* (a title one could never imagine Updike employing), Mailer explains, "there was no room for the old literary idea of oneself as a major writer ... All I felt then was that I was an outlaw, a psychic outlaw, and I liked it, I liked it a good night better than trying to be a gentleman" (quoted in Dickstein 124). Although Updike sometimes startled readers with graphic language and sexual situations in his fiction, as an individual, gentleman might be the most characteristic trait he possessed. Using a sports metaphor, which I think both men would appreciate, Mailer embodied boxing (if not a drunken fistfight out in the alley), while Updike golfed—the elegant swing and steely confidence of rolling in a clutch 12-foot putt.

Selfless as a Lens

Updike's journey, he says, began with "cunning private ambitions and childish fascination" to "make an impression," but evolved as his career unfolded to making the impression "a perfect transparency . . . selfless as a lens." Along the way, however, fame creates barriers to one's selflessness. Ironically, success becomes a double-edged sword—enabling the writer to publish more often, but at the same time, "clouds and clots our rapt witness to the world that surrounds and transcends us." (*Picked-Up Pieces* 54). Surely, given the author's attention to words, the religious language of "rapt witness" and "transcends" is intentional.

Here is a writer who sees craft as creed. Creating prose is tantamount to religious experience. Still, the process necessitates attention to base ends, such as marketing campaigns, appearances, and interviews that may sap energy from one's true calling, drawing on a potentially finite well of publishable words. Updike explains:

> A writer begins with his personal truth, with that obscure but vulnerable and, once lost, precious life that he lived before becoming a writer; but, those first impressions discharged . . . he finds himself, though empty, still posed in the role of a writer, with it may be an expectant audience of sorts and certainly a habit of communion. It is then that he dies as a writer, and becomes an inert cultural object merely, or is born again, by re-submitting his ego . . . to fresh drafts of experience and refined operations of his mind . . . To become less and transmit more, to replenish energy with wisdom—some such hope, at this more than mid-point of my life, is the reason why I write. (*Picked-Up Pieces* 54)

Yes, Updike is a craftsman, a professional, and a celebrity. His long, successful career affords scholars a unique opportunity to examine both his work and the many thousands of words devoted to his standing as an artist and icon, using one as a means of exploring the other. Participating in the mass media machine over a career spanning 55 years, Updike, perhaps more than any writer in modern American history, enables a full interrogation of what it means to be a writer through the rise and fall of the American Century.

Of all his esteemed contemporaries, Updike managed to remain visible and viable, maintaining a prodigious publication pace that few could ever match. At the heart of this effort stood two interlocking tenets: Updike's ever-present need to explain and a sense of professionalism that craved publication. Early in his career, Updike looked to the literary lights of the preceding generation for models of what it meant to be a writer, yet unlike those archetypes, he did not self-destruct or lose steam. Certainly a literary celebrity—twice appearing on the cover of *Time* magazine—he did not let fame's constant yearning for attention overtake his role as a working writer.

Although routinely celebrated as a craftsman and artist, Updike's professionalism, (perhaps a nod to his Pennsylvania work ethic) seems to be his most faithful pillar. He possessed an uncharacteristic need to publish and carved out a life that fulfilled that necessity. In encapsulating this oeuvre, one turns to Updike, commenting on E.B. White's 1971 National Medal for Literature: "A good writer is hard to talk about, since he has already, directly or by implication, said everything about himself that should be said" (*Picked-Up Pieces* 420). What is left for the next generation of Updike scholars is to explore those aspects of the man's life and experiences that draw out new analysis of his written work, or a call for the brand of literary biography Updike deemed most useful—one that provides deeper insight into what the author has written, the words on the page.

CHAPTER 3

Pennsylvania as American Ideal

> Yet for truth I still have my humanity and the stretch of history my lengthening life includes. Art does not belong only to the young, far from it; what does belong to the young is the future, and with it the confidence that your instincts will be vindicated by future developments. You know what is true in your bones.
> —John Updike, *Forbes ASAP* (2000)

Dear reader, please stay with me for a few moments as I gush over Updike and our shared Pennsylvania. My beloved declarations and the analysis that follows may pain those of you who embrace a deep and steadfast yearning for your own home state. Rather than beat around the bush, though, I will just come right out and say it: Pennsylvania is extraordinary. Thankfully, for the state and state of literature in the contemporary era, we had Updike to capture it for us.

The "truth" that Updike held in his "bones" referred to in the epigraph is based on his life in Pennsylvania. The fact that Updike returned—again and again—to Pennsylvania-based fiction throughout his life demonstrates how his "stretch of history" influenced him as a writer, thinker, and citizen. While some writers exhaust themselves of home and hearth drawn from their youths, Updike turned his love affair with the state into a national and even global tête-à-tête. One could reasonably argue that many readers grew to enjoy the surroundings, even if they had never stepped foot in the Keystone state. Imagine, for some 50 years, Updike may have been one of Pennsylvania's greatest tourism leaders and promoters!

Updike's first successes were almost all based on Pennsylvania, from the well-regarded "Friends from Philadelphia" to *Rabbit, Run* and

The Poorhouse Fair. Just like the high school reunions Updike faithfully attended for decades, he could never get out from under the yoke of Pennsylvania, if he even really wanted to. Of course, Rabbit's saga drew the author back once a decade. He also spent many years obsessed with James Buchanan, the only president to emerge from the state's hills and valleys.

Near the end of his life, Updike again returned to southeastern Pennsylvania. There is grace at the heart of the late work situated in Pennsylvania, like the story collections *Licks of Love* and *My Father's Tears,* a feeling that the state has simultaneously undergone tremendous transformation (perhaps even teetering on dilapidation), while retaining its former majesty and historic honor. Through Updike's eyes, a city like Reading (fictionalized as "Brewer"), which at one time seemed to glimmer in its newness and optimism, can (decades later . . . or perhaps a lifetime) be seen for its contemporary shabbiness, yet still retain its nostalgic ardor.

This chapter examines a slice of Updike's fiction set in and about Pennsylvania as a method for uncovering how the state's culture and surroundings influenced and informed his work. However, this idea should not be viewed as a one-way street, only benefiting the author. A kind of interdependence took place, particularly as the young writer returned to his native land over and over again for stories that enabled him to establish a reputation and livelihood.

Updike: Our Pennsylvanian

Pennsylvania is a land of contrasts. The most significant divergences reside on the state's opposing ends: Philadelphia and Pittsburgh. For a place not really that large geographically, Pennsylvania can almost be considered two separate kingdoms. Some sports enthusiasts simply draw a line down the center, Pittsburgh Steelers fans on the left, and Philadelphia Eagles fans on the right. It is impossible to root for both. Updike's hometown, Reading, however, though a bit closer to the eastern half, sits enough in the middle for there to be a nice mixture: rural beauty and city life; river and landlocked mountain; and a mingling of accents and ancestries making the meeting in the middle a state melting pot.

On the eastern half, one encounters stately colonial America at its finest, yet nestled within and surrounding the chaos and despair of a major urban center. From this perspective, Philadelphia is about an hour away, close enough for desired trips to the "big city" for professional baseball games and arts and cultural enrichment, but far enough removed to seem remote to one's daily life.

In the West, among the rolling hills and rivers, one finds the once-desolate steel towns surrounding great scenes of rural beauty. Along the banks of quick rivers sit hulking shells, seemingly abandoned where powerhouses of industrial might once clanged and crashed. Squinting in a vain attempt at looking back in time, one can almost see the barges filled with drab loads of metals and mountains of raw materials moving toward faraway markets. Even today, rusty disheveled barges push down the waterway, long rectangles of corroded steel causing deep ripples in the brackish water.

Rarely does Pennsylvania shine brighter, though, than in Updike's fiction. Not willing to create a mythical place, like his forefathers, he worked the land presented to him. Updike regales the state for its dull brick and weather-beaten steel, as well as its spring blossoms and winter lights. In accepting the National Book Critics Circle Award for fiction in 1982, Updike addressed the role of his home state, saying, "My native region of southeastern Pennsylvania . . . obligingly continues to warm my imagination with the impressions of humanity I received there" (*Hugging* 876). The interesting transition in Updike's statement is that the people he grew up with instilled a sense of "humanity" that stuck with him for the rest of his life.

The beauty in the author's Pennsylvanian worldview, writer David Heddendorf explains, is that "life for Updike was neither as beautiful as he might have wished it to be, nor as ugly as his critics seemed to wish he would make it" (489). Updike's world grew from a desire to be transparent, to find the authenticity in a scene or a situation that gave it meaning beyond one's circumstances. Heddendorf explains that Updike:

> [W]rote about ordinary people taking the world exactly as they found it. This was realism, I thought hazily, and it was everything beautiful, brave, and fine. In Updike I recognized the individual's baffled search for God, the stubborn clinging to faith, the persistent doubts and carnal thoughts of the average believer. Sin abounded. Epiphanies were few. This was a fictional world I could believe in. (487)

I initially came to Updike as a fellow Pennsylvanian. We both grew up in small towns, though Shillington is about 290 miles east of my hometown by car. Yet here was a famous writer reared in my beloved state. That fact alone drew me to his work.

Rabbit, Run hooked me immediately with its lyrical writing and imagery at the beginning of the novel of Harry "Rabbit" Angstrom playing pickup basketball. Years later, as a former high school basketball player, though not a superstar like Rabbit, I wondered if college were snatched away from me, if I might have ended up like hapless Harry—stuck in a loveless marriage with an irrelevant job and the deadly serious responsibilities that come with being a father. The opening basketball scene drew me in and urged me to find out what happened to this local star, so similar to the simple farm kids who I knew that excelled at sports, but had no academic future beyond high school.

On second reading, several years later, I yearned to read a fictional social history of the late 1950s and early 1960s. Of course, I again turned to *Rabbit, Run*. Rereading Updike's most famous novel spurred me on to more of his work. Thankfully, in the early (read: poor) days of my postcollegiate life, I discovered that nearly all of Updike's catalog could be found at used bookstores, the yellowing paperbacks often for no more than a 25 or 50 cents per book. Although the spines would soon crack and break on those little volumes of short stories and his early novels, they carried untold pleasures.

Many of these yellowing orphans still sit—lovingly preserved (when possible)—in my home office. If I picked up a duplicate, old hardback along the way, I could never get rid of the original, unless I shipped it off to a trusted recipient. In those early years, I attempted to read all of Updike's work, or at least as much as my miniscule bank account and the local public library allowed.

The beauty of Updike's work in my mind, first and foremost, centered on what I call a Pennsylvania sensibility. Regardless of setting, Updike's novels spoke to me as a fellow Pennsylvanian—either featuring characters I identified as similar to those in my own past or a narrative style that rang true to my ear. He captured the aura of the state and its timeless challenges, thus enabling a reader decades later to do more than just sense the implications, rather *feeling* them, like one does on the well-worn roads of home.

In addition, I felt readers could discover something fundamental from Updike. Consequently, for example, I learned more about my own mother–son relationship from *Of the Farm* and gained additional insight into the decade of the 1980s I grew up in from *Rabbit at Rest*. As I continued through his catalog, my eyes were opened to Africa in *The Coup*, the travails of Jewish writer Henry Bech, reintroduced to Nathaniel Hawthorne's *Scarlet Letter,* and the mystery of the 1960s in *Couples,* as well as numerous other short stories and essays.

As I learned to reread books as a writer, popular culture and history scholar, and graduate student, I once again honed in on the careful consideration of words and the power of lyrical writing. I studied F. Scott Fitzgerald, looking for his literary descendants—beautiful writers who the critics (often mistakenly) claim are all style and little or no substance. I believe Updike falls in that category, though each man stood as arguably the most famous freelance writer of his respective generation, they charted decidedly different paths. Yet the glib criticisms of "all sizzle and no steak" seemed pinned to each, regardless of the power of the work or the experimental nature.

In 2003, writing the Foreword for *Early Stories,* Updike admits the pull of the state on his early short fiction, revealing, "I arrived in New England with a Pennsylvania upbringing to write out of my system" (xiii). These early pieces "draw from the same autobiographical well," the same one he returns to again in multiple novels, later short stories, and nonfiction essays (xiii).

Updike loved Pennsylvania, but had to leave behind family and friends to blossom. As scholar D. Quentin Miller explains, "Updike's subjective geography has rendered his home town both the center of the universe and the place he had to flee in order to become the artist he is" ("Updike, Middles" 27). Updike could run off to live in small towns north of Boston, because the space gave him freedom that he could not possibly find in his hometown. Yet the gravitational pull on his worldview drew him back to the region for some of his strongest early work, ranging from various Olinger short stories to the early memoir "The Dogwood Tree."

Or, another way to look at it, as the Updike aficionado, memorabilia collector, and Reading native Michael F. Kline exclaims, "Updike had to leave, otherwise Reading would have tore him apart" (Interview). When pushed to explain this statement further, Kline describes the what-if scenario of Updike staying in Southeastern Pennsylvania, where the small-town fighting, prurience, and backbiting would have stifled him as an artist. Updike alludes to this idea in the 2000 novella "Rabbit Remembered" when Janice visits the West Brewer Diner. Sounding quite a bit like Harry, Janice anticipates her waitress's bleak future:

> [T]he marriage, the pregnancies, the heavy metals, the lost looks. The blazing beauty dwindled to a shrill spark, a needle of angry discontent lost in these streets lined with row houses and aluminum awnings and little front porches where the patient inhabitants sit and soak in the evening heat and wonder where it all went. (199)

However, let's not end this section on an imagined lifetime, but rather in exaltation of the life Updike lived. Moreover, let us examine Pennsylvania's role in his life and mind, which shaped this man and a served as a setting for so much of his work. The symbiosis worked, giving Pennsylvania its laureate and Updike his first and enduring magical universe.

Updike Creates Pennsylvania, Pennsylvania Creates Updike

On September 21, 2010, an ABC News/Yahoo! News poll revealed that only 50 percent of Americans believe that the American Dream "still exists," while 43 percent of respondents claimed that the American Dream "once held true," but is now a thing of the past. While the wealthy (57 percent) and educated (58 percent) still seem to believe in the concept, those surveyed with incomes below $25,000 yearly (46 percent) and with a high school education or less (48 percent) are less certain.

When reading about this poll and what it uncovers about the nation in 2010, my mind drifted to what John Updike might have thought about its conclusions. The pollsters defined the American Dream simply enough: the idea that "if you work hard, you get ahead." Yet a truer definition cuts deeper into the soul of the nation, exposing its complexities, dichotomies, and ever-present chaos. What it meant to be an American and pursue the American Dream served as Updike's stomping grounds throughout his long career. I wonder if he might have lamented the potential, imminent even, death of an idea at the heart of the nation?

In my mind, it is a short leap from the likely life and death of the American Dream to discussing Updike's deep love and constant return to his home state of Pennsylvania. The place—its people, location, topography, even its dirt, smell, and air—played an integral part in the author's conception of the American Dream.

Pennsylvania did not merely serve as a static foundational symbol or kind of representation for Updike. Including the state in his fiction, in a sense, supplied readers with a vision of the place, ultimately shaping their perspectives. In this regard, Updike stands as Pennsylvania's foremost chronicler. Pennsylvania helped define Updike as a writer, while Updike the writer simultaneously defined the state. Indeed, the imprint of Pennsylvania on the writer extends beyond the fictional worlds he created. One reads, hears, and sees the state seeping its way into Updike's interviews and nonfiction, pointing to his deep, lifelong love for Pennsylvania.

For Updike, however, there is an interesting dichotomy when it comes to Pennsylvania: the state represents a slice of the United States that he often relives through nostalgia, such as the notion that it was an ideal world for a child to grow up in. Yet it is also the state and Updike's small-town life that he fled as a young man, searching for broader experiences and the Harvard education, which would transform his life. The intricate relationship continued, even as he searched for a bigger life. Though he left the region, he never really let go mentally or physically. Certainly since his parents still lived in tiny Plowville and his mother stayed there after her husband died, Updike remained grounded to the region for much of his early writing career.

The importance of Pennsylvania in Updike's fiction certainly reveals the powerful influence the state wielded on him. Ultimately, this chapter delves into the inseparability attachment between the writer and his native land. My hope is that when Updike's archive at Harvard opens, researchers will be able to explore this topic in even greater detail. Certainly, the letters exchanged between Updike and his parents will shed important new light on the subject.

You've Got a Friend in Pennsylvania

Updike's famous 1968 interview with Charles Thomas Samuels in *The Paris Review* provides insight into not only the author's feelings about his ideal audience, locating his model reader—"not toward New York but toward a vague spot a little to the east of Kansas"—but also Pennsylvania's role in his fiction. Updike explains, "I am drawn to southeastern Pennsylvania because I know how things happen there, or at least how they used to happen. Once you have in your bones the fundamental feasibilities of a place, you can imagine there freely" (Samuels 26).

Later in that interview, when pressed about why so much of his writing tackles his childhood and adolescence, the author invokes other literary giants, saying, "I really don't think I'm alone among writers in caring about what they experienced in the first eighteen years of their life. Hemingway cherished the Michigan stories out of proportion . . . to their merit" (Samuels 28). He then adds both Twain and Joyce to the discussion.

For Updike, there is always a strong tie between what he writes and the writing process itself. In other words, there is a good reason for writing about one's youth, as he explains, "Nothing that happens to us after twenty is free from self-consciousness because by then we have the vocation to write. Writers' lives break into two halves. At the point where you get your writerly vocation you diminish your receptivity to experience" (Samuels 28).

Process is important to him, as is dedication to the craft. From his public comments about the noncreative aspects of being a celebrated author, such as book signings and interviews, one finds him less certain, yet willing to disclose and divulge, despite a lingering notion that sharing too much will somehow unduly draw from his personal (and possibly finite) fountain of creativity.

Studying Updike the person and Updike the writer—a distinction he sometimes used in analyzing his career—the researcher uncovers a professional dedicated to the craft of writing, mirrored by a deep commitment to writing as a livelihood. One sees this in a 1995 article he penned concerning his status as a short story writer: "More closely than my novels, more circumstantially than my poems, these efforts of a few thousand words each hold my life's incidents, predicaments, crises, joys. Further, they made my life possible, for I depended when young upon their sale to supply my livelihood" (*More Matter* 762). In Updike, craft and trade are inseparable.

If one accepts this connection between Updike's writing and the creative process as he so often described it, then a logical next question might be: did Pennsylvania actually matter? Can one imagine Updike writing about his early life regardless of where he grew up? While this possibility exists, I see evidence of what I call Updike's Pennsylvania sensibility in that he did not stop returning to Pennsylvania in his fiction, writing about the state right up to his death. I will return to this idea later in this chapter.

While it may be impossible to quantify what makes a writer, there is a mix of influences in Updike, and his home state certainly is one of the primary inspirations. In looking back at some of his work, one certainly gets the feeling that Pennsylvania is a character, yet it might have been more insightful to talk about how he creates Pennsylvanians in his work, rather than how he creates Pennsylvania.

Supporting the notion of Pennsylvania as a character, one sees the state most clearly in the areas he wrote about and continued to return to, including the urban setting of Reading and the rural farm in Plowville. What makes this notion interesting is the continuity Updike provides by placing his home state in context within his personal history and the actual history that takes place.

For example, Joey Robinson's visit to the farm in *Of the Farm* in the mid-1960s is updated and serves as a central story line featuring David Kern in "The Road Home" in the more recent story collection *My Father's Tears*. Thus, readers get to learn about this piece of Updike's history as it unfolds more than 40 years later. The Pennsylvania farm transforms from rugged, overgrown, and unwieldy to a highly efficient mechanized operation, symbolized by the Reichardt's growing hydroponic strawberries that require no dirt. Unlike any other writer, Updike continually plows his personal history, allowing the terrain to change over time. As such, it makes sense that he continued to return to his Pennsylvania boyhood, a time before he acquired a writerly outlook and the self-consciousness necessitated by the title "writer."

The Rabbit series also forced Updike to stay grounded in Pennsylvania. In *Rabbit, Run,* the character explores the city, often on foot. Decades later, in *Rabbit at Rest,* Harry is a snowbird and, after returning to Brewer from Florida, likes to bathe in the city by driving its streets. His outlook (perhaps mirroring Updike's?) is awash in nostalgia. He laments the loss of local businesses and trolley cars, even lampooning the old state motto: "You've Got a Friend in Pennsylvania." The reader finds that being back in the city "still excites him" as Harry wraps himself in his past, which is tied to the region.

A Pennsylvania Sensibility

In the mid-1990s, Updike penned an essay titled "Updike and I." The piece focuses on the relationship between Updike as a man and the writer/celebrity that the "real" Updike "created . . . out of the sticks and mud of my Pennsylvania boyhood" (*More Matter* 757).

The unnamed "I" in the short piece sees Updike as a "monster" and is horrified at facing "the rooms that Updike has filled with his books, his papers, his trophies, his projects." Yet the two are fused into a "sacred reality" that makes it impossible for one to act without the other (*More Matter* 758). Despite the strident tone at the opening of the essay, the narrator fears Updike abandoning him, a tinge of doubt at the core of many successful people who wonder—am I really that good or did I just get lucky?

Now a quick return to the idea of Updike holding a Pennsylvania sensibility. If you will, let me venture into a bit of ethnography. For me, a kid who grew up in a Shillington-like area in Western Pennsylvania, was a basketball star, and felt more than slightly out of place, something about *Rabbit, Run,* attracted me on first reading as a 10th-grader and continues to draw me to the novel almost three decades later. I have heard many similar responses from other Pennsylvanians, particularly at the first John Updike Society Conference held in 2010 at Alvernia University in Reading. However, when I journey into the text for close analysis, I have trouble identifying specific passages that I could label as examples of this idea.

What dawned on me recently is that I am looking in the wrong place. What I now believe is that this Pennsylvania sensibility is not tied to his descriptions of the state itself, which are plentiful in his work. Instead, it might actually be the characters themselves that bring about this feeling.

For example, though I shudder to think about this now as an adult and a father, but growing up as a basketball player and athlete, coaches like Marty Tothero, the lascivious and profane former coach from *Rabbit, Run,* were—if not commonplace—not outside one's detection. One might be lucky enough to not have to deal with a Tothero-like adult, but the whispers of coaches like him slipped across county lines and school districts. Moreover, certain students in school or recently graduated and stumbling toward adulthood resembled Ronnie, Ruth, and Margaret. And, most importantly, small-towns across Pennsylvania are filled with would-be Harry Angstroms, sports stars that shine brightest in high school, then lose their luster when the schoolboy career ends.

For a more pleasant typical Pennsylvanian, let's visit Updike's poem "In the Cemetery High Above Shillington" from the collection *Americana and Other Poems* (2001). Of Ellwood E. Coldren, he writes: "Can this mute rock/be Woody Coldren, who with booming voice/and flapping arms would lead us town tots through/a storm of carols Christmas morning from/the movie house's curtained, shallow stage?/He hid the sorrow of a soon-dead child/behind a plethora of public works" (31). Pennsylvania's rural towns and villages are filled with real-life characters like Woody, seemingly regular people who know everyone, always have a kind word at the ready, and serve as unofficial keepers of area culture via their institutional memories of daily trappings.

The other interesting point to note is that Pennsylvania also played a role in creating Updike. Perhaps, though, it would be more precise to say that Pennsylvanians created Updike. His loving, sheltered youth might not be considered typical, but it was instrumental in his development as a writer.

Watching the memorial service held for Updike at the New York Public Library and reading about his partnership in creating his books, one is struck by Updike's deep love for books, not only writing them, but also how they are manufactured, printed, and designed, even as a young boy. Let me tell you as a person married to a former middle school Language Arts and Reading teacher, this is not normal, even among the brightest young students.

Something took place in that household that developed this mind-set in Updike. And, at the Family Panel at the first biennial John Updike Society conference made up of Mary Weatherall (his first wife) and three of their four children (Miranda, Michael, and Elizabeth), attendees heard directly from the children that he and Mary replicated that idea in their own home. In fact, a slew of people could take credit for prepping Updike to enter the world of creativity.

At the same initial meeting of the John Updike Society, members toured numerous Updike sites in Reading, Shillington, and Plowville. Personally, I will never forget standing at The Pagoda atop Mount Penn and looking down on the surrounding area, attempting to piece together the streets where Rabbit and other characters lived. The ability to *see* Rabbit's life come to life brought Updike full circle for me. Suddenly, his Pennsylvania and my Pennsylvania were not separate entities some 300 miles apart—they were linked through the Rabbit novels and the understanding that no matter how much a non-Pennsylvanian loves Updike, one must be a Pennsylvanian to fully grasp its power over him and all of us who call or called it home.

Readers exploring the link between Updike and Pennsylvania have many opportunities, particularly in the Rabbit tetralogy and the Olinger short fiction. In addition, one might look at "The Walk with Elizanne" from *My Father's Tears*. In my mind, the story is quintessential Updike—exploring the themes that mattered to him toward the end of his career: aging, death, spirituality, friendship, lost love, and nostalgia.

In "The Walk with Elizanne," we revisit David Kern, one of Updike's many recurring, possibly stand-in, male protagonists as he attends his 50th Olinger High School reunion. Kern and his second wife visit Mamie Kauffman, one of David's classmates sick in the hospital with cancer. A former second-grade teacher, Mamie is described as "bubbly and warm," despite her illness (39). Rather than feel discarded, the stay in the hospital proves to her how many lives she touched: her former students fill the room with cards and artwork.

Updike begins the story with the Mamie scene to examine ideas around religion and spirituality at death. Mamie fights on, claiming of God, "He doesn't give you more than He gives you strength to bear," yet Mamie contrasts her dogma with advice received from reading a book by actress Shirley MacLaine, the kind of New Age mumbo jumbo that people are attracted to in the contemporary United States. Listening to her speak, Kern hopes that she will provide him with secrets revealing the key to dealing with death, but is deflated when she falls back on small-town philosophies and worn thinking.

David thinks back to Mamie as a high school student and time he spent with her mother after school playing gin rummy. She always told her daughter, "David will go places" (42). Mamie, who usually decorates for the reunions, also asks Kern to say something nice to Sarah Beth, who took over this time. It is clear from the exchanges regarding David's interaction with the mother and how Mamie urges him that Kern is and has always been a prominent member of their class. Later, at the reunion, Sarah Beth orchestrates an elaborate plan to introduce David to the mysterious Elizanne, a classmate who has never attended a reunion before. The narrator explains, "This woman with her bright stern stare was being presented as a treat, a delicacy, a rarity" (44). Kern is clearly the classmate that the women cater to and dote on, essentially filling the same roles their mothers occupied when David was a boy.

Updike also uses characters in the story to critique contemporary American popular culture, such as the contrast earlier between God and Shirley MacLaine. After meeting Elizanne's unnamed husband, Kern sees him as a proto-retiree, searching in his retirement years for "hardworking American leisure modeled on the handsome aging couples in commercials for Viagra and iron supplements." His outsider status pushed on David's sense of self-worth: "to whom they must all seem, David imagined, Pennsylvania Dutch hicks." Later, Sarah Beth reads Mamie's note to the class, in which she expounds on what she calls "the best of it," including "No drugs, no gangs, no school shootings, respect for our teachers, and faith in America" (45). This list represents the kind of pro-American middle-class ideals that many critics identified negatively with Updike, the kind of tenets that demonstrated Updike's overt conservatism. Yet Mamie's upbeat portrait contrasts with David's own feelings generated by looking at pictures from the past. In contrast, he sees, "The girls, too with their thickly laid-on lipstick and induced blond streaks, had a touch of killer—of determination to get their share of the life to come" (43). Mamie's flagrant nostalgia is juxtaposed with David's feeling about their aggression when younger to get theirs. Here Updike returns to a driving idea in *Rabbit, Run* that the young are always relentlessly pushing up and out on those older. This vicious cycle leaves Kern and Elizanne yearning to grab ahold of each other and their classmates as life vests as they drift out on a sea of old age. The reunion reminds them all of their young selves, but as the narrator later explains wistfully, "The Olinger High School Class of 1950 had given up on dancing" (46).

At the heart of the short story, however, is the touching tale of David serving as Elizanne's first kiss after he walked her home from school one day. Updike propels the story by making it just outside David's memory, so he does not fully remember its events, but is stirred by the romanticism and mystery of the day. The exchange draws him back to "their

Pennsylvania as American Ideal   49

younger selves, their true, fumbling, vanished selves" that seem simultaneously so distant, but also right in front of their noses (46).

Kern obsesses about the walk and the kiss after the reunion ends. Slowly, some details return, like an evening spent dancing with Elizanne. He could not, however, figure out why their relationship ended. As a result, the event became more central and entangled in his memories of Olinger. He even dreamed of her and hoped for a time after death, "until what they said, how they touched, whether or not he dared hold her hand in his, and each hair of the fine black down on her forearms all came as clear as letters deep-cut in marble" (51). David is still searching for answers and using the interaction with Elizanne as a fulcrum for thinking about what it all means: "Elizanne," he wanted to ask her, "what does it mean, this enormity of our having been children and now being old, living next door to death?" (52).

Perhaps I am too much of a romantic, but the splendor in "The Walk with Elizanne" is that Updike ends the story by taking the reader on the walk after keeping the memory hidden from the story's protagonist. With nothing more than a double space between the present and the past, the reader is suddenly transported. The writing is tender and the language perfectly captures the innocence of late 1940s' America.

The two teens—awkward and pure—recognize each other's specialness. Elizanne tells David that he will leave Olinger, while he comforts her when she says she talked too much, saying, "You didn't. It was like you were singing to me" (53). Updike captures the first kiss, showing the reader the beauty in its innocence and truth, as they entered "that warm still point around which the universe wheeled" (53). After they stop, she tells him that there is more she wants to say in the future. Kern assures her, "You will," stammering, "We have t-tons of time" (54). The youthful idea that time will always be there butts up against the weight Kern feels so many years later as an old man. He views life as mainly in his rearview mirror, but does not want to lose the ability to remember all of it, like the distortion these mirrors cause. The reader hopes that the dream sequence is just that—Kern's memory allowing him to relive this lost treasure. Whether it is that or merely a flashback, though, the story adds depth to the notion of youth and aging and the desperate tricks the mind will play in that delicate dance.

***

Returning, finally, to Updike, Pennsylvania, and my initial report on the American Dream in the new millennium, what big picture ideas can we draw? First, I think that the American Dream and Pennsylvania both served as driving narratives for Updike. During his lifetime, Pennsylvania remained a place where a small-town boy with real gifts and vivid aspirations could find a launchpad to greater accomplishments.

Yet, that said, Updike also bared the whole spectrum of the American Dream, which requires that some people do not succeed. As such, he can both celebrate Reading and take the city to task for its shortcomings. He can love Pennsylvania and simultaneously mourn its drift away from its status during the years of his idyllic youth. After a lifetime away, Updike puts Rabbit back in the heart of Brewer/Reading in *Rabbit at Rest*, extolling its nostalgic pull on his heartstrings: "Brewer, too, that torpid hive, speaks to him of himself . . . It still excites him to be among its plain flowerpot-colored blocks, its brick factories and row housing and great grim churches all mixed together, everything heavy and solid and built with an outmoded decorative zeal" (183). Even after Rabbit—Updike's main Pennsylvanian—passes, the author creates other characters that must return to the region, just as he himself did. Age may have prevented him from returning physically as often as his characters, but Updike's imagination flew back to Southeastern Pennsylvania regularly.

What I think we can conclude is that holding Updike to one perspective is impossible. Yes, Pennsylvania influenced him and remained a constant in his life of the mind. Yet there are as many—if not more—examples of work that have nothing to do with the state. Just as one cannot pin Updike down many topics, it is nearly impossible to quantify the influences that created Updike the writer. Someday, perhaps, maybe an enterprising scholar will digitalize Updike's entire opus and then use technology to calculate what total percentage of his work used Pennsylvania as a backdrop. This kind of quantification may be useful in thinking about his Pennsylvania material as a creative mother lode. Certainly, it is safe to establish though that being raised in Pennsylvania by Pennsylvanians created a foundation that allowed Updike to soar.

In his final month, Updike wrote a poem in praise of two classmates—Peggy Lutz and Fred Muth—who symbolized his lifelong love affair with Shillington and Pennsylvania. In the poem, the author thanks his friends and the town itself for providing all the content he would need to transform memory into a thriving illustrious career. In fact, he admits that the thought of Pennsylvania and the residents of his small hometown "brings tears less caustic than those the thought of death brings" (*Endpoint* 27). Updike's return to Pennsylvania as he dealt with the near-term end of his own life signals its importance in his universe.

The mental image of Updike in a hospital bed or at home, contemplating death this way, is nearly too devastating to consider. I tremble as I write these sentences, because I have met and spoken with his children and I mourn their loss, as well as for his many grandchildren. It makes me thankful that some of his ashes are at the family gravesite at Robeson Evangelical Lutheran Church in Plowville, where his parents are buried. In addition to the ashes, Updike's son Michael, a sculptor, crafted a slate grave marker for the site, which includes four versions of the author's signature, representing different phases of his life. These touching remembrances ensure that a piece of Updike will always remain in his glorious home state—a Pennsylvanian for eternity.

CHAPTER 4

Updike's Poetry

Had poetry paid as well as fiction, I would have written more of it.
—John Updike, 2006

Contemporary United States is an odd place—a land of extremes—filled with limitless contradictions, uncertainty, and bafflement. Yet one can approach the same crazy world with an aura of bemusement, humor, and self-deprecation. For some, this choice converts the chaos into good nature and anxiety into calm. The contradictions embodied in the United States and its people are as central to the culture as the closely held notions of freedom, democracy, and equality.

Americans, for example, demand the right to privacy, but then willfully outsource their personal information to such corporations as Google and Facebook. We see ourselves as the pillars of truth and justice, but look aside at the continuing horrors of racism, sexism, and homophobia. The Kinks, a British rock band, summed it all up in the hit song "Lola," about a young man's seemingly innocent crush on a transvestite, using his utter confusion as a symbol of the tumultuous 1970s, singing, "It's a mixed up, muddled up, shook up world, except for Lola." The song's seemingly normal narrator is the one befuddled, not the steady, secure Lola.

How do we get from a hit single about the mysterious Lola to modern United States and then on to Updike's poetry? The link is in the bare truth in the lyrics, exposing the listener to life's paradoxes and ambiguities. How many uptight, homophobic music fans, one might ask, have rocked out over the years to the Kinks' ode to transvestite love without ever picking up on its message? Moreover, what one realizes is that we are the ones in the midst of confusion—a "shook up world, *except* for

Lola" (italics added). Lola understands her/his place, while we struggle with what seems out of the ordinary or pretty much the rest of the world.

There is a link between great lyrics and great poetry. Both often explore humanity in concise ways, delivering unexpected truths along the journey. Updike crafted a career based on exploring the edges of what seemed like normal lives. He used images, ideas, and impulses that were ordinary to many, then poked and prodded at the blurry, less distinct areas he found outside the public sheen. Like a great song, Updike demonstrated that another story or version of it exists just beyond where *normal* ends. We all have private stores of experiences, lost loves, dreams, and aspirations that roil around in our lives, sometimes hidden, while other times exposed for the world to see. Like a man with X-ray vision glasses, Updike peeked into those cloistered areas and revealed much about the way people actually live their lives.

The grail for Updike was truth and accuracy. Poetry, fiction, and prose enabled him to combine faith, life, and art. In his memoir *Self-Consciousness*, Updike describes how as a boy he accepted faith, despite that "almost no one believed it, believed it really . . . I decided I nevertheless *would* believe" (242–43). Through that acceptance, he gained power as a writer "to describe life as accurately as I could." His focus, then, would be "attention to human erosions and betrayals." Updike's spirituality fueled the "small faith" that granted "artistic courage." According to the author, "My theory was that God already knows everything and cannot be shocked. And only truth is useful. Only truth can be built upon. From a higher, inhuman point of view, only truth, however harsh, is holy" (243). Though he calls poetry and fiction, "fabricated truth" and a "shelter," he determines that "Such writing is in essence pure . . . [yet also a]. . . dirty business; and good taste play small part in it" (243–44).

What emerges in Updike's poetry, I would argue at a greater extent then either his novels or short stories, is a dedication to his notion of "only truth . . . is holy" and what one must aspire to, regardless of its messiness. The power of this search, according to Updike, at times physically moved him. He explains, "In the days when I wrote poems habitually, I would know I had one, the idea of it, when my scalp crawled. When the skin on my head felt tight. My hand would shake and I couldn't write fast enough" (*Hugging* 864).

Imagine a writer as celebrated and widely published as Updike, by himself, his hands shaking as he composed a new poem. The vision is magical.

Given the debate over the last 50 or more years about authorial intention and the reader's place in interpreting fiction and poetry, it might seem a slippery slope to pin Updike's poetry to seemingly abstract notions of truth. Literary critic Wayne C. Booth, for example, discusses the "masks" authors create as they play with real selves versus created selves in fiction and poetry. He explains, ". . . if we probe the biographies and autobiographies of any great poet from ancient times to the present, we discover that the poetic self has emerged dressed up elegantly, exhibiting a sensitivity to life's woes and blisses that careful readers find themselves longing to possess—but that the FBP [flesh-and-blood person] has often violated in everyday behavior" (78). Yet Booth finds that poets' work is better specifically because they donned masks that helped them cleanse their writing.

Updike's poetry is full of authorial intent. One would expect this, given that Updike at his core is a man of ideas and opinions. There is more to his writing than fooling around with words to pay the bills, as he often ironically claimed. He says something important that must get out. Simultaneously, even in his most confessional poetry, there must be some masking done to hide away the writer's real feelings or true self. Updike certainly meant his poetry for publication, and that interplay between poet and audience exists, thus supporting Booth's ideas regarding masks and authorial intention. As readers, we too confront the work via many different guises, which transforms the piece's meaning over and over again.

In the same 2006 comment from *Poetry* that contains this chapter's epigraph, Updike says that he stuck with poetry "as the exercise of language at its highest pitch" (*Higher Gossip* 426). In this statement, one hears the genre's pull on Updike's soul as an artist. How could a dedicated wordsmith like Updike not be teased and tantalized by such a quest?

Yet I believe there is also a deeper longing than just for word games or the humming, tingles-up-the-neck feeling that writing poetry produces. There is truth there. Updike explained in a 1976 interview, "And so in writing, I try to adhere to the testable, the verifiable, the undeniable little thing. Somehow, I hope the pattern will emerge, and I guess I must have some such hope cosmically" (Plath, *Conversations* 99).

Reading Updike's poetry places his life on display—the beautiful, sometimes dirty, and dizzying search for authenticity—the kernels of faith, love, and longing for something bigger and meaningful. One senses this truthfulness at all costs feeling in "To a Dead Flame" (1991), which demonstrates Updike's optimism, despite the toll aging is taking on his physical self. Yet, the main point of the poem is to look back in glorified nostalgia at the affair he had with the now-deceased flame. Even though his current wife "hates this poem," Updike determines that men like him "must be allowed their private murmuring" (*Collected* 248). In this piece, Updike speaks to life's inevitable demise, various mysteries that overtake one as life unfolds, and the challenges people face as death seems closer and closer. These bits amount to truth.

***

Despite its importance to Updike personally, poetry is the area of his work least studied (and certainly read or purchased). The extant literature focuses mainly on his early poetry. In hopes of illuminating Updike's poetry from a different viewpoint, this chapter primarily examines his later writing, including his last collection, the haunting, brilliant *Endpoint and Other Poems*, published in 2009.

The broader discussion of Updike's poetry searches for the connections between the writer and his work: the recurring ideas, themes, impulses, and worldview contained within. As William H. Pritchard explains, "Updike's verse, both serious and light, had always been occasional, stimulated by a bit of travel, a daughter's graduation, a personal moment in life's progress" (*Man* 256). In the poems themselves, Updike refers to how and when they were written, for example, "in ballpoint, on a torn-off scrap of airline magazine" in the poem "Americana," written while Updike took a series of flights in the early 1990s (*Americana* 4).

And, as always with Updike, style is important. Donald J. Greiner, one of the few scholars to examine the writer's early poetry, indicates that even Updike's initial light verse puts his style on display: "Always lurking beneath the gaudy surface of the puns and play is a deep respect for language" (*Other* 4). The precision necessary for writing great poetry is evident in Updike's work, as well as the careful craft such efforts require. Creating poetry is not a side gig for him; rather he approaches its creation with reverence, even though the subject matter itself is sometimes irreverent.

The tricky wordplay at the heart of his light verse, for example, gave the young writer the opportunity to play with words and look for beauty where others saw only silliness. Though his formal poetry is often much more serious, it too necessitates a different style of using language to convey deep meanings. In Updike's poetry we often recognize similar foundations that reside in his fiction: the intricacies of daily life and the beauty in the struggle to live in a physical state that is constantly changing.

Americana

Published in 2001 and dedicated to his second wife, Martha (whom he strangely calls: "wife, adviser, fellow American"), *Americana and Other Poems* features an epigraph from Joseph Conrad's *Lord Jim* about how one's worldview can play tricks on the mind, essentially masking beauty in a veil of confusion. The jacket copy, which Updike probably wrote or at least approved, given his usual overseeing of such items, lists the subjects the slim volume will "take up," from the broad expanse of the United States itself to the many aspects of the "poet's life." As in so much of Updike's work, death is on his mind. The copy informs the reader "a light touch can be felt" in the author's "caressing of the living textures of things, and in his reluctance to wave goodbye to it all" (jacket flap).

Readers who have spent much time with Updike's more popular novels and short stories will recognize a similar kind of cadence in the *Americana* poems. One of the familiar themes is nostalgia. At times, there are just brief mentions. In "Near Clifton, Perhaps," the poet tells us that gas stations in Northern New Jersey have "no maps for sale" and the attendants within are loath to provide directions (20). On one hand, this lament seems nostalgic for current readers based on the ubiquity of GPS devices and cell phones that lead people to far-flung locales rather easily. The very notion of maps seems antiquated.

Yet for Updike, maps play a central role in his fiction (and perhaps in his real life). Reading these lines in "Near Clifton, Perhaps" with its teasing title, I am drawn immediately back in time to Rabbit's misadventures with the map on his aborted run and sage gas station attendant in *Rabbit, Run*. In his frustration, Rabbit balls the map up and tosses it aside. He also mentally chastises the attendant for giving the directions with a dose of suspiciousness and condescension. Similarly, in the short story "The Road Home" in *My Father's Tears*, David Kern wonders why the girl working behind the counter looks at him so strangely and is loath to provide directions. He relates it to Pennsylvanians not wanting strangers to feel too comfortable in their land. Perhaps one day, the use of electronic texts and database searching will enable the researcher to quantify how often Updike employs the idea of maps in his work.

The subtlety of Updike's literary technique is on display in the poem's final line, in which the reader can interpret the sorry state in many ways. One way of thinking about it is that it encompasses the poet's feelings about New Jersey, which keeps its details hidden. Another interpretation focuses on what people have done to the environment. Our collective sorry state results in a world full of overcrowded roads, which symbolizes man's great failure to rise above base consumer yearnings. Our plight, then, is wrapped up in traffic jams and wrong turns, not transcendent beauty (20).

Other poems in *Americana* take the reader back in time, and Updike teases the beauty out of seemingly commonplace events. For example, in "Before the Mirror," he reminisces on viewing a Picasso painting hanging in the Museum of Modern Art that the artist painted the year the writer was born. "The Hedge" remembers the way his mother and grandfather cranked an old-fashioned trimmer when attacking the dark green hedge that "enclosed the wide front yard" (28). These quick hits take the Updike aficionado back in time to eras that the author sees like they were unraveling right before his eyes. His mother's face—pink with exertion—and his grandfather's sweat-soaked clothes become snapshots for us, like sepia-toned photographs pulled from old scrapbooks or the Instagram photo application all the rage among Facebook users, which lets anyone turn a regular picture into one that seems vintage, pulled directly from an old scrapbook.

The most nostalgia-laden poem in *Americana* is "In the Cemetery High Above Shillington," which takes Updike far back into his personal history on a visit to the hallowed place in the 1990s. Walking a similar path as Updike did in 2010 at the inaugural John Updike Society meeting held at Alvernia University in Reading, the poem comes alive with stories drawn from Updike's youth and familiar names he later used in his fiction. The former takes the reader back to the white-haired Pappy Shilling, the son of the town's founder and through Updike's early years, racing a bicycle around town with his friends. The latter includes familiar Updikean friends, including Tothero and Olinger, a family name, rather than fictional city setting.

Endpoint

Published in 1969, the poetry collection *Midpoint* appeared at a time when the then-37-year-old Updike negotiated the profound life changes around him. Baffled by Vietnam protests, his appearance on the cover of *Time* magazine as the new voice of the adulterous American middle class, and the tremendous personal wealth the novel *Couples* generated, Updike turned to poetry.

As a result, he wrote "Midpoint," a long, autobiographical poem that took stock of his life to that point and then raised questions about some potential futures. Within the text, Updike included pixelated old photographs and use of bold type and varying fonts as a way of directing the reader's attention to key ideas. Seemingly always obsessed with death, the bold declaration that he had reached his midpoint placed the author in the middle, among the middle, and a man of the middle. Though he lived a couple of years past the predicted end, the novel put Updike's life into context, showing the nuance, care, and craft he applied to all his poems.

In the final section of "Midpoint," Updike casts a broad net. He moves from listing many of his literary heroes, including Kierkegaard, Barth, and Disney, among others, to outlining his philosophies, perhaps summarized in the line: "Our Guilt inheres in sheer Existing, so Forgive yourself your death, and freely flow" (*Poems* 99). Scholar William H. Pritchard sees a mix of parody and truth in "Midpoint," a method writers in the late 1960s used to poke fun at the form, while also engaging in its construction (*Man* 148–49). As a result, Updike could present views of life alternatively joyous and perhaps dreadful, but taken in their entirety as both confounding and gratifying. His playfulness throughout the poem is contained in its last stanza, where the author confesses that he was "Born laughing," but in the future, he "must impersonate a serious man" (*Poems* 101).

In contrast to the optimism and playfulness of "Midpoint," Updike's last collection of poetry—*Endpoint and Other Poems*—appeared about two months after his death. The timing of the publication, so quickly as readers and audiences still grieved Updike's unexpected passing, gives the book an added layer of eeriness and finality. It is as if the author finally got his say about death, which he had contemplated throughout so much of his life. Updike's success in this last effort, Pritchard boldly claims, writing in the inaugural issue of *The John Updike Review*: "there is nothing to rival 'Endpoint' in American poetry" (108).

"Endpoint" begins the collection and is a series of shorter poems that track key dates in Updike's life (usually on or around birthdays) from 2002 to the final days he lived (several dated December 22, 2008, a little more than a month before he died). Many of the pieces are filled with alternating bursts of nostalgia and dread about aging. He recalls his boyhood in contrast to old age in the first poem, "March Birthday 2002, and After," but also addresses the sick fear of flying that grips passengers when any plane seems to dip or drop too low, demonstrating the post-9/11 fear he wrote about so elegantly in *Terrorist*.

Updike returns to the atmosphere of the terrorist world a year later in "03/18/03." He laments that the new war contested in the dusty deserts of the Middle East is the fifth he has lived through, not counting the

Cold War. When he sees a ship trolling around the islands off the coast at night, he thinks back to the fear-induced days of World War II. His current house on the Massachusetts shore north of Boston—back then—would have served as a lookout station for German submarines off the Atlantic coast and had blackout shades tacked up on all its windows, to prevent it from becoming a target for what Americans considered the seemingly inevitable Nazi air raid on the United States.

Two years later, though Updike celebrates birthday number 73, he is more concerned about his fate as an author in an electronic world where people simply no longer read. He begins the poem, dejectedly, "A life poured into words—apparent waste" and laments both his own death and the death of physical print (8). Updike contrasts this vision of the future with his own past, when he fell in love with comic strips in the local newspaper. Soon, he is caught up in the production of books, even the very smell of them, and remembers holding *The Poorhouse Fair* galleys in his hands and seeing its vivid cover. Year after year, he adds more "spines" to the shelf of his growing catalog, a calm center to his chaotic (real) life, a madcap time, Updike claims, "I drank up women's tears and spat them out as 10-point Janson, Roman and *ital*" (10).

These words, Updike remembers vividly, though, were more than just the fulfillment of boyhood dreams and aspirations. The accumulation of words he fed legendary publisher Alfred Knopf and *New Yorker* editor William Maxwell were transformed into cold, hard cash. Paid by the exploration into his boyhood world, nostalgic recreations, and the dreams of the common man, Updike put food on the table and created a teeming life filled with a household of children, lovable chaos, and a place in small town Ipswich, a stone's throw from the mighty Atlantic.

In these poems at the end of his vaunted career, like those poems that served as milestones in his earlier life, Updike dropped the facade of authorial intervention and delivered the reader these reminisces straight from his heart. In "Midpoint," Updike might claim to act like a serious author, but in "Endpoint," the natural end is approaching, and one senses the author getting in his last licks at life, his bits on paper before the unknowing end.

***

At the 2012 meeting of the John Updike Society in Boston, two of Updike's close friends regaled the group with stories of Updike's life away from the computer and public appearances. Charlie Tsoutsouras played poker with the author and an evolving and revolving group of friends for many years. Dick Purinton golfed with Updike, and his discussion about his friend recreated a vivid image of Updike's competitiveness on the course, including his little cheer of "sweet" when he hit a good shot (reminiscent of Rabbit in *Rabbit, Run*) and how he chewed over missed putts long after the round ("Updike Friends").

Although the "Friends Panel" served as a highlight for Updike aficionados and scholars, the saddest moment came near the end when Purinton shared a heartrending conversation he had with Updike in one of his final days. Purinton recalled sitting with his friend, who turned to him and told him that he was angry. When Purinton asked why, figuring Updike needed a drink of water or something else to comfort him based on his illness, Updike instead looked at him and said, "I'm really mad now because I can't write anymore" ("Updike Friends"). Despite the anguish at the heart of this story, Updike readers can take solace in *Endpoint*, since Updike was able to reach out one last time. And if we agree with Pritchard's assessment, which I think has real validity, then this kindhearted, insightful little book of poems will at some point take its rightful place among the United States' great works of poetry.

CHAPTER 5

Rabbit, Run and American Culture

> I think there is an existential desperation which all men being mortal feel . . . Harry, having peaked so early, having tasted glory . . . finds he is not good enough to become a pro and like so many others of his ilk, he becomes nothing. Perhaps in that circumstance you're more aware of your own nothingness. Rabbit feels trapped, trapped by marriage, by a society which asks him to get a job, trapped within his own skin. He has a terror of being himself and not somebody else.
>
> —John Updike, from a 1983 interview

Beaming out from the cover of the November 7, 1960, issue of *Time* magazine—all toothy grin and thick, brushed back hair—Democratic presidential candidate John F. Kennedy looks much older drawn in portraiture than in actual photographs. The face as illustrated, full of deep wrinkles, contradicts the historical memory—and some commentators would claim the mythical legend—of JFK as an energetic, youthful hero.

The cover story inside, more closely following the typical Kennedy story arc, paints the picture of the young politician tirelessly campaigning in the final moments of the 1960 presidential campaign, including his need to nurse a sore hand from shaking hands and greeting the people lined deep to get a glimpse of him. The magazine described the frenzied masses as the "ecstasy of teenagers or the wild urge of the throngs to touch him" ("Democrats"). Despite the lines of aging displayed on the cover, the text portrays Kennedy as pure verve, bounding across 46 states, essentially willing himself to the nation's highest office.

Another theme emerges in the article as well, one that symbolizes the era and soon-elected Kennedy administration—the United States facing a critical watershed moment. According to *Time,* Kennedy is "a somewhat paradoxical figure who radiates confidence while he talks of grave troubles to come . . . brings a message of anxiety and discontent . . . with Depression fervor for welfare-state reform" ("Democrats"). From this perspective, what *Time*'s observers so correctly noted was the young candidate's ability to embody different messages for different audiences. He could be the arbiter of the nation's future, while at the same time standing as a celebrity or role model, a kind of political movie star whom people longed to see. In many instances, the image played the larger role, essentially overpowering the often-dour message that accompanied it.

Although the Kennedy campaign engineered the atmosphere of anxious change to benefit the candidate's message and image, a belief took hold that the transition from the 1950s, symbolized by patrician President Dwight D. Eisenhower, to the unknowns of the next decade necessitated a vigorous chief executive who would act boldly and strategically.

Kennedy pulled together these multiple guises under an aura of cool confidence, personifying the *it* factor that voters desired. With movie star looks, money, a famous name, and a beautiful, cultured wife, Kennedy used his celebrity status to counterbalance the somewhat dim picture he painted of the threats confronting the nation after eight years of Eisenhower's rule. As an image-maker, Kennedy benefited from portraying himself as the kind of youthful, vigorous leader the nation needed as it began a new decade.

Ironically, in that same issue of *Time,* far back in the Arts & Entertainment section, is the magazine's review of *Rabbit, Run,* sternly titled "Desperate Weakling." Obviously, a review in *Time* magazine during that era went far in determining a novel's initial achievement, especially in an issue with Kennedy on the cover that would be widely read. Yet the resulting essay is so ineffectual that readers were probably either more enticed to read the book after seeing the review or left scratching their heads in wonder. It is as if the unnamed reviewer simply cannot make sense of the book or its unruly protagonist. Clearly, the reviewer wants to both revile and rejoice Rabbit, while simultaneously applauding and scolding Updike too.

As a result, the reader is confronted with hedged language, such as the explanation that *Rabbit, Run* is a "depressing and frequently sordid story [but written] with a true novelist's power." The coded language of "a true novelist's power" accentuates the young author's accomplishment, but diminishing it as well, since the novel is labeled "sordid." Furthermore, Updike's "too-explicit sexual scenes are often in the worst of taste, but his set pieces describing Rabbit's crackup, his confrontations with wife, family, mistress and imploring minister show some of the surest writing in years" ("Desperate"). The tangled nature of the *Time* analysis reflected the novel's initial reviews in general.

This insight might surprise contemporary readers, given the book's place on high school and college reading lists and the praise it generally has received from critics and literary scholars. For example, the high regard includes *Newsweek*'s catalog of "The Top 100 Books of All Time," a meta-list drawn from a variety of all-time best lists to develop a conclusive inventory. The compilers determined *Rabbit, Run* placed at number 77 (*Newsweek*).

Interestingly, one of the sources used to create the list was *Time*'s "100 Best Novels," which included the book, paired on its website along with the original review. Given such a mixed assessment, the magazine's editors must have elevated the novel based on the power of the tetralogy and decades of positive critical reevaluation.

At the heart of the uncertainty of *Time*'s original reviewer is discomfort with Harry "Rabbit" Angstrom. The assessment ultimately laid the challenges at Rabbit's feet, explaining, "The real weakness of the book is Rabbit's own. Not many men, no matter how desperate, are as devoid of inner resources. For all its excellences, it would have been a bigger book if Rabbit had been a bigger man" ("Desperate"). Obviously, the reviewer could not have foreseen that the thin novel would expand into a treasured tetralogy covering Rabbit's life, death, and aftermath over the next 40 years. *Time*'s writer simply seems to miss or overlook the *it* factor Rabbit possesses, instead describing his story as a "revolting zigzag course of a weak, sensual, selfish and confused moral bankrupt" ("Desperate").

Upon further analysis, however, one sees a link between the Kennedy image gracing the cover and the mystified review of *Rabbit, Run* inside. Examining the connection from a contextual viewpoint, a relationship forms that ties together the era and its stark contrasts between the Eisenhower 1950s and soon-to-be Kennedy 1960s with Updike's fictional character, simultaneously antihero and everyman. At this watershed moment in the days leading to the pivotal 1960 presidential election, a veritable revolution was about to occur. To his credit, Updike anticipated this turn while writing the novel in 1959. Its publication in the fall of the following year made it even timelier.

Politically and culturally, Kennedy symbolized the gray areas emerging in the modern era, while it probably seemed to the preceding generation that the whole world might implode. Rather than simply the righteous progress of the American Way, Kennedy represented contrasting notions of strength and glamour, power and celebrity, and progress and resolve. The zigzag that the *Time* writer interpreted as a weakness actually can be viewed as a potent new way of examining the burgeoning Camelot era. Writing in 1977, Updike noted the notion of the book's speed, focusing on Rabbit's running through the use of present tense writing, "To emphasize how thoroughly the zigzagging hero lived in the present . . . Such are the feelings of my angst-ridden Everyman, fertile and fearful and not easy to catch" (Updike, *Hugging* 849–50).

From this vantage point, Rabbit is the fictional personification of the challenges modern man faced in the transition from one decade to the next. Unlike his father's generation, he would rebel against entrapment and how society assumed (or demanded) men should act. Writing the novel in 1959, Updike captured the specific moment in time that portrayed the upheaval about to take place in the United States and around the world. No one could have concluded that this lighting strike would occur in a fictionalized rendering of Reading, Pennsylvania, within the small world of a kitchen gadget pitchman. Under this guise, perhaps zigzagging is more than some inability to decide on a path, but like a rabbit pursued by a fox, a matter of life or death.

***

Updike himself burst onto the national literary scene in the mid-1950s, publishing stories and poems in *The New Yorker,* taking a staff writer position at the magazine, and then debuting individual books of poetry, short stories, and an acclaimed first novel in short order. By the end of the 1950s, the young author already displayed exquisite talent across an array of genres—a trait that continued for the rest of his career.

Yet despite Updike's impressive output, none of his early projects would qualify as a signature work, such as Norman Mailer's *The Naked and the Dead* or J.D. Salinger's *The Catcher in the Rye.* The post-World War II impetus toward deep specialized knowledge, combined with increasing consumerism that turned every product into a consumer good, established certain authors as forces in the literary community and compelled the rest of the world to pay attention. In modern marketing terms, Updike needed a blockbuster to cement his place among the literary elite.

While he did not stampede into public view based on best-sellerdom for his first novel like many budding literary lions of the day, the young author's critical success in his 20s produced an unexpected silver lining. Rather than be forced to create under immense pressure or labor to meet

Table 5.1 Sales of the Rabbit Tetralogy—Hardcover and Paperback

Title	Hardcover	Paperback
Rabbit, Run	37,560	1,931,121
Rabbit Redux	59,580	1,063,089
Rabbit Is Rich	87,164	1,192,004
Rabbit at Rest	93,224	204,887

Sales figures through 1996 from Knopf. "In the Beauty of the Lilies: Marketing Plan." Winter 1996.

unrealistic expectations—the burden faced by most prominent first-time writers—Updike could craft his second novel. By contrast, Mailer faced intense scrutiny while writing his second novel *Barbary Shore*, which compounded his own uneasiness and conflicted feelings about fame and its consequences.

Although Updike faced financial worries after leaving the staff at *The New Yorker* and essentially becoming a full-time freelance writer, or as he wrote "free-lance," moving his growing family to small-town Massachusetts (and a timely monetary grant) afforded him the time and lifestyle to construct *Rabbit, Run*. As a result, he took chances with the novel: telling the story in present tense (considered a novelty at the time) and using risqué language to depict sexual scenes (some of which was later cut at publisher Alfred Knopf's personal request under the watchful eyes of a corporate attorney). Luckily, neither readers nor his publisher placed Updike in a specific category after his first novel, which may have resulted if *Rabbit, Run* had been his first book. The fickleness of the modern publishing industry may have increased demand for him to produce an immediate sequel, or at least one with the chance at commercial success.

Instead, according to scholar William Pritchard, the young writer produced an "aggressive book . . . [that] assaulted readers" and perceived as "new and disturbingly immediate in its portrayal—some saw it as a very hostile one—of American life" (*Updike* 46). *Rabbit, Run* solidified Updike's place as a chronicler of Middle America (I argue that this label served, in some respects, as a burden for the young writer), yet the very notion of writing about an American everyman at the crux of the transformation from the 1950s to 1960s caught the reading public's attention. If Rabbit's young life seemed hostile, well, it as least captured something fundamentally at hand in the culture. Furthermore, while Updike once specifically identified *Rabbit, Run* as an "Eisenhower [book]," what he does so well is put his finger on a moment in time—a lightning strike that occurred in the jagged flow from America in the 1950s to 1960s (*Picked-Up* 482). From this perspective, then, *Rabbit, Run* is the slide from Eisenhower to Kennedy, illuminating both eras while also simultaneously striking a new path.

With incredible skill and literary aplomb, Updike's greatest strength at this early stage of his career is creating a central character that readers might find repugnant, but steeping him with enough recognizable attributes or interesting ideas to make the journey manageable. Accentuating Rabbit's warm, furry parts allows Updike to diminish the assault that confronted readers in contemplating adultery, prostitution, bullying, hatred, parental neglect, and the accidental death of a newborn.

The most enduring question about *Rabbit, Run* may be in considering how Updike made such a loathsome individual so gripping. Echoing his literary hero, Vladimir Nabokov with his signature novel *Lolita,* Updike infuses Rabbit with attributes that are identifiable. Moreover, he does not make Rabbit a monster, like Nabokov's Humbert Humbert. Scholar Robert Detweiler labels Rabbit a "nonhero [who] runs compulsively but aimlessly through an industrialized wasteland, dogged by a lust that distorts his relationships with all others but that at least blots out the pain of the . . . deadly boredom of daily life" (34). For Detweiler, the Rabbit portrayal "in the ironic mode" and not "an entirely despicable man" reveals Updike's skill, because the character is otherwise, "irresponsible, undependable, and gutless" (38). Rabbit's complicated and conflicted nature serves as an example of the quintessential Updike hero, though one must use that term lightly.

In these contrasts, Updike zeroes in on something ultimately remarkable in the portrait of an average family in suburban America. Focusing on Rabbit specifically, this chapter examines the traits that make him uniquely American from a textual analysis perspective, but does not pretend to be exhaustive in summarizing the novel. Instead, particular emphasis is placed on context. As mentioned earlier and expanded upon later in this chapter, Updike's introduction of Rabbit took place in a cultural time frame that enabled the figure to represent the nation at the time of his creation and also carry echoes to today's world.

You're Still Fighting

Analyzing *Rabbit, Run* after repeated readings reveals nuances that are not necessarily apparent at the outset. The sometimes-prostitute Ruth Leonard, for example, transforms from a central, yet somewhat secondary, player into a pivotal character. Examining her more closely, she becomes almost a kind of oracle or seer. This assertion, though may strike Updike's critics in a peculiar way, given that he often faced criticism for creating demeaning female characters. A new look at Ruth, from my perspective, demonstrates that this denunciation is exaggerated.

Ruth seems to be Rabbit's true soul mate. Unlike all the people in his circle of friends and family members who continually allow Rabbit to slip through their fingers, Ruth is the lone figure in the novel that scrutinizes his actions and tells him when he is wrong. Yet she also falls prey to Rabbit, returning his love, even though she senses the danger in his lack of accountability, which both attracts and baffles her. It is as if she is willing to nuzzle up to this big, white rabbit, despite its potential for rabies or hidden sharp teeth. Ruth's existential thinking enables her to live for the moment, to do what is necessary to get through the day, yet Rabbit's hopefulness—his *it* factor—allows her to ignore the fact that one bite might ultimately kill her.

Because Ruth is able to see the authentic Rabbit hidden underneath the layers of angst, her insight adds new layers to the story. Ruth's explanation for why she finds him attractive holds a possible secret to Rabbit's likability throughout the novel, despite his egregious personal life and its tragic consequences.

After a night and a morning of making love, Rabbit needles Ruth into confessing why she likes him. Ruth finally admits, "Cause you haven't given up. In your stupid way you're still fighting." Knowing that Ruth "gets it," Rabbit finds that "pleasure spins along his nerves, making him feel immense" (89).

This quick statement reveals a great deal about Rabbit, as does his response, which is to "settle right in" to a new domestic relationship with her. At this point in his life, Rabbit is not a serial adulterer. When Ruth admits that she likes Rabbit and then surprises him with the depth of her insight about what he sees as the beauty in himself, he knows "He has her" (89).

Unfortunately, for Ruth, Rabbit will use the disclosure against her, regardless of its veracity, since the reader is never completely certain that the world-weary young woman really does love him. By admitting she likes Rabbit, thus increasing his ego, Ruth provides him with the tools to exploit her. He needs her approval to fire his confidence, even though—in a rather vicious circle—it is that seed that enables him to take advantage of her, just as he does others in his personal circle.

For example, later, when he returns to her after running from the baby's burial, Rabbit guesses from her reaction to him that she is pregnant.

The acknowledgment breaks down her defenses and he uses the moment to "push her ahead of him into the room," though he emerges from an attempt to hold her with a scratched neck. As a battle of words ensues, Ruth begins breaking down the kinks in his character, yet they never really faze him, since "he feels she has imagined this encounter so often that she is determined to say everything, which will be too much" (278).

At one point, Ruth the seer laments Rabbit's self-absorption, wondering "Why don't you look outside your own pretty skin once in a while?" Later, she accuses him of having "the touch of death . . . Mr. Death himself" (278–79). However, when she admits that she did not have an abortion and that she visited her parents instead, Rabbit feels, once again, regaining power over her—"of being by nature her master, of getting on top of her" (279).

Even though Ruth sees into Rabbit's true self, she does not have the power to change him and knows it. She asks him why he cares about the baby and he cannot give a concrete answer, yet what he says speaks volumes: "I don't know any of these answers. All I know is what feels right. You feel right to me. Sometimes Janice used to. Sometimes nothing does" (281). Ruth counters by demanding that he divorce his wife or she will have an abortion, but he knows she is bluffing. Rabbit feels the act is staged and it sickens him.

In the end, Ruth, not Rabbit, is the one trapped by pregnancy and Rabbit's refusal to leave his worthless marriage. He skitters away, zigzagging back and forth, while she suffers under the responsibility of raising the child alone. By conning Ruth into believing that he cares (or maybe actually convincing himself in the process), Rabbit plants her firmly in the ground. She undergoes a life-altering transformation to motherhood, while Rabbit continues thumping through the bush.

Although Ruth cannot capture Rabbit, or even keep him from skittering away when she needs him most, everything she says about him is true and will eventually haunt him for decades. Ultimately, her power is revealed in raising their daughter Annabelle and her eventual reconciliation with Nelson Angstrom in the novella "Rabbit Remembered." The siblings will rejoice in the love that their shared father could never fully deliver.

Fearful and Not Easy to Catch

Could Rabbit really be the American Everyman? It took time (and the completion of the tetralogy) for this idea to become clearer, just as it took further digging to see how deeply Kennedy embodied parallel traits. While vastly different, the two iconic figures held similarities that would emerge over time, fleshed out in subsequent novels on one hand and through archival research and interviews on the other. It is almost as if Updike creates in Rabbit Angstrom the kind of man Kennedy may have become if stripped of all the advantages he had as the son of one of the nation's richest and influential men.

Although the most striking feature binding the two seems to be their comparable sensuality, the deepest shared belief is actually the lust for life that guides them, the fundamental understanding that destiny holds greater things in store. Simply put, JFK and Rabbit are both stars. The stages are different, given their respective backgrounds, but they both personify the notion of doing something "first-rate" that Rabbit has trouble deciphering for Reverend Jack Eccles in *Rabbit, Run*.

While Rabbit never carries out his run to glory that he senses fate has in store for him, he is also no "desperate weakling." Instead, what the reader glimpses in *Rabbit, Run*, and emerges more completely over the course of the character's life, is his *it* factor, whether it is charisma, confidence, magnetism, or some other label for that god-given star quality that some people naturally possess. One of the factors that makes Rabbit riveting—despite his often-drab surroundings and somewhat mundane life—is that most readers have experiences with these kinds of individuals at some point in their own lives. We all know that person who always comes up roses, regardless of where they fall. With Rabbit, Updike provides closer inspection to one such life, like the best-written reality show ever on air, the proverbial look into our neighbor's medicine chest or most closeted secrets.

The other characters in the novel catch glimmers of this and it makes them nuts. They do not understand how Rabbit gets away with his actions, not even putting up much of a struggle to get him to conform. Ruth, the one person he seems to actually care about in *Rabbit, Run*, chides him, but ultimately cannot figure it out:

> "Oh all the *world* loves you," Ruth says suddenly. "What I wonder is why?"
>
> "I'm lovable," he says.
>
> "I mean why the hell *you*. What's so special about *you*?" . . .
>
> "What in the hell makes you think you don't have to pull your own weight?" (135, italics in original)

A few moments later—exasperated and on the verge of tears as she reflects on the secret that she is pregnant—Ruth asks Rabbit, "Don't you think you're going to have to pay a price?" His response, after Updike includes a long internal monologue on Ruth's state of mind, encapsulates Rabbit's new worldview: "When I ran from Janice I made an interesting discovery . . . If you have the guts to be yourself . . . other people'll pay your price" (141). Literary scholar James A. Schiff chalks this up as "Rabbit's instinctual response to life," explaining:

> Rabbit does what others consider doing but ultimately do not or cannot do because of convention and responsibility. Refusing to censor or stifle impulses that are normally restrained, Rabbit does what feels good . . . he does not suffer strong doses of guilt because of his behavior, nor does he draw severe punishment from his creator, Updike. Though others are wounded and scarred by his actions, Rabbit in many ways goes unscathed. (*Revisited* 34)

Creating a character like Rabbit who could virtually get away with anything—often in the middle of repugnant deplorable situations by 1960 standards—reveals the skills of the young author in terms of writing and analyzing cultural ripples all around him.

In terms of portraying Rabbit as a man driven by his libido, Updike in some respects anticipates the sexual wrangling that took place behind closed doors in JFK's life and the free love era of the later 1960s. Historians have so thoroughly uncovered the depths of rampant marital betrayal that took place behind the public image of Kennedy that the mental equation of him as "president" + "adulterer" is forever linked in the public eye—one cannot envision one without the other.

The unbridled adultery and sexual shenanigans of men with enormous power, such as Kennedy and, later, Bill Clinton, has turned infidelity into a seminal facet of the American male character, both in reality and in its representation within the broader popular culture. Thus, at least for contemporary readers, Rabbit's actions seem less out of the mainstream than they did in 1960.

On one level, power is at issue. Updike deftly reveals the struggle for control being waged within *traditional* American families and between men and women. Conversely, though, the public image of JFK and his nuclear family mimicked those in the wider society, what actually took place behind the scenes mirrors Rabbit's travels. Rabbit is Kennedyesque and Kennedy is Rabbitesque. These similarities became palpable as historians and journalists exposed Kennedy's hidden life.

At least some of the initial and lasting popularity of the novel must be based on how the author examines the public versus private sides of middle class existence. As literary scholar Donald J. Greiner explains, like most people, Rabbit is more than what appears on the surface and Updike succeeds in presenting this complexity:

> Rabbit Angstrom personified his man in the middle, the always hopeful quester through the bumps and grits of the mundane, the regular guy stuck on the horns of "yes, but." *Rabbit, Run* continues to disturb readers because of Updike's refusal to damn the deep-feeling yet shallow-thinking adulterer, yet it is now clear that, when read as a whole, the Rabbit tetralogy . . . focuses more on Angstrom's stubborn-headed belief in American exceptionalism than on his never-ending pursuit of the next willing woman. (*Novels* 181)

Updike rather vividly points out that like most middle-class Americans, Rabbit believes in the nation as a kind of paradise. Even when the world around him appears shabby, the character holds faith, a clutching to the American Dream that takes some of the sting out of his vile behavior.

The Secret of Life

In the epigraph at the beginning of this chapter, Updike comments on Rabbit's sense of "nothingness," which leads him to feel "trapped" in nearly every facet of his life. Today's readers might find the traps holding Rabbit from feeling some sense of personal satisfaction or acceptance with his life built upon a foundation of self-created drama. Throughout the novel, it seems as if Rabbit is his own worst enemy, often unable to put into words what he thinks.

The most stunning incident of Rabbit's inability to explain himself takes place at Rebecca June's gravesite. During Eccles's sermon, "Rabbit's chest vibrates with excitement and strength; he is sure his girl has ascended to Heaven." He feels the power of the collected family members at the grave combine to "give his unbaptized baby force to leap to Heaven," yet he is unable to transform his sensation into worlds. It seems he wants to tell his wife and family that Rebecca June will be okay and is in a better place. However, when he opens his mouth to convey this feeling to Janice, instead he blurts out, "Don't look at *me* . . . I didn't kill her . . . You all keep acting as if *I* did it. I wasn't anywhere near. *She's* the one" (271, italics in original).

As one can imagine, the crude manner of transitioning his feeling into words is met with outrage. Rabbit wants to tell Janice that he forgives her, but instead leaves everyone flabbergasted. Realizing that no one understands him, Rabbit despises them: "His face burns. His embarrassment is savage. Forgiveness had been big in his heart and now it's hate" (271). In Rabbit's mind, they all turned against him. Consequently, he feels caught in their judgment and must run away. Rabbit flees the scene, only his fellow-wanderer Eccles in pursuit.

Later, descending down Mount Judge and wandering the streets of Brewer, again thinking to himself what he cannot put into words, Rabbit more clearly assesses what took place: "That lopsided kink about Becky is gone, he has put her in Heaven, he felt her go." Rabbit then comes to the crux of the outburst with Janice and their families, saying, "If Janice had felt it he would have stayed. Or would he?" (277).

Interestingly, in many exchanges like these, Updike's narrative voice becomes clearest and also most baffling. On one hand, we have the lucid, insightful narrator/wordsmith who excels at the written word, while the central character is stymied by his lack of getting words out, despite his day-to-day work as a salesman and his ability to speak fairly intelligently throughout the novel. Rabbit is good at following the MagiPeel script, which he uses to sell the worthless product in his dead-end sales job, but cannot meet the same standards when communicating with people in his personal life, particularly if his emotions are involved.

Simultaneously, Updike then blurs the line between narration and what may be Rabbit's internal analysis, thus leaving the reader with a contrasting sense of Rabbit. According to Schiff, "Updike merges his own sophisticated resources for language and observation with the seemingly cruder working-class perceptions of Rabbit . . . a blend of artfulness and crudity, lyricism and vulgarity" (*Revisited* 30). As a result, the reader wonders: is he the offensive, ex-jock, sex-driven 20-something or is the reader to interpret the narration as the *real* Rabbit, smarter than he seems and astute in his ability to analyze situations?

Obviously, Updike's literary technique plays a central role in the initial novel and the tetralogy as a whole. This fuzzy feeling the careful reader gets in attempting to understand Rabbit leads some critics to wonder where Rabbit ends and Updike begins. The evidence on the page could lead one to a variety of conclusions. "In other words," explains Pritchard, "from the first paragraph on there is a writerly presence here, making something out of Rabbit that he can't make out of himself, on his own" (*Updike* 49). Since much of Updike's work is autobiographical in nature, the question is fair.

***

Given the enduring popularity of *Rabbit, Run*—an important text for high school and college students, as a research piece for scholars and commentators, and for general readership—the question remains: why Rabbit? How can such a seemingly vile character represent so much of what it means to be American in the contemporary era? Scholar and novelist Marshall Boswell explains it succinctly, "Rabbit is intellectually limited, narcissistic, and even cruel—and yet—he remains mysteriously irresistible to the end . . . the novel's considerable and lasting power" ("Updike, Religion" 49). The complexities of *Rabbit, Run* and Updike's willingness to play with and interrogate faith, ambiguity, and nuance increase its power.

Additionally, there is a contextual aspect of Rabbit's attractiveness in the way we have interpreted the novel's context from a cultural perspective. The labels people usually apply to the 1950s center on portraying the era as either a happy fabulous time or one of tranquility under the docile stewardship of President Eisenhower. By contrast, the 1960s are viewed as turbulent and chaotic, represented by the counterculture and Vietnam War. Given these kinds of shorthand ways of viewing the era from a nostalgic viewpoint, Rabbit then personifies not only the disquiet and restless spirit permeating the culture as it carried the nation from the postwar era into seemingly chaotic depths, but also the residual patriotism of the earlier decade. The sureness of fighting World War II, the Korean conflict, and recovering from the Great Depression fell out from under the nation, replaced by the imprecise haze of Cold War and technology catapulting the country into the New Age. Uncertainty ruled the day, whether it emerged in the menace of nuclear weapons or the pace of life hastened by technological innovations, like the television.

Rabbit resists many of these forces, yet they are embodied by his drunk "dumb mutt" of a wife (as he remembers her when young reflecting back on his life), pregnant, yet boozily transfixed by The Mickey Mouse Club and its child Mouseketeers, shooing Rabbit from cutting off her view in their cramped, suffocating apartment (*Rabbit at Rest* 469). Stuffed somewhere between the greatest generation and the subsequent baby boom, Rabbit and his ilk cannot navigate from the same road map as their predecessors or approach life with the vigor and vitality of those, as Rabbit assesses them, "The kids keep coming, they keep crowding you up" (9).

Even Janice, Rabbit's wife and the character that launched the first shots of feminist criticism at Updike, does not understand her place in the changing society or what it could be. She is as confused as Rabbit, lost in her own mind as much as in her role as a dutiful daughter. When faced with Rabbit's runaway from her home, she retreats to her parents and virtually back to an image of her teenage life, despite the psychological turmoil it caused at the time. She outsources Nelson to her own mother, despite the mental damage she received at her hands earlier in life and runs off to the movies with a girlfriend from high school.

At the same time, Updike is able to make Janice seem immature or at least a lackadaisical parent and wife, but he also allows the reader into her thoughts, which makes her struggles palpable. The young novelist adds an additional layer to Janice that enables the reader to find her somewhat sympathetic for much of the book. As a result, rather than throw the novel across the room after she "accidentally" drowns the newborn, readers recognize the circumstances that caused the tragedy. It may be impossible to fully comprehend or forgive Janice here, but Updike creates a portrait of a young woman in over her head and on the edge. Chaos can provide clarity amid the storm or simply ratchet up the intensity and feeling of helplessness.

Observers can also look to Updike for some indication of why he believes Rabbit is an American everyman, since the author discussed the character at length. For example, in a self-interview with his literary alter ego Henry Bech published when *Rabbit, Redux* appeared, Updike spoke about writing future Rabbit novels, hoping he could spend additional time with "my ex-basketball player and fellow-pilgrim" (*Hugging* 875). The "fellow-pilgrim" moniker reveals Updike's kinship with Rabbit and indicates a spiritual connection between the two. In the same mock exchange (a contrivance in which Updike could write as little or as much as he desired, even discussing his general dislike of interviews), Updike says that the aim of his fiction is "bringing the corners forward. Or throwing light into them, if you'd rather. Singing the hitherto unsung . . . let literature concern itself, as the Gospels to, with the inner lives of hidden men" (*Hugging* 873–74). The challenge remains, though, in what it is specifically or generally that makes Rabbit so captivating.

Updike unleashes another clue in a 1980 interview, discussing his goal of portraying middle- or working-class American life, despite its tragedy, in hopes of uncovering, "the secret of life" (Thomas, "Is Updike" 151). From a reader's perspective, the potential for discovering this secret, even if it is drawn from a base source like Rabbit, in many respects makes the quest compelling. When the journey is enhanced by Updike's poetic writing style and vivid descriptions of the world around us, the path is pleasurable, even if the actions taking place on the page are less so. Furthermore, if one accepts Updike's fixation on portraying real life in the real United States, then both the triumphs and tragedies must receive attention. This outlook, as a matter of fact, mirrors the rise and fall of all life, from the micro-level of our own families and lives to the life span of universes.

In the end, faith may be the most conclusive answer to this tricky question. Leaving Ruth for the last time, Rabbit struggles under the weight of decision making, virtually paralyzed by his inability to act. In moving along the dirty Brewer sidewalks, however, Rabbit experiences an epiphany. "Goodness lies inside," he thinks, "there is nothing outside, those things he was trying to balance have no weight." In other words, Rabbit essentially absolves himself of the mess he has created in his own life and in the lives of those around him, similarly to how he would receive such absolution from a clergyman or a higher power.

He is left with a "black space in the middle" and his lack of answers makes Rabbit "infinitely small and impossible to capture. Its smallness fills him like a vastness" (283). Rabbit can fill that "vastness" with the weight of infinite space or God, but either way, he finally recognizes that his life centers only on what he can control from within. And returning to the prophetic monologue by head Mouseketeer Jimmie that he and Janice watched on television earlier in the story line, in accepting this epiphany, Rabbit dutifully fulfills the charge to "know thyself" and is finally happy (14).

Though God is not mentioned directly, this sequence takes place in front of a dark church and the reflections of streetlights. The hazy light, sifting through trees and sky, lends a mystical pallor to the scene. Yet in juxtaposing the dark house of worship with the manmade streetlights, Updike comments on how everyday life overpowers faith. Or, in other words, even though the church gets a person once a week, we still have to live in the everyday world the other six. The majesty of the scene perhaps enables Rabbit to marry the spiritual and material worlds, but he will determine what is reality.

Rabbit's happiness is tangible as he imagines the street as a mighty river and the row houses "seem to twitch and shift in the corner of his eye, alive." Then, as an unshackled wild rabbit might do, he sets off running into the unknown. "Ah: runs. Runs" (284).

CHAPTER 6

Chronicler of American Sexuality

> In admiring another, and in yearning to make our flesh one with the other's, we are stepping out of our skins into a kind of selfishness and into a sense of beauty . . . Humanly enough, some sense of the forbidden . . . gives lust its savor, its keenness. Such is the confusion of this fallen world, where sins lie intermixed with the seeds of being.
> —John Updike, 1993

Decades ago, during my early graduate school days—long before the Internet, e-mail, or cell phones smaller (or lighter) than a brick—faculty members held end-of-the-term parties, particularly as spring budded around us and the chaos of the preceding semester seemed to slowly fade. At these events, some grad students attempted to fit in with their mentors, putting on their mismatched thrift store clothes that served as formal wear and drank wine. Others acted more typically student-like and purged their own semester worries in a sea of alcohol.

On campuses around the world, these kinds of get-togethers still mark the end of the term. A great deal of gossip is generated, at least that is, enough to get the faculty and grad students through to the fall semester when the whole process begins again. In our department, however, any potential public debauchery could not hold a candle to the spat that everyone waited for: the inevitable fight between a self-described highbrow professor and his decidedly up-from-the-streets colleague regarding the state of modern American culture.

Thankfully, it did not take much of a catalyst to initiate the quarrel. Every time they crossed paths, an intellectual bloodbath ensued. Highbrow's argument built on the supremacy of the American arts scene, from the roots of jazz to the latest literary fiction. He painted a convincing portrait of American artists building on and then further developing European interests that spoke to surging upper middle class tastes.

Many audience members, I recall, were quite taken with his position. Highbrow's declarations provided us all a bit of sophistication and its companion, intellectual snobbery, letting us know that we were more cultured than the working-class rabble who filled the small town that housed our large university and the sons and daughters of blue-collar families that filled our classrooms.

Lowbrow, however, would let his adversary ramble on for a bit, and then, zap! He produced his trump card: the estimate at the time (the early 1990s) that pornography was a $1 to $2 billion dollar industry in the United States. I can still see the sly smile on his face and hear the uptick in his voice: "How do you explain the size of the porn business, given its position in polite society, larger than the Hollywood movie industry?"

From there, the roller coaster took off up and down man-made mountains. Within minutes, each professor abandoned good taste and went after the other viciously. Crowds grew and then peeled off in tangential discussions. We stood around yearning for a bloodbath in our own graduate school angst and in hopes of venting our own frustrations in the intensity of the argument.

In the end, I remember that each professor held his own and courted others to one side or the other. Still, growing up poor, the lowbrow argument seemed more credible. Yet this was the first time many of the graduate students (and I suspect, some of the faculty) were confronted by the intellectual questions derived from American popular culture, particularly what could be construed as its unseemly aspects. Personally, what it taught me is that people maintained public personas and private lives—each mattered—and that both aspects should be held up to investigation, interrogation, and exploration.

This notion that all aspects of life should be put under a microscope, including lifestyles and cultural patterns, powered Updike's work from the start. He understood that people were simultaneously attracted to and repelled by artistic expressions of sexuality, but like those people stunned by the magnitude of the pornography industry, unable to sweep it away or explain it in a manner that put pornography's very existence into a tidy package. Instead, Updike used sex not only as a means of portraying so-called normal life represented in his fiction, but also as a way to reveal the way sex transcends normality.

While the media fixated on Updike's graphic sex scenes, particularly given the widespread close-mindedness of the general public, one could almost hear the author exclaiming: "This is what constitutes real America; here are its authentic people, consumed with the same feelings, obsessions, and desires; and this is the very embodiment of what makes us who we are." At the same time, Updike's protestations had a religious/spiritual component: God saw all. Nothing he or any other human being wrote about people and their sex lives could surprise Him. As a result, if an author were to really interrogate what it means to be alive in the modern world, then sexuality must be part of that picture.

By exploring human sexuality in all its forms, Updike gave voice to the parts of society that were generally ignored or only considered in private. He explained his goal in early short stories to demonstrate how "tiny details . . . acquire the intensity of proclamation." Here Updike claims, "Things turn symbolic; hidden meanings emerge." Yet where life and fiction meet, one finds, "The blurred sexuality of this playful moment . . . ominous, for it is carrying the participants away from their childhoods, into the dizzying mystery of time" (*Odd Jobs* 135).

It seems natural—in retrospect—that Updike's goal of exposing Middle America to a truer version of lived life in the late 1950s would cause him to focus on sexuality, particularly coming out of that era. In those early days, he explains, ". . . the material was fresh, fresh to me and fresh to the world, and authentic. By authentic I mean actual" (*Odd Jobs* 135). Few ideas, if any, could squeeze past sex in the thinking of teens and young adults. Therefore, sex, thoughts about sex, and sex's role more broadly in society are at the heart of Updike's early fiction and novels, though most notably comes alive in *Rabbit, Run*. For Updike personally, his real-life role as a young husband and father must have influenced his thinking about sexuality and its outcome: producing children.

While Updike achieved literary fame with the early successes of his novels and consistent flow of poetry and prose in *The New Yorker*, *Couples* (1968) catapulted him into the broader public eye. The novel's overt sexuality and the notion that here was a big book addressing a zeitgeist moment in American society culminated with Updike's appearance on the cover of *Time* magazine. Suddenly, the then 36-year-old author came to represent the mysterious, sexual face of the United States. Who could forget the blaring *Time* headline: "The Adulterous Society?"

The idea of casting an author within a larger, scandalous cultural milieu coincided with the growth of celebrity culture in the United States. The *Time* cover image and accompanying article served to both examine and sensationalize the idea of adultery. Tying the notion to Updike enabled the magazine's editors to send a message to its readers: by linking a respected literary figure to a shocking topic, we have legitimized it and provided a forum for added discussion. Coincidently, by doing so, they also sell more magazines. *Couples,* then, served as a third-party validator for the *Time* exposé while simultaneously providing endorsement of the novel for middle-class audiences. *Time* got its juicy story and Updike received his big best seller.

Updike continued to investigate relationships, marriage, and adultery throughout his career in his novels and short fiction. Although he did not want to be labeled simply as an author who focused on sex and sexuality or suburban adultery, the tag stuck to some degree, at least among the traditional book-buying public. There is plenty of evidence that Updike did not want the label or the attention *Couples* received, from fleeing Ipswich to spend a year in England after publication to his writing about negative aspects of literary fame.

Updike's examination into America's middleness, however, necessitated that he address sex, despite how it might typecast him as an author. At the end of his career, Updike broke new ground, openly writing about sex among older characters. Considering how much he eventually published regarding sexuality among aging adults, future investigators will certainly find a wealth of material in his work that helps them really understand the evolving notions of sexuality in Updike's generation.

This chapter examines Updike's role as a more visible public figure as he became the apostle of a new sexual undercurrent, first in the then-controversial scenes in *Rabbit, Run* and certainly after the publication of *Couples*. The very notion that, in a nation founded on personal freedoms like the United States, people's feelings about sexuality run the gamut from hung-up to outraged is astonishing. Looking at Updike's work and placing it within the cultural context of the period will shed new light on one of his many lasting contribution to American literature and society.

Couples and Middle America: Sex and Culture

In my mind, *Couples* is an enigma. Similar to reading *Rabbit, Run* today, it is difficult to imagine the uproar *Couples* caused in 1968 based on its sexual content, particularly when that year is presented to subsequent generations as a watershed moment in American history when everything that previously happened suddenly changed. Through mass media and popular culture, contemporary audiences are more or less programmed to view 1968 as an orgy of sex, hippies, drugs, rock music, and warfare in Vietnam.

The modern reader might also question how the sex in the novel could have been so scandalous. In comparison with today's network and cable television fare, the average situation comedy contains as much sexuality and sexual innuendo as *Couples,* while most Lifetime movies (while not as explicit on-screen) focus on similar themes with even more outrageous (and often deadly) outcomes. Almost every new series on premium cable channels like HBO and Showtime has more illicit sex than Updike's novel. Yet looking back on its era and what took place in the nation at that time, there is little doubt that *Couples* served as a catalyst for significant cultural transformations on the horizon.

One could write entire books on the genius of *Couples*. Many scholars have produced thoughtful, close readings of its might. Donald Greiner, the dean of Updike studies, calls the novel, "a serious account of an effort by upper middle-class Americans to establish an erotic utopia" (*Novels* 144). In describing the 10 couples at the center of the novel, Jack De Bellis explains, "Their interconnections are amusing, surprising and instructive, making *Couples* a deft social analysis by America's literary authority on domestic affairs" (121).

Looking at the timing of the novel and the stroke of luck of the *Time* cover, one wonders if *Updike* planned or purposely wrote *Couples* to capitalize on the frank subject matter and the era itself. Surely, novelists want to write great books, but they also have sales in mind if they want their careers to flourish. A similar vein runs through other creative industries. Directors and actors often distinguish between pet projects and potential blockbusters, just as songwriters and musicians attempt to write chart-toppers.

In subsequent interviews and essays, Updike himself provided many clues and a great deal of background about his own thought process when he wrote the novel. Some of Updike's missives appear out of the blue, but contain multitudes. One example is the 1971 commentary on the short story "The Indian," which appeared when the story was reprinted in a small journal, *The Blue Cloud Review* (and later reprinted alone in the collection *Higher Gossip*). In a reflective mood, several years after *Couples* launched and threw his life into chaos, the author provides deep insight into his frame of mind.

Although focusing on "The Indian," Updike makes an aside about *Couples,* informing the reader that he first transformed the real-life Ipswich into the fictional "Tarbox" in the story. He then discusses the reason that this is important for the novel, explaining that Ipswich/Tarbox, "for all its charm seems to me to be the arena of the Decline of the West." Next, Updike reiterates this notion, revealing, "readers of my novel *Couples* would do well to have this little preliminary evocation of Tarbox in mind" (*Higher* 468).

The idea that a sleepy, charming New England town, tucked in and among mysterious salt marshes and whipped by the biting wind off the Atlantic, represents "the Decline of the West" is provocative. When Updike wrote *Couples* in the late 1960s, one could imagine many events or issues that might truly lead to the West's downfall, most notably the potential escalation of Vietnam into a world war, thus signaling a possible nuclear holocaust. Tiny, patrician Ipswich, Massachusetts, seems an unlikely catalyst for culture's demise.

Despite these fears, only several years removed from the Bay of Pigs fiasco and Kennedy's staring down of Khrushchev over placing warheads in Cuba, not to mention Kennedy's assassination, the idea that adultery and casual sex ("the post-pill paradise") would destroy Western society signals the psychological and moral complications Updike worked through in the novel. He is certainly placing a tremendous amount of pressure on tiny Ipswich as "the arena" of civilization's decline.

Perhaps Updike experienced some sort of epiphany as he sorted out the story, as he claimed, in church—the same, real-life spot of the church that burned to the ground in Ipswich and served as the deciding blow in Piet Hanema's downfall and rebirth in *Couples*. Did the dizzying societal and cultural transformation rocking the small, salt-slathered town—just as they shook the nation as a whole—foretell an epic end of the world or, like the couples in the novel, would these changes merely destroy families and friendships? The larger issue at hand is whether Updike got it correct. Is there a link between relaxed societal constraints personified by the sexual freedoms of the 1960s that remains important today?

In *Picked-Up Pieces,* Updike remarks that "The book is, of course, not about sex as such: It's about sex as the emergent religion, as the only thing left" (486). Putting the two remarks together, then, we are left with the notion that the changes taking place due to the sexual revolution emerge as the only religion left to cling to, yet also have the capacity to destroy it all. In a 1968 interview, Updike explained, ". . . in this novel I was asking the question, after Christianity, what? Sex, in its many permutations, is surely the glue, ambience, and motive force of the new humanism" (quoted in Greiner, *Novels* 148).

While sex might have been viewed as the "glue" of the late 1960s, at the same time, it was both venerated and condemned for being "free," given away too easily, which led to all kinds of breakdowns, from the "traditional" nuclear family to a sense of community that existed prior to the onslaught of divorce. Updike's former Harvard roommate, the renowned historian Christopher Lasch, writing in *The True and Only Heaven* (1991), would seem to have been backing Updike's decision to place the West's decline at Ipswich/Tarbox's door. Lasch explains, "To see the modern world from the point of view of a parent is to see it in the worst possible light" (33). He then lists the evils that progress wrought, including "obsession with sex, violence, and the pornography of 'making it,'" "our refusal to draw a distinction between right and wrong," and "our reluctance to judge or be judged" (33–34). At the center of *Couples* is the disruption that results from individual choices, basically ripping apart communities formed on a kind of intimacy and trust that replaced religion as society's real cement.

Sexual freedom, in other words, liberated individuals. But as Lasch demonstrates, it also carried consequences. The most pointed outcome was that the family and family values that developed out of the remnants of the 1960s and early 1970s became a political matter still hotly contested today. Given the dogmatism of the political left and right in the current political warfare, the battle over *values* will continue as a central focus into the foreseeable future.

For Lasch, conservatives used the idea of family values to further solidify the preeminence of consumer culture in modern life. Once could certainly argue that the nation still confronts this idea. He explains:

> Under Reagan, the inner logic of the market became fully explicit: idealization of the man on the make; a pursuit of quick profits . . . a widening chasm between rich and poor . . . all in the name of "family, work, neighborhood, peace, and freedom." (516)

Therefore, what Updike had in mind in describing the breakdown of families and communities based on sexuality as a new religion (and the only one remaining) has essentially evolved (some would argue, devolved) into a nation more or less obsessed with sexuality as a political football. The destruction Updike witnessed in small-town Ipswich could have struck him like a divining rod, the first tremors that a watershed moment stood on the horizon. In this light, *Couples* is a significant benchmark in comprehending contemporary American history.

Sex and Complications in the New Millennium

One of the most painful and troubled relationships in Updike's 2006 novel *Terrorist* is between Ahmad and his mother Teresa, an Irish American free spirit, nurse's aide, and part-time painter. Rather than respecting her for raising him as a single parent, even if in difficult situations, Ahmad scorns her for driving off his father and, in his eyes, whoring around. Ahmad's inner thoughts regarding his mother spill out as he sits behind the wheel all day, driving around northern New Jersey, and delivering furniture, though the unnamed narrator creeps into the story as well, leaving the close reader wondering where one ends and the other begins.

For example, at the beginning of one representative passage, "Ahmad sees his mother as an aging woman still in her heart, playing at art and love" (168). However, he reacts negatively to the thought that a new lover drives her to act young when she is clearly not. "Playing at art and love" triggers the boy's near past, a time of unsure manhood in a home with no father to serve as a guide.

Instead, Ahmad recounts his negative exchanges with a plethora of ex-boyfriends who vied with him for dominance, even though his age prohibited him from serving as a true threat. Each suitor, he hears in his mind: "*She may be your mother but I fuck her,* their manner said, and this too was American, this valuing of sexual performance over all family ties" (168, italics in original). The phrase "Ahmad sees" presented in the previous paragraph leads the reader to assume that the monologue takes place within the boy's mind. However, several sentences later, the text shifts to "Ahmad does not hate his mother; she is too scattered to hate, too distracted by her pursuit of happiness" (168–69). The intensity of the emotion has multiplied rather quickly, but the reader still cannot be completely sure whether this is Ahmad's thoughts or the narrator setting the tone.

Whenever their relationship is viewed through the lens of the Koran, the voice is Ahmad's. The reader receives a glimpse into the boy's thinking as he analyzes what he has learned versus what he sees in his mother. Another voice emerges, however, that appears distinct: "For some years it has been awkward, their bodies sharing the limited space of the apartment. Her ideas of healthy behavior include appearing before her son in her underwear or a summer nightie that allows the shadows of her private parts to show through" (169). While this section grows more intimate, the narrator seems to take over, even to bring in Teresa's point of view about healthy behavior. The narrator continues to add context to the mental imagery, but via some distance, explaining, "When he rebukes her attire as improper and provocative, she mocks and teases him as if he is flirting with her" (169). Perhaps Updike uses a more detached voice in this section to touch on difficult topics, in some way shielding Ahmad from them. As the thoughts become more intimate, Updike continues moving between Ahmad's views and editorializing.

Interestingly, this section is not the first that addresses the Freudian aspects of Ahmad and Teresa's relationship. Earlier, at the boy's high school graduation, Teresa and Jack talk about him. The exchange reveals the depths of her ignorance about her son, particularly when she waves off his religious training as "this Allah thing" that he did by himself. To her, the search for God equates to a search for his absentee father. Teresa resents this thought—even if it is only true in her mind—particularly for "a father who didn't do squat for him." Summing up her thoughts, Teresa explains (as much to herself as Jack), "But I guess a boy needs a father, and if he doesn't have one he'll invent one. How's that for cut-rate Freud?" In response, Jack thinks of her sexually, seeing the mention of Freud differently: "Freud, who encouraged a century to keep on screwing" (117). Bringing aspects of Freud into the novel has two purposes, first allowing Updike to foreshadow the relationship between Teresa and Jack and, ultimately, linking her son and her sexual partner in a closer relationship. Then, tacitly slipping Freud into the narrator's intimate editorializing enables the author to expose the tension between mother and son.

Ultimately, the link to Freud is rejected, though the reader might feel that the rebuff is argued a bit too vehemently, as if the thinker is trying to convince himself. Again, however, one cannot be sure who is doing the thinking: "Praise Allah, Ahmad never dreamed of sleeping with his mother, never undressed her in those spaces of his brain where Satan thrusts vileness upon the dreaming and daydreaming" (170). The reference to Allah leads one to believe that these are the teen's thoughts. However, the next sentence clouds that interpretation, concluding, "In truth, insofar as the boy allows himself to link such thoughts with the image of his mother, she is not his type" (170). In the process of deep thought, people do not qualify with sayings such as *in truth* or refer to themselves as "the boy," which suggests the narrator has slipped back into the text to contextualize the emotion-laden passage.

The discussion of sex and sexuality earlier in Updike's career juxtaposed with this example from *Terrorist* demonstrates a move away from sexuality as the driving force in his stories to its use as a peripheral catalyst. Even here, however, sex remains important as human beings navigate their lives and evolution as individuals and part of the larger humankind. The characters at the heart of *Couples* jump from one sexual encounter to the next, symbolizing a new freedom experienced as birth control pills gained broad use. Sex propels the novel. In contrast, sexuality is a significant aspect of *Terrorist*, but not a critical plot device.

88   John Updike

Certainly, Ahmad's budding sexuality lends to his overall confusion in his move to manhood, but sexuality is more pervasive in twenty-first century America, thus less of a focus. These examples reveal Updike's insight and analysis as a cultural historian able to adapt and change to replicate current vibes.

Updike's Sexual Language

Updike is almost universally praised as a stylist, even by critics that view his use of language as a matter of style over substance. Even his harshest critics find a certain joy in a writer so committed to the craft. Oddly, however, for such a lyrical writer, there is a peculiarly Updikean use of dated, nostalgic, and sometimes explicitly offensive words and phrases that litter his novels. Considering that many of the same terms and phrases appear in the author's works dating back to the beginning of his career, one must assume that he employs them intentionally. What the reader cannot infer, though, is why.

This question takes on greater significance when one considers that many of these odd choices are outright offensive; even in today's everything-goes society. Certainly, ignorance is not the answer. Updike is no stranger to the wars regarding political correctness and its consequences on language use over the past several decades. He is also aware of the implications of the Internet on exposing people of all ages to a broader range of mass culture than ever before in human history. A man whose life is consumed by words cannot be granted leniency in understanding the transformation of language over time.

For example, in *Terrorist*, Updike uses the dated, offensive phrase "hot little twats" (43) to describe the potential conflicts that might arise in today's high school environment when female students are in private offices with male guidance counselors and authority figures. In these cases, the potential for charges of sexual misconduct transfers the power from teacher to student. As a result, male teachers and other school officials rarely conduct serious or off-the-cuff discussions with female students behind closed doors. One wonders, though, why a writer who focuses on the use of language, as if every word is meticulously crafted, would use such a charged phrase.

Could it be that Updike employs the phrase as a not-so-gentle dig at the female critics that have doggedly attacked his works as sexist over the years? In this scenario, Updike the author could be purposely thumbing his nose at potential detractors. Updike uses the phrase to castigate all women who use their sexuality to gain favors.

In the novella "Rabbit Remembered," Updike also uses the word when Ronnie Harrison, Janice's then-husband and Harry's lifelong nemesis, decides that no one in the house is allowed to contact Rabbit's long-lost daughter Annabelle. He booms, "I for*bid* . . . anybody getting in touch with this twat" (*Licks* 221, italics in original). Coming from Ronnie, who has been portrayed as a brute and ignorant across the decades, the word is a slur, meant to denigrate the girl and what she represents.

There is another interesting element to Updike's use of language and phrases that modern audiences might find offensive. One assumes that most editors would either change the phrase themselves or negotiate with the author for it to be modified. Questions are then raised regarding the role of the writer as part of the editorial process. Maybe the simplest answer is that once an author reaches the heights of an Updike, no editor holds the power to truly edit or request changes. Given that Updike had strong ties to his editors at Knopf, perhaps his relationships with them and the consequences on his work will be revealed as archival collections open to public view.

Additionally, from a stylistic perspective, it is even difficult to ascertain exactly who is calling out the female high school students as potential "hot little twats" in *Terrorist* (43). It is a passage that the reader could assume is taking place inside Jack's mind, since it occurs between two instances of the guidance counselor talking to Ahmad. However, Updike never specifically indicates that the thought is actually a thought of one of the characters.

The passage might be explored with more authority as an example of an intrusion by the unnamed narrator. The section begins: "He [Jack] stands and on impulse shakes the tall, slender, fragile-seeming youth's hand, which he . . . would never do with a girl these days—the merest touch risks a complaint." The end of the piece reveals Jack startled by Ahmad's weak, damp handshake, an example of the narrator describing the scene from an omniscient viewpoint (43). Yet encased between Jack's dialogue, it blurs the line.

The phrase takes on extra importance because it concludes the first meeting between Jack and Ahmad, the novel's two central characters. Jack clearly holds a position of authority over the high school student, but they jockey for moral high ground. In the battle between the fervent Muslim youth and world-weary Jewish teacher, the power of Ahmad's belief tilts the exchange slightly in his favor. The boy's ability to argue for his belief system sparks an interest in Jack, which extends the conversation, even though he has already labeled the teen a "lost cause" (42). Several fatherly words, a firm handshake, and kind farewell enable the reader to witness a strange bond forming. Actually, both characters qualify for the shorthand "lc" that Jack affixes to the boy's file. What the reader sees is a battle: the boy's misguided faith versus Jack's empty worldview.

More troublesome in terms of Updike's language choices is his insistence in using the word "cunt" repeatedly in his career when referring to female genitalia. The simple fact is that "the c-bomb," as it is now called in popular culture lore, is arguably the single most offensive word in the English language. One might even postulate that the word is beyond offensive, making any use of it obtuse and nonsensical. Yet Updike drudges it up again and again, more or less sticking it in the eye of all critics and readers, regardless of gender. Certainly, Updike understands this, which suggests that using it is calculated.

In *Terrorist,* the use adds nothing to the story line of the evolving and devolving affair between Jack and Teresa. The woman forces Jack to talk about hers, a sort of odd power play showing her dominant role in the relationship, reversing traditional power roles. "Tell me about my cunt, Jack," she says. "I want to hear it. Loosen up." However, when he derides the discussion as "grotesque," she lashes out, saying, "Why, you prim prick? You Jewish priss. What's grotesque about my cunt?" (160). The testy conversation continues, eventually devolving into the inevitable argument over commitment that takes place in the midst of affairs.

Examining the section, however, one realizes that the exchange centered on Teresa's vagina could have been deleted and still maintained the same level of importance. The tension is not lessened if the offensive word is taken out. In some respects, actually, it would strengthen the exchange of emotions, since the word is not used, even by men in their 60s and women in their late 40s. It is a name that someone in the contemporary United States might call another person as a derogative remark, but it is not used as an erotic term or some kind of mangled pillow talk.

There are other odd, outdated terms that suggest Updike's fondness for them and insistence that they remain. In the previous scene, the argument leads to discussion about the fight after it ends. Jack and Teresa each mention that they hate it when they "quarrel," another old-fashioned word that is not commonly used in modern society (162). Instead, given today's fast-paced, technology-driven lifestyle and hyper-violent forms of mass culture that fills people's daily lives, when they argue, they use "fight." The word "quarrel" just does not sum up how people relate in a society built on sensationalism and emotion.

Another odd word choice occurs when Jack thinks about the 9/11 terrorists, who combined computer skills with religious fanaticism to form a new kind of threat. Thinking to himself, he complains, "Those *creeps* who flew the planes into the World Trade Center had good technical educations" (27, italics added). The use of "creeps" is interesting here, both as a counter to the stronger language used in the popular media to label the terrorists and due to the outdated word itself.

The watered-down notion of "creeps" is in stark contrast to President Bush himself and members of his administration calling terrorists "murderers," "killers," and other harsh names meant to persuade viewers and listeners to think of them in similar terms. "Creeps," rather than "murderers" or something similar suggests that Updike is asking the reader to soften his view. He may also be hinting that the novel takes place in a distant future where the strident rhetoric of the Bush administration is no longer relevant.

* * *

As these numerous examples demonstrate, sex is a complicated subject in Updike's work. When he dipped into relationships early in his career, readers found his frank scenes shocking (a notion that is kind of peculiar for contemporary readers numbed by cable television, the Internet, and film). This jolt, however, had a silver lining of sorts, transforming him into the bard of the American middle-class bedroom. The more graphic the better, which spurred more people to buy his novels.

For authors, even among those considered in the handful of the best in the world, sales equal power—the clout to write about whatever one chooses. Updike's sex books sold amazing numbers: *Rabbit, Run* nearly 2 million copies by 1996 and *Couples* some 4.4 million (Knopf). Examining what went on in the nation's bedrooms, behind the closed curtains of a noontime tryst or among husbands and wives playing with the idea of finding themselves by exploring the body of another, made Updike wealthy. He did not want to be typecast as merely a best-selling male novelist who writes about sex, but the nod to best-selling status much be acknowledged as important for him as an artist and professional.

Updike continued to shock his fans—some of his sex scenes grew more detailed, while others used language and description that drew attention for either working well or not working at all for readers and critics. But change lurked underfoot. The very notion of sex changed as the decades progressed, which troubled the novelist. Mingling sex with death rattled Updike. In 2005, he described the twenty-first-century United States as a place foreign in his mind. His America remained the semirural one of the early 1950s, not a place where "sex without condoms is flirting with death by AIDS" (*Higher* 470). It is as if sex and sexuality are pillars in Updike's worldview, foundational ideas that got blasted away while no one was looking. The change held deep ramifications.

American sexuality—so often repressive, calling back to our Puritan roots—remains a central theme, whether considered from a political perspective (e.g., religious conservatives demanding an end to funding for women's health clinics) or a cultural one (females of all ages wearing tight, tiny clothing that expose as much skin as possible). What Updike figured out early is that we do not have any answers to our sex problem in the United States, but we sure do want to know as much as we can about what is going on in other people's bedrooms.

Updike got out ahead of the zeitgeist and packaged sex up neatly for middle- and upper-middle-class readers. He gave them that look inside the medicine cabinet that reality television has provided viewers for the last 20 years and the Internet accelerates via blogs, pictures, and the shameless self-satisfaction and me-centered displays posted on Facebook. That Updike grasped this transformation out of the air and rode if across the decades, in some senses, validates his decision early on to focus on the people around him, in some ways like him, and those that toiled to simply live a fulfilling life.

CHAPTER 7

Rabbit Lives and Dies

> The past, Proust pointed out, is Paradise. We cannot help revisiting Paradise, and the writer has his own magic carpet woven of words to take him there. I feel nostalgic about almost everything I have experienced—people I knew, brand-name products I consumed, movies I saw, books I once read, certain tints of weather that return to me unexpectedly. It is marvelous, to have lived, and the longer one lives the more marvelous it seems.
> —John Updike, from a 2005 interview

It is a hot July day and I am standing on a dark, wooden boardwalk with my wife and seven-year-old daughter. Less than 10 feet away is the cliff of a 65-foot waterfall. We watch as the water slides almost lazily over the sandstone shelf and drops to the bottom. That water had no sense of the chaos it would shortly become as it transformed into a light mist and white-water blend. From high above, we watch the plunge and resulting crash, and a dizzying sense of vertigo takes hold. At the bottom of the gorge where the water from Brandywine Falls churns is layer upon layer of Bedford and Cleveland shale. This soft rock, which forms the base of the falls, is some 350 to 400 million years old.

Losing myself in the giddy view of water crashing downward and sunlight filtering through the mist, I think of Updike and how he routinely captures moments like these in his work. What might he think, standing here looking down on nature's creation—the same perspective God might have—earthward and eternal?

At the base of Brandywine Falls, the shale itself is bewitching. The difficulty of contextualizing hundreds of millions of years is more or less beyond the mind's eye. History's timeline is so vast that it jumbles into a set of mostly incomprehensible numbers. Then, again, I think of Updike, exposing what so many consider the so-called mundane aspects of life, recognizing the timelessness in how human beings interact with one another. That nondescript rock, even from a short distance blending into one uniform site, holds a past, a present, and a future. The shale forms a foundation for so much beauty, yet is nothing more than rock.

Looking more specifically at Rabbit Angstrom, Updike's most famous creation, I pull the fictional character along in my mind and consider his timelessness. It is impossible, though, to think 400 million years ahead, but if American literary history as we now know it is stretched out, like two ends of a rubber band, only a handful of characters achieved iconic status: Hester, Huck, Gatsby, Lolita, and Rabbit. As James A. Schiff explains, Updike created a uniquely American story that "embraces and celebrates, rather than denigrates, his country." Updike's ability, Schiff says, to "give the mundane its due," enables us to take his work for granted, just as we underestimate the shale's role in the beauty of the falls ("Other Writers").

I use Brandywine Falls and its intriguing rock formations as a way to discuss big history with my daughter, examine the far reaches of our comprehension, and consider how we might make sense out of it all. Then, I think about how appreciative I am that Updike has presented us with life as life through Rabbit. Like that shale foundation, Rabbit has a past, a present, and a future for readers.

Rabbit's Transformations

Rabbit's ostensible evolution over the course of the tetralogy is a sore spot for certain readers. For some critics, it seems the main character's viewpoints and thoughts too closely mirror his creator's. That is, Updike drifts in and out of playing Rabbit . . . or perhaps it is vice versa. In the face of this assessment, though, the obvious question confronting the series seems to center on whether or not an American male living in roughly the same time frame would or could have transformed as Rabbit did. Over the course of his fiction life, Rabbit essentially transformed from a profoundly immature 20-something in *Rabbit, Run* to the somewhat wiser, yet still self-centered and reckless, individual at the center of *Rabbit at Rest*.

Certainly, Harry grew over the course of the books, but also contained dichotomies. For example, Rabbit holds contrasting ideas about racism against blacks and Jews, despite his experiences with black history as experienced in *Rabbit, Redux*. Is it conceivable that an average

American like Harry Angstrom could undergo such a lifetime's worth of metamorphosis? While this author sees transformation, some scholars find the final Harry portrayed in *Rabbit at Rest* less than satisfying, which adds ambiguity to any kind of overall evaluation of the character.

Charles Berryman, for example, explains, "his conduct in the final volume tends to match the nihilism of his thought that 'nothing matters very much,' together with its equal, 'we'll all soon be dead.' . . . Any reader who has followed the adventures of Rabbit for more than fifteen hundred pages is apt to feel at least a bit disappointed by the banality of his end" (20).

Others find, however, that there is more at play on the topic than meets the eye. Scholar Matthew Wilson claims:

> Updike transforms Rabbit from the traditional solitary American male character fleeing society and women as representatives of that society to a man integrated into society and surrounded, almost comically, by women; the final novel, *Rabbit At Rest*, transforms him again into a man isolated from his family and society, but his isolation is not a return to an earlier mode of being because Harry has developed an almost acute historical consciousness. (6)

A commentator, naturally, might retort that the more important issue is whether Rabbit developed a historical worldview, or if this is simply a case of Updike intruding into the character's universe. Given the decades-long sweep of the tetralogy, Updike's role as both a historian and fiction writer must be evaluated.

Critic D.T. Max reasons that Updike's "special genius," which propels the Rabbit novels and his other work, "is that he has the disposition to fulfill the roles of novelist and social historian" (249). Certainly, Rabbit's historical sense could be viewed as too finely tuned, and nothing more than an intrusion by Updike. Yet are not historical markers how people determine their own place in the world? The "where were you when . . ." question helps people understand their lives in context with the eras in which they live, the past built around family and family stories, and the broader sweep of American history. Max explains, "Updike's novels give us a view of our times as rich, human and entertaining as they really were. He can create a wholly satisfying fictional universe and tell us about our own, taking us on an inner and outer journey at once" (249). The fact that Rabbit captains this historical ship does not make him a mere hologram of Updike. Better, the character provides Updike a way to talk about American culture and society the way the people all around us actually experience it, whether agony and pain or happiness and contentment.

Perhaps more intriguing is the change in Rabbit, not necessarily as an amateur or observant social historian, but rather when one tackles the novels from the standpoint of a provincial young adult forced into the wider world (or like the Forrest Gump character, aimlessly bumping up against history and his times, which he usually does not comprehend). Contextually, as the world flattened over the course of the second half of the twentieth century, it seems more than necessary for Rabbit's worldview to broaden simultaneously. Whether or not he would have preferred to let the world into southeastern Pennsylvania, globalization forced the world in regardless.

For example, while the first novel is hyper-focused on the confines of Brewer and the small, nearby Pennsylvania towns, Rabbit's physical and mental future takes him far from the hills of his home state. Although he spent time in Texas in the army, when he returns to Brewer, he recalls the enemy being the local high schools he played against as a basketball star. Rabbit's view of the world does not extend much beyond several adjacent counties, shrinking actually to fit his depressed mood as his spirit deflates.

As Rabbit ages and becomes a productive member of society—rich, even—he begins to move around the country more freely, which replicates the upper middle-class experience for Americans nationwide in those later decades. Rabbit, for example, finds that his youthful vision of Florida as a kind of Valhalla is a mirage, but at least he gets there. He finds certain happiness in the routines established in the Sunshine State retirement condo community, but eventually he feels trapped by the smallness of his life there.

In *Rabbit Is Rich*, financial success and admiration from the community combine to change Harry. That old sense of self-worth returns, which has been starved since he last felt adulation from worshiping crowds as a high school basketball star. As a result, Rabbit takes on an air of authority. He is viewed as a town leader. With that new position (after decades of living a third-rate life), he assumes the mantle of social critic and commentator.

In contemporary America, this kind of transformation has less to do with a strong sense of historical consciousness and is more a factor of money and influence. Small towns across the country are filled with similar families and individuals, who actively construct a power base built on business acumen. Harry inherits his power from "old man" Springer via Janet's new ownership of the car lot. In turn, these kinds of local leaders climb the social hierarchy, make the right charitable donations, run civic organizations, hold political offices, and take other steps to solidify their place at the top of the food chain. The shiny business card, sparkly new car, country club membership, and an increasingly conservative outlook are the status symbols that the newly powerful Harry instinctively grabs.

Watching 175-plus entities float by in the 2012 July Fourth holiday parade in small-town Stow, Ohio, I could not help but think about Harry leading the parade as Uncle Sam in *Rabbit at Rest*. While there were the expected marching bands, Girl Scout floats, and civic groups present, the overwhelming number of participants comprised a virtual phalanx of city, county, and regional politicians. Convertible after convertible showcased a 40-something running for county auditor or the 60-year-old, multi-term councilman up for reelection in the fall elections. This seemed to me a quintessential Updikean moment that revealed a community (one of countless like it nationwide) full of Harry Angstroms.

Harry's transformation over the course of the Rabbit novels, despite the grumpy analysis of a handful of critics who think Updike oversteps his authorial bounds, is essential in defining what it means to be an American in the late twentieth century. Rabbit's moves mirror and respond to the way the nation itself undergoes constant sociopolitical and economic change. Rabbit must respond to the world around him, which is a vastly different place in each book. Thematically, according to Donald J. Greiner, Updike alters his everyman to parallel how aging and culture change people over time: "Questing in the first novel, mired in the second, he is secure and almost smug in the third. Life can be good in the middle forties with golf partners ready on Saturday and a wife who has never looked better" (*Novels* 89). Rather than view Rabbit's transformations as Updike's tidy packaging of his own thoughts and opinions, one should examine how people like the fictional character faced the extreme changes wrought by the contemporary world. The Rabbit tetralogy is then seen as a quest toward some epic vision of the American Dream by an ordinary man who stumbles toward the sketchy ideal of what may constitute a life well lived.

Rabbit Dies

Young Rabbit Angstrom listens as Keds "snap" and watches as the ball clanks off the "crotch" of the rim at the opening of *Rabbit, Run*. Thirty years later, an overweight Harry, on a self-imposed exile in Florida, lumbers, playing one-on-one with a black kid 40 years younger, shooting at a bent, beaten-up basket. Yet stars have a feel for the game. Despite his flagging heart and old man's body, the ball finds the hole. He plays on, ignoring the desperate distress signals his body sends out. If this were a film, the audience would be yelling "stop" at the screen. Harry, though, keeps it up, through the pain.

The inevitable collapse takes place as Rabbit "bursts from within." The narrator informs the reader, though, that the boy "catches the ball on its fall through the basket" (506). Rabbit may or may not have realized that the game would cost him his life, but he won. That ball dropping through the basket served as both a final exclamation point and a return to an earlier era. He made his last shot, just like countless superstitious players all over the world, essentially admitting that you cannot die without having made the final one.

Although the basketball game and concluding scene in the hospital where Harry dies bring *Rabbit at Rest* to a fitting close, it is after his solo flight to Florida that Updike reveals the deep-rooted nature of Rabbit's character. Finally making the trip by himself, which he bumbled on his initial run decades earlier, Harry enters the Sunshine State in off-season, when the other snowbirds are all with their families up north. Being alone allows him to piece together ideas about his life and circumstances. Although this section of the novel is one that critics could call Updike out for slipping in too easily, there is a summation aspect that needs made and Harry (alone) has the breathing space to think, despite his uneasiness with life's silent, slow moments.

Women and their roles in Rabbit's life fill much of his thinking. Running into a female neighbor in the condo hallway, he realizes, "All his life seems to have been a journey into the bodies of women" (468). Later, he cannot help calling Janice back in Pennsylvania, even though he tells himself he won't and calls her a list of familiar names, like "dumb mutt," and internally chastises her for attempting to run everyone's lives (469). In this era before the ubiquitous cell phone attached to one's hip, there is no answer, which alternatively makes Harry angry and self-pitying.

What scares Harry more than the silence of his time alone in Florida with his wife and the rest of his family back north is the creeping doubts that slip into his mind about what his life has meant. Unlike his younger days, he does not talk about spirituality, God, or the elusive *it* he once yearned to discover. Now, Rabbit looks inward and down, like a rabbit searching for a place to nest. Cautiously, he determines, "His whole life seems . . . to have been unreal, or no realer than the lives on TV shows, and now it's too late to make it real, to be serious, to reach down into the earth's iron core and fetch up a real life for himself" (469). Rabbit no longer wishes to look up to the heavens for answers; his life has proven to him that such answers (and prayers) go unnoticed.

To emphasize these points, Updike uses late 1980s popular culture as bookends to contextualize Harry's earthward thinking. Prior to the internal argument, Harry attempts to pass the time by watching television, which leaves him restless. Really, though, this state is more closely akin to depression. The television families epitomized by reruns of *The Cosby Show* and *Roseanne* leave him despondent. The zaniness of these unreal lives vectors too sharply with his own, which deteriorates into "nothing at all but boredom and a lost feeling, especially when you get up in the morning and the moon is still shining and men are making noisy bets on the first tee" (468). Harry is not interested in participating anymore and it turns him fretful—a rabbit more caught than ever, the net feeling more and more like a noose at each new sunrise. He spends his days ever more lonely, eating frozen meals and searching the cable channels for "something worthy to kill time with" (470).

Harry's descent into depression and slide toward death are foreshadowed by the second part of the popular culture bookend—his/Updike's lengthy commentary on the violence and hopelessness that flashes across one's screen, like rapidly flipping channels with the remote. Harry sees danger all around him and proclaims: "this time of year is full of violence," which he lists, including an impending hurricane and a cop who kills his own dog with a crowbar (469). Updike's explicit descriptions amplify Rabbit's own angst and feelings of desolation.

There is no longer a road home for Rabbit. Although he cannot admit it to himself, he needs Janice, but feels that her silence from Pennsylvania means that she will never forgive him the elicit affair with Pru, his daughter-in-law. Without his Janice—his symbolic heart—Harry obsesses over each beat of his real battered, drained heart. He thinks, "[T]here is a nest of purple slithering half-dead thoughts he cannot bear to put his face in. There is a whole host of goblins, it turns out, that Janice's warm little tightly knit body . . . protected him from" (472). As the time lapses without her, Harry's heartbeat grows weaker. She is not there to monitor him, watch the foods he eats, or talk through his anguish. The search for action leads him to the dilapidated court in the black section of town and to his ultimate demise.

What I read in this seminal moment of *Rabbit at Rest* is Updike's tribute to the power of women, particularly Janice. She is the one, it turns out, who serves as the foundation of the tetralogy, growing into a new character that still has doubts and frailties, but soldiers onward.

By contrast, Harry remains the rabbit, skittering though life avoiding nets and entrapment. Yet the critics who heaped heated scorn at Updike for the lack of growth in female characters sit on their hands, instead of admitting that their initial readings may have led to hasty evaluations.

Rabbit's Ghost

In 2000, as he had at the start of each of the preceding four decades, Updike returned to literature's most enduring character, producing *Licks of Love*, a book of short stories that contained a sequel to the tetralogy: "Rabbit Remembered." Prior to publication, as marketing buzz escalated, some observers and critics wondered whether the author would reveal that Rabbit somehow survived the heart attack on the hot pavement of the Florida basketball court at the end of *Rabbit at Rest*.

While many readers would have welcomed another dose of Rabbit on the page, Updike instead carried the saga forward, focusing on the survivors. As a matter of fact, Updike called the former possibility a "violation, a contradiction of *Rabbit at Rest*'s final, promissory word, 'Enough.' . . . a jimmying-open of a closed box" (*Due* 643). Instead, Updike focused, more or less, on the ghost of Rabbit and how such ethereal beings influence the world after death. Furthermore, although Updike's readers might have coveted more Rabbit, critics reacted coolly to the collection. One reviewer likened it to the popular soap opera *Days of Our Lives*, instead calling the novella "Hares of Our Lives" and criticizing its characters for not "growing and developing . . . Their lives are as meaningless as they have found themselves to be" (Curran 150). Other commentators find the story itself too upbeat. Scholar Peter J. Bailey, for example, says, "the novella occasionally runs the risk of overachieving plot consonances and of thereby trivializing the tetralogy it sequelizes" (220–21).

Updike, however, clearly reveled in returning to the aftermath of Rabbit's death and the Brewer landscape he knew so well. This chapter's epigraph, for example, points to the author's nostalgic feelings about his Pennsylvania boyhood region, the locale of "Rabbit Remembered." Even though the area has not aged well, Updike approaches it with not only a mix of nostalgia and warmth, but also a bit of trepidation.

One might counter the unenthusiastic critics, however, by focusing on what the relationship means to the larger novel cycle. The virtual rebirth that takes place through the reconciliation of Annabelle (Rabbit's long-lost illegitimate daughter) and Nelson (his much-maligned son) symbolizes a brighter day on the horizon for Brewer/Reading. The hope they carry into the future together as brother and sister may in some respects double for Updike's wish that America's small cities might too survive.

The story also brings the siblings together to demonstrate that they are able to live on and grow despite the family problems they endured. In commenting about this new relationship, Updike had the spirit world and its sway in mind, saying, "Rabbit's ghost presides, not quite palpably, over this long-deferred meeting of his children" (*Due* 644). While containing physical and psychological traits inherited from their father, as an adult, each child is able to overcome Rabbit's ghost. Furthermore, it is via their new lives as siblings that they can find inner peace, overcoming their internal demons. The relationship promises the joy that they never had with their shared father.

Updike's joy in writing the novella also shows in the way he tied up various loose ends, even returning to reexamine many marginal characters. For an author as preoccupied with the subject of death for many, many years, writing the novella may have also served as a kind of a final exclamation point on the tetralogy. Updike later explained it as a process of putting final words to paper: "packing my bag, it may be; at least my desk, as I write these words, is otherwise ominously clean" (*Due* 644). The finality of "Rabbit Remembered" meant something to its author. He explains, "In *Licks of Love* the details are lit by love, love for what we can no longer have" (*Higher* 469). Later, in 2005, answering questions posed by a French publication, Updike says, "I did feel . . . happy . . . to be back in Rabbit's territory, even with my hero only haunting it . . . I loved watching Annabelle and Nelson get together . . . riding with them into the new millennium . . . in the shell of a once thriving small-city downtown" (*Higher* 470).

The notion of survivors or surviving is apt in describing what is left of the Angstrom clan, now that its heart (and head) has been felled. At the onset of the story, Updike quickly fills the reader in on the 10-year interval, relaying weighty information: Janice is now "Janice Harrison," married to Rabbit's nemesis Ronnie; Nelson lives with them in the long-suffering Springer family home; and Pru and the children left him and returned to Ohio. The scene begins with Annabelle, an odd, young woman appearing at the door, claiming to be Rabbit's illegitimate daughter with Ruth (Leonard) Byer.

Although the link in the peculiar family reunion between Janice (who is no longer an Angstrom) and Annabelle (who never was) is not ascertained right away, Updike sprinkles the meeting with details that clue the reader into her true identity. Physically, Annabelle mirrors Ruth, full-figured and broad, with similar hair, "raggedly short . . . mixed of light-brown and darker-brown and gray strands." Strains of Rabbit also filter in her demeanor and language. Thus, Janice finds "something pleasant and kind and calm about the girl." When talking about Ruth's recent death, Annabelle explains that her mother "didn't like hospitals, they made her feel penned up," words one could imagine Rabbit using (180).

Dedicated Rabbit followers will find significant transformation throughout the sequel, particularly as Janice develops. On one hand, she is still self-centered, thinking, that Annabelle's appearance is an "innocently disgusting intrusion" bound to "disturb her peace." For her, life is different: "With Ronnie being so steady compared to Harry, she has known peace" (182). When she thinks about her former husband, though, she still swoons a bit and even develops a rationale for the appalling way they treated one another.

Ten years with nothing but memories of Rabbit has softened the sharp edges of their actual lives together. "She can't think any more that Harry was all to blame for their early troubles," she thinks, "He had been just trying life on too: life and sex and making babies and finding out who you are." By contrast, her time with Ronnie, she finds, "Second marriages were lighter. You just expect a little companionship, a little fun that harms no one else" (195).

Janice has changed, but the process is not complete, nor does it move into the realm of absurdity. Updike deftly reveals depth in Janice merely hinted at in the earlier novels, but she still retains consistency. At times she is still obtuse and drinks too much, yet she has toughened too. She is haunted by Rebecca June's long-ago death and her careless parenting of Nelson, but finds strength in the ensuing journey.

Rebecca June

The Everyman Library's publication of the complete tetralogy, *Rabbit Angstrom,* provides today's readers the opportunity to swallow the series whole (though an imposing 1,500 pages), rather than in 10-year increments, like when initially published, something like the current craze of buying a complete television season on DVD for a specific show to watch straight through, rather than in each weekly installment. What emerges from such a reading of the tetralogy is the powerful influence Rebecca June's death has on Rabbit and his immediate family.

While some current or future readers might question the authenticity of using such a tragic episode as a plot device, in the late 1950s and early 1960s, accidental childhood death in the United States stood as a national problem of epic proportions, particularly when compared with other first-world nations. In 1960, for example, the number of accidental childhood deaths in the United States reached 30.1 per 1,000 live births. Despite the technological superiority the United States prided itself on, 10 years later, the figure only dropped to 25.7, larger than Ireland (23.4), the United Kingdom (21.8), France (19.2), and Japan (17.8). In 2010, the number declined to 6.7, yet that still ranks the United States 42nd in the world in the category. Given Updike's penchant for research and broad reading habit, it is entirely probable that he drew the idea for the baby's death from research (Rajaratnam; World Bank). Like so many times in his career, Updike seemingly drew upon a crystal ball for source material and found a topic applicable to his fiction.

What has not been emphasized enough in Updike scholarship pertaining to the Rabbit novels is the way the baby's death haunts Rabbit for the rest of his life. From my reading, it seems as if Rebecca June's presence takes hold of Rabbit and becomes the most important force in his life, in some ways replacing his self-image as a basketball star or forcing it to the side. In *Rabbit at Rest,* for example, some mental reference to his daughter takes place on a daily basis and influences everything else around him, whether it is his relationship with his living offspring, Nelson, or his young grandchildren.

One of the many successes in the Rabbit series is Updike's depiction of the debilitating consequences of accidental child death. The loss of his daughter reveals to Rabbit that the elusive *it* he searched for in discussions with Reverend Eccles and on the golf course in *Rabbit, Run* does not exist. In *Rabbit at Rest,* a much older Rabbit thinks, "when he went back to the apartment alone there was still this tubful of tepid gray water that had killed her. God hadn't pulled the plug. It would have been so easy for Him, Who set the stars in place. To have it unhappen . . ." (10). In the same novel, as Rabbit lay dying, Janice is overcome with emotion at the sight of him in the hospital full of wires. The only grief she can equate it to is the loss of Becky: "a crashing wave of sorrow and terrified awareness of utter loss like nothing ever in her life except the time she accidently drowned her own dear baby" (510).

In her brief life, Rebecca June served as Rabbit's *it,* the one thing outside of basketball that was "first-rate." Her demise becomes the central fulcrum in Rabbit's unconscious and the reason why he cannot find fulfillment. The baby's death is a dark cloud permanently hanging over this little clan, frequently permeating their innermost thoughts and haunting Rabbit and Janice as they struggle to cope with life afterward.

My Only Friend, the End

What do we make of Harry "Rabbit" Angstrom after some 1,500 published pages at the dawn of five sequential decades? It may seem like a bit of a cop-out, given the complexity and length of the reader's journey with Rabbit through the rise and fall of the American Century, but there is no quick answer. We are simply to wrestle with Rabbit, use the character as a kind of compass for interpreting our lives and the lives of those around us, and then move on.

As readers, we ingest Rabbit, devouring his significance through analysis of ourselves and absorbing what we can via intense, close reading and experience gained from the long journey via the written word. In a 1997 interview with Charlie Rose, Updike discussed his journey with Rabbit, explaining, "people really loved that character." Yet to stay true to the story and character, he had to have Rabbit die: "That is my duty as a novelist, to see him through. I thought that kind of man might come to an early end" ("Interview").

Rabbit is not a dry run, print version of Homer Simpson, just some oafish buffoon whose existence is meant to simply parody the ills of modern society. Updike's character, though at times seeming a cousin of the cartoon patriarch, demands that we address the complexities and tribulations of a society lurching forward without a map toward the future or a sound memory of the past. Though the use of present tense from a writer's perspective propels the narrative forward, Rabbit has a nostalgic, yet shockingly strong sense of the past. As we have discussed, baby Becky is an anchor tied to Rabbit's neck, keeping death lurking at every corner. He cannot escape the past, despite today's agony, ecstasy, wealth, or sex.

Updike rejoiced in the totality of the Rabbit universe and in his role as creator (and destroyer), explaining, "This is a man's life; a life ends." As for his own part, he told Rose, "Writers are cruel. Authors are cruel. We make and we destroy." Yet every fictional character takes on some real form when he or she appears in print. Updike acknowledges this fuzzy line between fiction and reality, declaring, "I loved him, he was good to me. He was a brother to me and a good friend. He opened me up. As a writer I could see things through him that I couldn't see through by any other means" ("Interview").

In creating a realistic character in Rabbit, Updike had to see him through, and the end could not be easy, though it is given a heavy dose of grace via Updike's lyrical prose. In other words, according to James A. Schiff, Rabbit chose to live a certain narcissistic life that "has gotten him into trouble, and ultimately there will be a price to pay for his self-indulgence" (*Revisited* 58). The teenage boy that Harry challenges to a game of one-on-one that ultimately takes his life is nicknamed Tiger. The lonely Rabbit meets his end at the hands of a stronger, younger predator. He wins the game, but loses his life.

One can almost imagine a picture of Updike, sitting alone in his office, multiple desks, a typewriter, a computer, stacks of page proofs and books that must be reviewed, conferring with Rabbit. They huddle together, like men do when they are concentrating and onto subjects demanding privacy and care. Perhaps Rabbit is whispering parts of his story in Updike's direction, gesticulating a bit when making an apt point. Updike, demur, serves as confidante and counsel. The subject is sage; the author is interpreter, creator, and friend. This is Updike saying: here is a life, an American life in full. Yes, a life.

CHAPTER 8

Between Writer and Reader: Updike as Critic

> I never set out to be an essayist or critic. My mother didn't raise me to be one. My notion of being a writer was that you write the stuff—fiction, poetry, whatever; you invent and you don't waste your energy on criticism. But then when I began to receive criticism in the press, it seemed to me that I could do better than this.
> —John Updike, 2001

In November 2007, *The Atlantic* celebrated its 150th anniversary with a special cover story assessing "The Future of the American Idea." The collection of essays featured an all-star cast of writers, scientists, public intellectuals, and politicians. Befitting his place as the nation's leading essayist/literary critic, Updike launched the short vignettes, basing his idea on the "individual," the collective people who are trusted to "act in their own enlightened self-interest, with a necessary respect for others." Empowering people through individual liberty, Updike claims, is what will guide the nation as it deals with the multitude of threats posed by those outside the American system. It is no surprise that his reading of the ideas central to the nation revolve around "buoyancy, good nature, and mutual tolerance of its people," since these tenets also describe the author as both a literary and a cultural critic ("The Individual" 14).

Updike outlines his thinking regarding how one should go about writing reviews and other essays in the 1975 collection *Picked-Up Pieces*. During his first two decades as a critic, the author created an internal "code of reviewing" that included understanding an author's intention, quoting from the work enough to give the prospective reader a sense of its style, describing the book through quotation, not giving away the ending, and attempting to understand why a book failed, if it did so, within the author's entire body of work. Summing up his thoughts, Updike explains, "The communion between reviewer and his public is based upon the presumption of certain possible joys of reading, and all our discriminations should curve toward that end" (*Picked-Up* 14).

This chapter provides a closer examination of Updike's nonfiction and essays, particularly in the new millennium. In some respects, I hope that it stimulates further work on the author's catalog in these areas, similar to the call James A. Schiff made in *John Updike Revisited,* titling a chapter: "Updike Ignored: The Contemporary Independent Critic." Schiff's book is the starting point for an explanation for why Updike's nonfiction has not received relatively much consideration through the 1991 collection *Odd Jobs.* William H. Pritchard also addresses the challenge in *Updike: America's Man of Letters* (2000). Now that the total number of nonfiction works has topped out at 11—through 2011's posthumous *Higher Gossip*—perhaps scholars will now turn to the essays, reviews, and personal pieces with more determination.

Updike as Critic

Submerged in Updike's nonfiction, the reader is happily pummeled by waves of fulfilled intellectual curiosity. The overpowering, almost shockwave concussion, rocks one to the bones and reverberates around a seemingly simple question: is there anything Updike did not *know*? By *know,* I mean more than just possessing the raw ability to write about a topic authoritatively. Instead, Updike leaves the reader with the impression that he might just be the first person to ever chew over a given issue.

At the end of a nonfiction piece, whether a rumination on one of his literary contemporaries or impressions of an afternoon yearning for transcendence on the golf course, one is left stunned, full, thankful, and perhaps on the path toward intellectual exhaustion. Quite often, a reader might simply conclude, "there is nothing more I can learn about this subject."

Ironically, despite the general familiarity with Updike's nonfiction among critics and the general public, no one has tackled the 11 books of essays and criticism (as of early 2013) with the vigor that scholars have investigated his fiction, though various academics have called for a deeper examination, including Schiff, Pritchard, and Donald Greiner. While one imagines a legion of American literature doctoral students at this very moment plodding through the millions of nonfiction words Updike produced, the likelihood of that scenario is far-fetched.

Currently, Updike does not seem particularly hot as an academic topic in English departments, either among faculty or within graduate student populations. The trend is toward more seemingly cutting-edge topics, such as queer studies, diversity, multiculturalism, cultural studies, and the like. Nor is the single-author study much appreciated, both factors keeping Updike's nonfiction work in the background. His complexity, audacious scope, and brilliant style are not enough to draw young scholars or graduate students to his work in the numbers that it should: maybe for no other single reason than that to get the once-in-a-lifetime tenure track position or tenure, the aspiring student and scholar must do scholarly research that fellow academics will judge as valuable. If Updike is mostly outside this circle, then his long-term reputation might flag.

Personally, although divulging such ideas reveals my own bias, I believe that one could center his or her academic career solely on Updike's essays and criticism. These scholarly days would be spent gleefully and happily churning through the mountains of insight, wit, and analysis the author produced over his 50-plus year career. At the end of that work, however, I think one could forcibly make the case that Updike is the most important critic of the twentieth century. No one possessed the range Updike displayed on a regular basis.

Scholars who already study Updike and write about his work will not find my declaration of the writer's greatness as a critic and essayist outlandish, nor will those who have read clearly superior pieces, for example, the slim volume recently reissued by The Library of America: *Hub Fans Bid Kid Adieu* (2010). Making such a decisive claim, though, is backed by thousands of pages of prose that is consistently outstanding, from the earliest *New Yorker* essays collected in *Assorted Prose* to the posthumous *Higher Gossip*.

In comments about his nonfiction, Updike trod a typical self-deprecating path, labeling the work, "my daily exertions" (*Due* xvii). Even this seemingly unassuming phrase in itself, however, is a mini work of art. Doesn't *exertions* seem so fittingly Updike, in the way it slides off the page with that exuberant *x*? Then there are the mild to overt sexual overtones of daily exertions, in which the mind boggles with just what it is that he intimates by using those words.

It is as if the nonfiction pieces were Updike's mental exercises. He put himself through these paces to remain intellectually fit on one hand and make the money necessary to live on the other. Perhaps one could liken this to F. Scott Fitzgerald's need to pump out short stories for ready magazine markets to pay the bills and provide the time to work on novels. Fitzgerald, however, usually belittled this work, determining that many of the stories were subpar. While Updike hints at the nonfiction being merely freelance work, there is more to its role within his worldview as a writer.

The mocking tone Updike uses to discuss himself as an essayist and critic also veils how vitally important the essays and criticism were in his comprehension of himself as a writer. Updike loved words, the idea of being a writer, and getting into print. Otherwise, why would he have spent so much time contributing to minor publications, college reminisces, and revisiting his oeuvre via new introductions and forewords? The nonfiction flood that poured forth constituted Updike's efforts, in his words, "to enter in some guise into the mass of printed material that hung above the middle-browed middle class . . . like a vast cloud gently raining ink" (*Due* xvii).

In accepting the National Book Critics Circle Award in Criticism for *Hugging the Shore* (1983), Updike depreciates his skills, labeling himself, "a free-lance writer who writes on occasion about books, bringing to the task a rusty liberal-arts education, an average citizen's spotty knowledge of contemporary issues, and a fiction writer's childish willingness to immerse himself in make-believe" (*Higher* 421). The obvious question, despite Updike's self-deprecation, is what percentage of typical freelancers or "average citizens" get to publish in the *New Yorker* or any number of other lauded publications? Clearly, this part of Updike's writer persona served as a way for him to make sense of himself, because the common labels he applies in modesty are far from the lofty status of the artist that exists in the real world. One senses that something deeper was at work within Updike that necessitated this kind of downgrade of his fame.

Updike internalized the stated desire to be in print—which I have called elsewhere a mix of his commitment to professionalism and dedication to craft—to the point that it seemed more or less addictive. In analyzing Updike's rationale for so much critical work, James A. Schiff explains, "Of course where there is pleasure there is often compulsion or obsession: Updike appears driven, for whatever personal reason, to record his impressions of everything he reads, observes, and experiences" (*Revisited* 179).

Updike's boyhood dream of seeing his name in *The New Yorker* and following in the footsteps trod by other literary greats created in him a compulsion. It is as if the outpouring of words never ceased to amaze him, even after the words ran into the millions published across fiction, prose, and poetry. In his later years, Updike seemed almost surprised that old age did not slow him down. The ink never ran out, even at the end of his life. Since his death, there have also been a handful of posthumous works. Like all great writers, one imagines that there will be additional volumes of letters, story collections, and perhaps even some of his unpublished fiction in some form or another.

Style

Over a five-decade career, spanning millions of published words, there is an Updike literary style that readers immediately recognize. His technique is a mixture of visions—drawn from a range of influences, from his childhood dream of being a cartoonist to a fascination with flow, whether musical or in the fluidity of the golf swing.

While it may seem odd to discuss Updike, nonfiction, and style in the same sentence, since the reader usually encounters such terminology referring to his fiction, I believe that his nonfiction style is just as penetrating, thoughtful, and intentional. Quite frankly, it is impossible to imagine a linguistic stylist as deliberate in his use of language as Updike.

I tackle the notion of Updike's style at several points in this book, because it is a critical element in appreciating his oeuvre—a constant in his work, whether he wrote a postcard to a friend or a published essay at the request of a national or regional publication. Even when reading Updike's speeches, the commentator finds a certain Updikean lilt and turn of phrase that seems perfectly written. Using a baseball metaphor, perhaps style in some ways is similar to a batter's swing. The bat is merely a tool to hit the baseball, and anyone can fool around with it. Yet it is the way the mind works and the body responds that determines success. Anyone can swing a bat; it takes an expert to hit major league pitching. From this perspective, Updike's style is as beautiful as the swing of his hero Ted Williams.

Over and over again, interviewers attempt to get at the heart of Updike's style, and one can almost sense his frustration in pulling the words together to do so, too much of a stately Pennsylvanian and reserved New Englander to demur. In an interview conducted in the mid-1980s, Updike likened writing to creating ideas and characters "fitting" together, "a kind of music that the images make together" (Plath, *Conversations* 185). Sensing the musicality and visual aspects of Updike's work enables the reader to gain a broader understanding of the linkage between content and literary device. The musicality of his written work connects his prose and fiction as a kind of glue or the dark matter that holds together events between the pages that take place in the reader's imagination as it interacts with the writer's words.

The words themselves are not haphazard. As a matter of fact, one cannot imagine a writer more exacting with word choice than Updike. Taking this notion at face value, however, forces one to then examine single words and short phrases as deliberate devises that propel the writer's voice. There is also a competing sense that Updike simply could not explain how he crafted such beautiful prose.

For better or worse, many commentators contend that Updike's most enduring feature is his style, particularly in his fiction. In the late 1980s, for example, literary scholar Harold Bloom based an entire book of criticism on this notion. However, unlike the general (and nearly universal) praise heaped on Ernest Hemingway and F. Scott Fitzgerald for creating their own unique literary voices, critics do not arrive at a consensus regarding Updike. A review of academic and general criticism finds some individuals praising Updike for his ability to write lyrical prose, with words that seem to dance off the page and phrases that evoke new ways of interpreting life's most minute details. Others, however, believe that Updike's style serves as camouflage that masks otherwise empty plotlines. These critics essentially invoke the old adage: "all sizzle, no steak."

This opposing viewpoint is reflected in the well-known *John Updike* volume in the "Modern Critical Views" series edited by Bloom. Famously, Bloom set the tone for years of ensuing Updike criticism, labeling the author, "A minor novelist with a major style" who "hovers always near a greatness he is too shrewd or too diffident to risk" (7). Several of the essays in the collection drive home the same general point.

It is interesting to note, though, that Joyce Carol Oates and Cynthia Ozick, two fellow fiction writers and cultural critics, are much more evenhanded in their assessments published in Bloom's book. Could this indicate a divide between how fiction writers approach other fiction writers versus how academic critics examine them? Oates, for example, may be one of the few writers in the world as prolific, for as long a period, as Updike.

Furthermore, how does Updike's style in fiction relate to his nonfiction voice? From my perspective, it is difficult (if not impossible) to break one from the other. Perhaps the biggest difference is that fiction necessitates a certain risk-taking that is less obligatory in essays or criticism. Updike also imposed rules on himself as a reviewer, for example, that he would have never done (or at least not as blatantly) as a fiction writer.

Beauty

Crisp, insightful, and provocative, Updike's essays strike the same note found in his fiction and poetry. In me, that internal feeling is akin to a sense of rightness or otherworldly majesty. Searching for a way to describe his prose, I am drawn to sports analogies, since they are so often employed in describing a model of perfection.

Perhaps an apt comparison is with another famous New England legend—Larry Bird. The Boston Celtic's jump shot seemed to fly on a magical arc, lifting up softly from his fingers, hanging in midair, and then accelerating as it zipped down through the hoop. Updike's essays give the reader that same feeling of triumph, the fist pump after sinking a long putt for birdie or the *yes* exhaled when the hometown slugger knocks one out of the yard. Updike and Bird also shared a single-minded dedication to practicing their respective crafts, the work and sweat that the public does not seen, but takes place day after day.

As a literary critic and historian, Updike applies the same intensity to nonfiction that he used to drive his fiction. For example, in a foreword to Kirk Curnutt's *Coffee with Hemingway* (2007), Updike is able to convey the nation's literary grandmaster like few ever could. Updike writes about Hemingway:

- A sense of life's tragic brevity always lies beneath the surface of his taut dialogues and evocations of nature (*Higher* 74).

- The man was a bearish celebrity when literature still bred celebrities; his work remains a touchstone of artistic ardor and luminously clean prose (*Higher* 74).

Each of these sentences demonstrates Updike's ability to understand other writers. Then, he passes that analysis on to the reader. As a result, we feel the depth of Updike's skill as a literary critic, while simultaneously sensing that there is extra power here, since Updike may stand alongside an icon like Hemingway. As a scholar, Updike garners my esteem based on his deep, thoughtful reading of the text. One never gets the sense that he has shirked his responsibility via a cursory reading or not interrogated the work and its author earnestly.

In a 1988 speech assessing writer Raymond Carver reprinted in *Higher Gossip*, Updike strikes a note that speaks to Carver's brilliance and points to what all artists should strive to achieve. In summary, Updike explains that Carver's writing "[D]isplays the loftiest qualities: honesty of vision, integrity of workmanship, and a warm and humane desire to celebrate, to bring the news, as he himself expressed it, from one world to another, in a style that reveals 'the fierce pleasure we take in doing it'" (80).

In both the commentary on Hemingway and the words about Carver, Updike is at his literary best when examining the work of fiction's greats. As one artist to another, he understood the effort required to produce writing at this distinguished level. Thus, as a reviewer, he proffered the reader a glimpse inside the craftsman guild that most of them could never observe or even imagine. Some might even go as far as to claim that only a great artist with a deep sense of humanity can assess or evaluate the work of another creative luminary. No matter how much one studies fiction, the production of the kind of writing widely regarded as among the best is a space reserved for a small number of greats.

In the New Century

In *Due Considerations,* his last nonfiction collection published while he lived, Updike includes a short essay "My Philadelphia," written at the request of the editors of *Philadelphia* magazine, one of the hundreds of hyper-local or -regional tomes that fill a large corner of supermarket and bookstore racks around the nation. In the 1998 piece, the esteemed author recalls the great metropolis from the eyes of a small-town kid from far-away Shillington, "mostly a rumor from beyond the horizon" (667).

Ironically, many of Updike's readers come to his nonfiction from a similar vantage point. For them, his criticism, in many respects, represents an enormous (maybe even mystical) city located at a great distance from his novels and short story collections. When people who read literary criticism and prose literature either search out or stumble upon Updike's nonfiction, however, they soon realize that they are in the hands of a masterful and compassionate thinker. Whether the subject at hand is a new novel emerging from Russia, an exhibit at the Metropolitan Museum of Art, or a reappraisal of a long-dead great, in Updike's hands, the topic will be explored with grace, diligent research, contextual clarity, careful analysis, and stylish prose.

Taken as a whole, then, Updike's many books of collected prose represent the life's work of America's greatest literary critic. Yes, you read that correctly: the nation's preeminent literary critic—ever. While hints of this status have started to emerge from academics and journalists, it may take a big book on the collected works to make the case, since the whims of academe usually determine which artists wear such subjective crowns. Yet one can hardly deny the power of the millions of words and thousands of pages of published nonfictional prose that Updike produced over his lifetime.

Updike and September 11

In Updike's eyewitness account of the 9/11 terrorist attacks published in *The New Yorker,* the reader at once confronts the now-familiar Updike style: "Suddenly summoned to witness something immense and terrible, we keep fighting not to reduce it to our own smallness" (*Due* 117). On the surface, this one-sentence hook appears direct. On subsequent readings, though, the sentence virtually twists and crackles on the many hidden meanings contained within.

On one hand, there is the carefully chosen verbiage: "suddenly summoned," "immense and terrible," and "our own smallness." This delicate and playful, yet powerful, language is Updike's calling card, particularly among the magazine's readers quite familiar with the author's style. However, the sentence also reveals an interesting exploration of Updike's use of technique to suggest substance. For example, how does one read "suddenly summoned," without quickly wondering who it is exactly that is doing the summoning? Is it the "four-year-old girl and her babysitter" calling from "the [apartment] library" (*Due* 117), or is it Updike's feeling that some higher power summoned him personally to witness the carnage? Drawing on the latter, one could infer that in some manner Updike explains or rationalizes his entire career as extracting from divine intervention. Analyzing five decades of interviews with Updike, one consistently finds that he regards being a writer a profession, approaching it as if a trade position. Who then summons the craftsman to craft? For Updike, this question has (literally) loomed above his work from the start.

The second half of the sentence is just as cagey, first with the imprecise *we,* which could be the intimate audience of two—Updike and an individual reader—or the broader *we,* as in the American people. Furthermore, the *we* is "fighting not to reduce it to our own smallness," yet is not the most biting criticism of Updike's fiction that he is little more than a fancy navel-gazer, writing beautiful sentences about imaginary worlds that stretch no further than his own arm's reach?

This must be a counterpunch at that stable of Updike critics, for in the next sentence, the "we" transforms to "where I happened to be" (*Due* 117). As *we,* it appears that Updike is already watching the terrorist attacks through the eyes of a writer and possibly addressing critics who might appraise his interpretation. The turn to *I*, therefore, reveals that he is processing what he sees from the vantage of a writer and beginning to reduce the event to his own smallness—exactly what he worries about in the first part of the sentence.

Continuing, Updike's voice—which I argue that he uses seamlessly whether writing fiction or nonfiction—is as much an essential facet of the article as the events he addresses. The reader finds the following words and understands that this is Updike and could only be Updike: "at first glance, more curious than horrendous: smoke speckled with bits of paper curled into the cloudless sky . . . strange inky rivulets . . . burst into ballooning flame . . . as on television, this was not quite real" (*Due* 117). Anyone familiar with Updike's nonfiction realizes that the author is not capable of delivering a straight journalistic piece, nor would his *New Yorker* readers desire that from him. There is a relationship built between Updike and his audience, yes, and the foundation of that union is literary technique.

***

What Updike did as well as any critic writing in contemporary society (and perhaps ever) is to look at each book as a work of art. He then assesses it with care, even if he does not think it holds up to the work of art label. Scholar Morris Dickstein explores this notion, saying, "The test of a critic comes not in his ideas about art, and certainly not in his ideas about criticism, but in the depth and intimacy of his encounter with the work itself—not the work in isolation, but the work in its abundance of reference, richness of texture, complexity of thought and feeling" ("Rise" 64). Updike understands and respects the commitment necessary for a person to buy, read, and think about a book and the valuable role a reviewer plays in this potentially sacred exchange.

In both reviews and essays, Updike took great care in approaching, analyzing, and assessing his topic or work of art. As his reputation as a nonfiction writer grew, he also employed the same attention to his own writing, collecting ephemera that some readers would find extremely interesting, despite the potential that other critics might find it self-indulgent. Answering this challenge in *Due Considerations* (2007), Updike replies, "[W]here else would I put them, in final form? A drop of truth, of lived experience, glistens in each. They underline the personal note that all essays and criticism, even those lacking a single first-person pronoun, contain" (xxii). The author realized, even in the face of potential disapproval, that the craft of writing always called for a concurrent shedding of blood and sweat that made even the most innocuous work important. As a result, the interested reader who wants to dive into Updike's criticism can start at any point in the writer's career or, alternatively, go right to the end of these books, each since *Assorted Prose* containing a collection of Updike-specific material, from the self-interviews with Bech to the special forewords he wrote for limited edition printings of his fiction, poetry, and nonfiction.

Under any circumstances, however, Updike's nonfiction is a treasure trove for both readers and literary scholars. While Updike's status as one of America's greatest novelists might never be usurped by his standing as a critic and essayist, I believe that the key to understanding the writer is found in his nonfiction. What better key than the thousands of pages of collected work to plumb the depths of Updike's life and work?

CHAPTER 9

Master Storyteller

> Stories are meant, like other forms of writing or communications, to bring light. And a story justifies itself if it clarifies our own lives, even in a small detail; if it makes us see and feel any more sharply. I think that this sharper seeing, this extra vision which a writer brings, might work social change of a subtle sort.
>
> —John Updike, 2001

Commenting early in the new millennium about short stories, Updike emphasized several important words and phrases in the epigraph above: "light," "clarifies our own lives," "see," "feel," and "social change." These ideas about what writing can do—the power it possesses as a source of context and "subtle" modification in the reader's life—is central to reading Updike's short fiction.

Unlike some writers who thrive on bombastic plots or poke around in life's darker corners to find a way to connect with readers, Updike mastered a delicate balance of plot, characterization, dialogue, and emotion that left one slightly roughed over and forced to contemplate meanings, nuance, and transcendence. Updike's short stories display brilliant use of the form and demonstrate how a writer can move from addressing the personal or particular instance and then connect it to the most fundamental questions that plague us as people. Certainly, the finest stories selected from his catalog combine to rank him as one of the best at the craft to ever live.

An Updike aficionado who plans to capture the writer's particular brand of magic must make countless choices across many genres. These are serious concerns: what work to include and how much should or can be left untouched. Honestly, any attempt at comprehensive coverage is futile, certainly given the writer's own word count limits, which serves as a central facet of today's publishing business, not to mention the waning ability of contemporary readers to sit through book length collections. Attempts at breadth would take a lifetime's effort, not only in the deep dive required to analyze such powerful work, but also in terms of simply reading and rereading it all.

One certainly faces the challenge of climbing a Mount Kilimanjaro-like amount of work when appraising Updike's short fiction. Though he produced fewer stories in his last decade than earlier in his career, Updike is regarded as one of literature's very best short story writers. This chapter examines particular, representative pieces from Updike's approximately 17 volumes (there are potentially more that could spring to life based on additional posthumous collections).

One could literally spend an entire lifetime reading and analyzing Updike's short fiction, its various cycles and recurring characters, scenes, and outcomes. The recognition must also be made, though, that many academics have undertaken much of this work over many decades. Robert M. Luscher, for example, has provided Updike scholars and critics with masterful analysis of the author's short fiction.

As such, this chapter focuses on Updike's ideas about writing short stories and some of his recent work in that area, particularly since these pieces have received less scholarly attention. Close reading of Updike's short fiction provides insight into his craft—how he actually put words together on the page to evoke a particular feeling—focusing on literary technique, form, and the elusive notion of style that his admirers and critics both use to describe his writing. I end the chapter with an extended examination of the story "The Long Road" reprinted in the posthumous collection *My Father's Tears*, which I believe demonstrates much of the author's dynamic presence as a short story writer, while also addressing themes consistent across his entire career.

Torn from the Fabric of Your Own Life

Updike once recalled that his short stories were "composed really in a rather desperate fashion." He likened the grind to produce them to a sporting event, explaining that, "you show up on the field and hope something nice happens, but you're never sure it will." As in describing so much of his work, Updike took great pains to reveal that the production was never easy or simple. There is a cost—a price paid and risk taken for the creative process—as if one must open a vein or undergo some other painful form of bloodletting to achieve grace. Updike explains:

> It's torn from the fabric of your own life, often in what seems a perilous and even illicit way. But you're hoping to make out of the rubbish, the quotidian rubbish of your own life, a few objects that will somehow be worth examining and treasuring, as in archaeology, later. (*Updike in Cincinnati* 61)

Similarly, in January 1995, Updike proclaims:

> More closely than my novels, more circumstantially than my poems, these efforts of a few thousand words each hold my life's incidents, predicaments, crises, joys. Further, they made my life possible, for I depended when young upon their sale to supply my livelihood. (*More* 762)

For Updike, his life is central to the stories, ranging from the Pennsylvania boyhood to his later marriage troubles, travels around the world, and aging. While those critics who call for authors to take on many or all of society's challenges might deem the everyday aspects of such a middling life unworthy of close examination, it is in this endeavor that Updike uncovers the dignity of modern existence, even in its most sordid details.

There is something particularly magical in even the most commonplace, routine patterns of daily life. As a result, Updike's work demonstrates the complexity of an American era lived within a broader, multifaceted world. Rather than denigrate the common person, he celebrates the intricacies, interactions, and chaos that represents a lived life in the modern world. The gems hidden in the fields of these seemingly mundane daily rituals hold life's true beauty and grace. Updike took great care in unearthing all of life's mysteries.

In the future, what might surprise audiences that did not grow up reading Updike's work or engage with it while he lived is not only his ability to write so well for so long about aging in contemporary America, but also his ability to generate stellar work long after most writers might have lost their edge. Other writers choose to overlook age, many not imagining that their ideal readers age too. Some do not write about the subject as a central theme because they do not want to be deemed irrelevant by critics and their reading publics. As Updike himself so masterfully described in *Rabbit, Run*: the world focuses on those it deems coming up, not the ones being pushed out. There is no love lost for old people in the United States, ironically, even as the baby boomers grow older.

While we are pushing and pulling at topics and issues, clearly there is room for debate regarding Updike's late stories. Updike's critics may not agree with my general perception, especially since he wrote fewer and fewer short fiction pieces toward the end of his career. Yet in examining these works, one discovers wonderful links to themes, ideas, and characters that make the Updikean universe complete.

Scholar Robert M. Luscher explains that Updike's later short fiction, "reiterated the themes of art's potential transcendence over mortality" ("Marriage" 117). In his post-new millennium work, Updike not only created new ideas out of the societal transformation that took place as the United States lurched toward some new post-9/11 and post-hegemony status, but also simultaneously reexamined older ideas about his Pennsylvania boyhood and young adolescence that made the era of the 1950s come alive all over again.

Updike's oeuvre has exerted such a powerful spell on me personally as a reader (and I am sure many others steeped in its history) that I sometimes have difficulty making distinctions between its characters and their creator. The various novels and short stories have weaved into a unified universe. Like interlocking shapes that may seem blurry up close, but then gain perspective as one takes in the whole picture, Updike returns to ideas that time works over, engaging with topics that are fluid, like a landscape that may seem static, but is in fact always transforming. When I encounter a short story, I am relieved to find characters that seem like old friends.

There are also recurrent episodes that Updike readers will immediately identify in numerous stories that help the author reconfigure and reexamine topics across decades. As a result, readers notice that some characters in Updike stories:

- Are forced to live on farms by their mothers
- Live with their parents and grandparents
- Focus on how jittery and out-of-place fathers seem
- Are in unhappy marriages, search for a way out, despite children involved
- Live far away from where their parents and grandparents die

While these specific circumstances might draw a reader to another story among Updike's massive story catalog, the transformative aspect of recycling this material is that it does not feel depleted or shopworn.

However, I am fully cognizant that critics of Updike's work and the themes he chooses to give prominence to might balk at my statement, which absolves him of shortcutting his work via recycling specific events and reminiscences.

For example, in the recent story "The Road Home" from *My Father's Tears,* David Kern visits the family farm he rents to a local farming family and thinks, "Only he had escaped" and laments, "Ancestral soil, and to him was just mud" (173, 178). As readers, we have been to this place with Updike before—physically and emotionally—across numerous stories and novels, from *On the Farm* to "Flight" and "Pigeon Feathers." If Kern were nothing more than a one-dimensional character, there would be room for criticism of Updike's using him in the story at the end of his career. Yet close inspection reveals that the author shows Kern growing and changing as a result of the time lag, just as a person in real life would undergo changes as decades passed and new perspectives took hold.

Given that Updike participated in so many interviews, discussions, and articles about his work, he left a long paper trail that provides valuable insights regarding his thoughts about his stories. In *Updike in Cincinnati,* for example, the author comments on the nuts and bolts of short story authorship, saying:

> A critic has to assume that the author had a tremendous array of choices, of sentences, words he could have chosen. You could have written these words and not those words; another sentence could have followed this instead of the one that did. But, in fact, to the writer doing it, what you turn out is more or less what you can't help turning out, and this is all you *can* turn out. So that it's not as if you have very many choices at all, and what seems to be a pondered device is really just the author's own helpless voice. (58)

Updike's explication of the writing process—a deeply personal aspect of his private life—reveals how traditional criticism might be turned on its head. This style leaves nothing back, like a dragster running on pure octane until the fuel cells are empty. Perhaps, then, criticism should move away from concerns about word or plot choice to a higher-order conversation about authenticity and truth. Without the choices Updike alludes to in the passage above, writing takes on a more desperate tone, as if the author is choking on very specific words and phrases that must be ejected. Anyone who has ever choked understands that helpless feeling afterward, a mix of relief and fear. Updike seems to be equating this feeling to churning away at short stories, which is a frightening thought, given the amount of pain and suffering this would necessitate.

From this perspective, the "light" mentioned in this chapter's epigraph equates to the very words that appear on the page, which illuminate the extent of what is possible. The writing act, as such, is not akin to producing a set of geometric cutouts that can be shape-shifted and pieced together to form some greater whole. These are words bled onto the page, stained into the fabric of a piece like real blood from a seeping wound. Writer and literary critic David Lodge emphasizes the centrality of language, explaining, "The novelist's medium is language: whatever he does, *qua* novelist, he does in and through language" (ix). These bursts, then, are an end in themselves, representing all that a writer can say. For more on what Updike had to say and how he told his stories, we turn to a controversial topic among Updikean scholars and critics—his legendary style.

Style

A constant challenge in holding Updike up to scrutiny is the divisive concept of style. Depending on the commentator's perspective, style is either incredibly central to a writer's craft or a nuisance that somehow adds sizzle, but little steak to the literary meal. Perhaps style as a concept is too closely associated with rhetoric, thus viewed as persuasion or propaganda, rather than poetic or lyrical.

In a 2008 essay, David Heddendorf explains that Updike's foes find him "too in love with his universally admired language," which he counters is part of the popular misconception about the author. Instead, Heddendorf views Updike as "immodest" and anyone who labels him otherwise, holds, "both an uneasiness with the magnitude of Updike's talent and a confusion about modesty itself" (108). Surely, no other contemporary American writer has had more ink spilled regarding his writing style than Updike. It is one of the formulaic (some would argue, banal) criticisms one often finds in newspaper and magazine reviews that seem set out to take a shot at Updike.

I suppose one way of thinking about style differently is comparing ideas about style with the music aficionado's preference for singer or song or perhaps singer versus guitarist, which happens in many groups with the vocalist writing the lyrics and the lead guitarist writing the music. Perhaps a writer like Updike is akin to Bob Dylan or Mick Jagger, while a novelist dedicated to plot or story is similar to Keith Richards or Elton John. Do you love the Rolling Stones based on Mick's voice, lyrics, and stage presence or Keith's licks, melodies, and raunchy riffs?

Looking at Updike, critics often turn for or against him based on their ideas about style (or at least about *his* style). Whether indirect or not, a quick look at how critics interpret Updike's style leads into one of two pretty distinct camps. Time and again, one finds critics in virtual death matches over the role of style in Updike's work. They use the topic as a primary catalyst for determining his significance.

Scholar James A. Schiff equates style with Updike's focus on popular culture, explaining, "Few writers have made as great an effort as John Updike to capture what it feels like to be an American living in the twentieth century" ("Updike, Film" 147). In other words, the author's ability to capture life's nuances in its everyday grace not only sets him apart, but also infuses his style with beauty. Literary critic James Wood, arguing against Updike's style is representative of his negative reviewers, explains: "He is a prose writer of great beauty, but that prose confronts one with the question of whether beauty is enough . . . his fondness for an expensive phrase obscures, because it marks the moment at which he inserts himself oppressively." More derisively, Wood also calls Updike's prose "lyric kitsch . . . sentimental and false" (*Broken Estate* 212).

Considering the countless (millions?) words he carefully crafted, Updike often danced around style. *Odd Jobs* contains a reprint of his 1985 Herman Melville Lecture on the Creative Imagination sponsored by The Writers' Institute at Albany, New York. In the address, Updike described what he perceived as the fundamental connection between imagination and style: "Creative excitement, and a sense of useful work, has invariably and only come to me when I felt I was transferring, with a lively accuracy, some piece of experienced reality to the printed page" (135). He continued, explaining, "The wish to do justice to the real world compels language into those semi-transparent layers that make a style . . . some perception about the nature of reality seeks embodiment" (136). Thus, if one takes the author at his word, the desire to portray reality faithfully drives style.

In many ways, Updike's thoughts about subject matter and style mirror those of Michael Chabon, a writer often compared with his older contemporary, because of his seemingly effortless lyrical prose. Chabon examines honesty in fiction and the way that concept drives style. "Literature, like magic," he claims, "has always been about the handling of secrets, about the pain, the destruction, and the marvelous liberation that can result when they are revealed." Anything outside truth telling, he explains, becomes work "pallid, inanimate, a lump of earth" (155). The novelist must "celebrate" his mastery over subject matter to bring to life something amazing (156).

In 2004, for the book *The Sound on the Page: Style and Voice in Writing* by Ben Yagoda, Updike provided a modification of his vision of style, explaining, "Style as I understand it is nothing less than a writer's habits of mind . . . the very germ of the thing . . . Just as one's handwriting tends to come out the same every time, with certain quirks of emphasis and flow, so does one's writing" (133). Examining Updike's work after his death, writer Larry Woiwode compared him with other greats, saying, "The only comparisons to his silken and often seamless prose, though no comparison really quite fits, are Henry James and James Joyce and Marcel Proust, with a dash of Henry Green. It is that good" (85–86).

Interestingly, in the aforementioned rather brief, yet meaty, examination of his own style, Updike primarily focuses on the topic as it relates to his novels, mentioning several by name and what extra stylistic push propelled the work. For example, he had a desire "to write the way Jackson Pollack painted, in long stringy loops" for *Seek My Face* (164). In the Yagoda book, the only mention of his short fiction is when he juxtaposes the "freewheeling and uninhibited" prose of *Rabbit, Run* with his *New Yorker* stories (163). Updike's comparison seems almost apologetic, explaining that the novel contrasted to the stories via a "conscious effort to escape the me who writes in the past tense and tends to get mired in elaborate backward-looking syntax" (163).

In the Foreword to *The Early Stories* (2003), Updike pays homage to J. D. Salinger and Ernest Hemingway for inspiring his short fiction, along with a list of others. However, Updike found his own style and honed his unique talents via the thoughtful, revelatory voice of *The New Yorker*. To do so, though, he had to get out of New York City, where he felt suffocated by "agents and wisenheimers." Instead, the young writer needed to be among the people, "immersed in the ordinary, which careful explication would reveal to be extraordinary" (xxi). He recalls with nostalgia the role the *New Yorker* played in his life, not only providing an intellectual home for his work, but also financing his first automobile and modest Ipswich lifestyle. He wonders what would have become of him if legendary magazine editor William Shawn "had not liked my work?" (xvii).

With Updike there is always a strain running through his remarks that mixes these two ideas: the craft as profession and the creative life. With the publication of his short fiction, the money he earned afforded him and his family a middle-class lifestyle. His efforts, though, focused on more than just earning a paycheck. As a writer, he set out to tell stories that simultaneously confronted the fulcrum of humanity, the rationale that "Death and its adjutants tax each transaction," as well as its opposite, that "our hearts expect happiness, as an underlying norm" (xvi). It is in the middle that he found these scenes, at once profound and eternal, full of the grace and terror of life in the United States through these muddled times.

One cannot, however, disavow the fact that Updike built his early career on the sale of short fiction to *The New Yorker*. To fully comprehend the centrality of the magazine for him, today's reader must imagine a world where the short story was not widely discussed in college classrooms, like it is currently. An aspiring writer did not have countless classes or entire degrees based on the form. Without as many channels on the television and fewer distractions, magazines filled space with a great deal more short fiction than in today's magazine industry.

Though he could look back at the classics, Updike had little instruction on where to go in terms of form or style. Instead of the "crisp, wised-up, decisively downbeat stories" prevalent at the time, Updike decided to chart a different direction, explaining, "A good story could be ambiguous, the better to contain the ambiguity of the world" (*More* 764). Settling in small-town Ipswich, the young writer's career took off: "I was hip-deep in neighbors and friends, children and pets; I gossiped, I drank, I played golf, I attended church. This was life, and I shaped and polished off odd fragments of it to send away in brown manila envelopes" (*More* 764–65). More telling, Updike admits, "A good story was, basically, one that they accepted. Yet nobody on the editorial staff ever instructed us how to write one" (*More* 765).

Updike not only set about creating his own short fiction style, but his second (or was it third?) full-time career as an essayist and reviewer prompted him to read and reread literature's greats. Perhaps looking at several comments about Fitzgerald's and Hemingway's style will provide some guidance in comprehending his own.

Updike actually sounds like he could be describing his own work in discussing Fitzgerald. For example, Updike explains, "his style is hard to parody, blended as it is of poetry and aperçu, of external detail quickly transmuted to internal sensation" (*Higher* 72–73). Meanwhile, he calls Hemingway's "apparently simple style," a "thoughtful product of modernism in its prime." And since Updike acknowledges Papa's influence on his own early work, one should not wonder at the glimpses he offers, explaining, "A sense of life's tragic brevity always lies beneath the surfaces of his taut dialogues and evocations of nature" (*Higher* 74).

Given Updike's incredibly close reading of American literary greats and his ability to write so convincingly about the strength of their work, it is no wonder that we find influences in his writing, particularly in the short fiction. Maybe Updike's most succinct explication of style—though it came in his acceptance speech for the 1963 National Book Award fiction prize for *Centaur*—states: "Fiction is a tissue of literal lies that refreshes and informs our sense of actuality . . . word by word, to be accurate, we put ourselves on the way toward making something useful and beautiful and, in a word, good" (*Picked-Up* 34).

The (Long) Road Home

Despite the recognition that the baby boomers are the largest segment of the U.S. population and have the most disposable income, contemporary American popular culture has been slow to respond to ageist stereotypes. In a society that favors its popular culture perpetually directed as 18- to 35-year-old males, there is little room for seasoned celebrities, despite the occasional success of a Clint Eastwood or the Rolling Stones. A star can still shine once he or she gets past 60 years old, but more often than not, at least some reaction will be based on the star who has *still got it*, despite aging.

Furthermore, while it is becoming more common for people to lead productive lives and experience healthy retirements for decades longer than their predecessors, we are still more likely to see older people portrayed as infirm or feebleminded. We trot out an aging star and treat him like a walking nostalgia act, essentially throwing a bone to the boomers, while at the same time we tacitly insist that actresses that display even minimal signs of aging undergo extensive plastic surgery and chemical injections. The basic unfairness of this situation means little when the popular culture machine demands youth and vigor. There is always another young pretty face to step up and into the spotlight.

Updike's decision, then, to provide realistic depictions of what it means for an individual to age and continue evolving as a person is important and instructive. In the later short stories, he renders aging protagonists filled with complexity and a certain measure of wisdom that demonstrates life's inherent ambiguities. Reviewing two of the author's later collections in *The John Updike Review,* Luscher exclaims that *My Father's Tears* contains stories that "rank among Updike's finest, distinguished not only by their style and control but also by their poignant and self-conscious attention to preparation for death" (119). These are not perfect characters; they live within their pasts, still searching for meaning, and strive to address the present, even though the future is uncertain.

On its surface, "The Road Home" from *My Father's Tears* appears to be a straightforward story of a man who returns to the Pennsylvania area of his youth to check on farmland he rents to a local farming family and to have dinner with a few aging high school friends while he is in town. Because this is an Updike piece, though, the reader understands—even anticipates—the multiple layers it contains. The author exceeds these expectations by creating David Kern and the story's other characters with depth and a sense of complexity. Updike's telling also includes more than a little critique of modern culture and its consequences.

David opens the story in a rented Nissan and steady rain, each disorienting him from the once-familiar Pennsylvania of his youth. More telling, though, entire small communities have been obliterated, "vanished behind a garish stretch of national franchises and retail outlets" (170). The world David knew is gone: Philadelphians surge in, while he himself could not leave quickly enough as a young man. Yet once he is oriented correctly, the former resident recalls every nook and cranny of the road, including its signs. Thus, while much of the surface changes to meet the twenty-first century, David's awareness of its bones demonstrates that infrastructure remains. The wash of change in the form of consumerism, Updike tacitly reveals, is mere gloss covering the aspects of one's homeland that matters, the paths and trails developed in youth as building blocks toward adulthood.

The site of his land and its homestead flood David's mind with memories of his mother, even stretching back to stories she told of her youth living on that exact same farm. These glimpses deliver pangs of guilt, not only in that he did not fulfill her wish that he someday live on the land, but also in the infrequency of his actual visits. As David drives, however, he feels "his ancestors all around him," simultaneously though he is thankful that he had "escaped" from rural Pennsylvania (174).

Reichardt's farm and all its newfangled equipment to maximize the land for profit—for example, hydroponics used to grow strawberries year-round—show Kern that every facet of life is receptive to or transformed by innovation, even farming that takes place minus the dirt, its most traditional necessity. Farm patriarch Enoch Reichardt is David's age and proud to show off the updates, even as they slosh and slide in the rain in the farmer's large black Ford sedan. Here Updike might be nodding toward the value of older machinery and its solidness—juxtaposing the big Ford cruiser with the delicate innovations and science that makes the farm more productive.

The give-and-take of progress is all around David as he visits his mother's beloved land. "Ancestral soil," David thinks, "and to him it was just mud" (178). The change in the land saddens him, not only in that he let his mother down somehow, despite not selling out to further development, thus saving her beloved farmland, but also in that change is the real constant, not the people making or adapting to change. There is a dichotomy in his reaction: nostalgia for the land, versus his desire as a young man to leave the area to make his own way.

Enoch chides him about someday living on the land, as his mother wished. Kern cruelly adds that he someday might, turning the farmland and its updates into "my big front yard" (178). The jibe seems unnecessary, since Enoch is only attempting to show that the land is being put to good use, but Kern's response reveals an adversarial relationship, perhaps harking back to his feelings about the land and his mother. The potshot at Enoch also suggests that Kern holds onto old notions of ownership. He owns the land, while Enoch merely rents it.

"The Road Home" is a kind of love letter to Updike's mother via the farm and to his father, since the second half of the story takes place in and around Alton, which Kern calls his father's "territory" (179). One of the first landmarks he notices as he drives away from the farm is a bridge that his father helped build while working on a road crew during the Great Depression. David reveals his father's deep connection to the area, thinking that he "never crossed this bridge without imagining drops of his father's sweat as part of it, dried into the concrete" (179). In this brief scene, which one might pass over without much thought, Updike demonstrates the deep roots people have to their communities, even if children move away. People are bound to the land and these ties run deep, even encompassing the very foundations of the communities themselves.

His mother's farm is mutable and changes with its latest inhabitant, just like the old sandstone farmhouse, which has had numerous tenets since she passed away. David's father, on the other hand, is marked by permanence—a bridge is a necessity and the stones used to construct such a landmark are more or less eternal. Yet the city itself slides into decrepitude, a decades long fall that David characterizes by "throwaway men—working-class males whose craft or occupation had withered away and left them with nothing to do all day but smoke cigarettes and wait for a visit to the local bar to ripen into a permissible activity" (179).

Alton is a dying city, its failure symbolized by the closure of Blankenbiller's Department Store, one of its venerable institutions, which is being torn down and surrounded by construction fencing. In surveying the scene, the narrator adds a criticism of the modern United States, stating, "A dying city . . . and they keep putting up banks" (180). Now the store location existed as nothing more than a giant, debris-filled hole, just like Kern's memories of the city and store—awaiting death, his own future hole in the earth.

Although Updike wrote in 2006: "Now 'stories of senility' are about the only ones I have to tell. My only new experience is of aging, and not even the aged much want to read about it," his stories about aging are innovative and instructive for a culture that pushes old people aside (*Higher* 5). Kern feels older, but not old, which he equates with his parents' generation. Yet Updike reveals how the character reacts to situations, like asking the hotel desk worker for directions, with trepidation usually equated with older people: "Uncomprehending, but afraid of appearing senile, he docilely nodded and went to his room." At the same time, however, Kern singles out his former classmates for inviting him to an early dinner, based on their "age and frailty" (182).

At dinner, David sits among childhood friends, some who have aged quite a bit, including Sandra, a woman Kern "loved" since kindergarten (186). What the scene reveals is that Kern is considered the "returned prodigal." They want to make him happy, so they have him sit next to her, despite her difficulty hearing. But his status as the center of attention falls victim to the everyday—the local politics and daily existence that his friends relive "buried beneath a silt of decades, of thousands of days spent in this same territory, maturing, marrying, childbearing, burying parents, laboring, retiring" (187).

David runs out of gas in the competition with the combined mountain of life that has taken place in Alton without him. Unlike Rabbit Angstrom, the basketball whiz who the youngsters had never even heard of, Kern is remembered, but finds that his "prodigal" role is not enough to stay in the spotlight. In his mid-20s, Rabbit is aware of being pushed up and out. In his 60s, however, David is already out. And though treated like a returning hero for a moment, he still feels like the precocious boy from his youth. When he says goodnight to Sandra, he lacks confidence. After a brief peck on the cheek—unfortunately on the paralyzed side of her face—he adds "an absurd gesture . . . a thumbs-up" (189). The reader can sense Kern's burning embarrassment, not sure how to act among these lifelong friends who have gone on living without him for decades. He is the outsider, even while filled with past memories and experiences of life in their shared hometown.

The foursome clambers into an SUV, but not before they demand that David follow them back to the hotel. The convoy traverses the outskirts of the city, which causes David to both catalog the changes and engage in some nostalgic feelings about places he used to visit, like a local all-night diner that kids frequented in his day. In disbelief, David marvels at the group dropping him right at the hotel front door, as if he had never been there before, like "some out-of-town moron." Yet, to them, he is an outsider, even if in his mind he yells, "I know where I am now! I'm here" (192). For those who stayed in Alton, there is only here and not here.

    David, despite his history in the region and attachment through land ownership, is little more than an absentee landlord. He cannot be part of "here" any longer. His connection to the land of his youth is broken, just as it is for his departed family members and soon will be for his friends. The changing landscape of booming suburbs and dying city accentuate that progress is at the helm. People merely tag along behind, tethered by a thin wire of memory, which is slowly replaced as one's brain is overfilled with a lifetime's activities and events. Kern searches for the past beyond the new cloverleaf overpasses and faded street signs, just as he did in the farmland and fields of his youth that were only there in vague outline. David cannot control the destruction of his history. What he considers change, others would deem evolution.

CHAPTER 10

Radical Departures: Updike as Experimental Novelist

> The man is happy, hidden. The sea breeze blows, the waiters ignore him. He is writing his memoirs. No, I should put it more precisely: Colonel Ellelloû is rumored to be working on his memoirs.
> —Updike, ending of *The Coup* (1978)

The never-ending desire to oversimplify life's complexities in modern American culture leads to generalizations that fuel arguments, but does little to explore an issue or individual's complications. This reductionist thinking is based on how the creators of popular culture and mass communications think about audiences: an embedded notion that they are generally too simpleminded, uneducated, or ignorant to understand anything that speaks to life's intricacies and disjointed moments.

An outcome of this tendency is creating an environment that excels in and celebrates specialization. As a result, it is much better to lock in on information, as the old saying explains, "a mile deep and inch wide," by trotting out so-called experts on any range of subjects or to fall back on old ideas. The downside of the creation of a talking head society is the urge to label everything and everyone as a means of finding the most common denominator or creating a shorthand label in the nanosecond consumer mind-set oftentimes places things in boxes where they do not belong or do so without providing the context that displays nuance.

Much of this thinking is also tied to rampant consumerism, which serves as the grease in the hyper-capitalism system that needs goods and services to be available and easily acquired. In an attempt to capitalize on marketing dollars in hopes of creating buzz, everything from Michael Jordan (MJ) and Jennifer Lopez (J-Lo) to *Sex and the City* (SATC) and Burger King (BK) is shortened to its simplest terms as a method of strengthening the brand, appealing to some general notion of hip, or simply competing with the millions of blips darting across a consumer's internal display at any given time. Often celebrities become little more than sign systems in an attempt to sell products: a brand, a character trait, or even an idea, all in the name of consumerism. How many billions of dollars have Tom Hanks and George Clooney generated, for example, by fitting into the consumers' idea of an archetype?

If one accepts the idea that these sign systems are created to generate consumer demand, then the oversimplification must have ramifications. In many respects, the often-used moniker "suburban chronicler" or its many derivative offspring placed on Updike created an image of his fiction that betrayed or mischaracterized much of his oeuvre. If nothing else, these labels reduced his work to an idea that might have existed in the mind of a book reviewer or critic, but does not hold up to reality, or at least only touches on part of what he wrote.

However, the notion that those within Updike's inner circle also attempted to create a brand around his work, or that he himself participated in this effort, adds additional layers of intricacy to the idea. Crowning Updike the king of Middle America, therefore, helps establish him as a brand and provides audiences with an easy way of identifying with that brand. The authenticity of the label seems less important than the means of using it to sell goods. And while this may appear duplicitous, Updike also warrants some of the criticism for using the moniker too. Many times in his career, he spoke or wrote of "middles" and his role in illuminating them in his fiction. It seems as if every interviewer felt compelled to ask Updike one or several obligatory questions about his role in explaining suburban America to readers. In the literary marketplace, writers exist as both creators and brands. Therefore, Updike needed a way to tie the brand to his work in a way that harried book buyers could relate to and use when making purchasing decisions. There is a fundamental link between the writer as creator and the writer as a brand that can be bought, sold, and marketed that is critical here and discussed at length at various places in this book.

Without disregarding or diminishing Updike's great corpus within the confines of contemporary suburban America, there is a compelling body of work that shoots the author off into a different direction—fiction that shows Updike eagerly exploring new ideas about structure, reality, time, mythology, and space. Certainly, this idea begins at the launch of Updike's writing career. His first novel was the futuristic *The Poorhouse Fair*. The next year, *Rabbit, Run* appears, filled with overt sexuality (for the era) and its present-tense point of view. Then, he follows with

The Centaur, overlaying Greek myth on the father–son relationship. Thinking about Updike's work this way, perhaps it is not too much of a stretch to claim that he is an experimental novelist who also wrote suburban fiction, or one who wrote experimental fiction based on ideas at the heart of mainstream America.

Examining Updike's experimental fiction, from his earliest novels to those that followed later, more innovative gems, such as *A Month of Sundays* (1975) and *The Coup* (1978) to the science fiction *Toward the End of Time* (1997), this chapter considers Updike's role as a writer expanding the boundaries of traditional fiction, a label most critics place (and force) on him. These works, among other important novels in his catalog, reveal Updike taking risks. For example, scholar Jack De Bellis discusses the novelty of *The Witches of Eastwick,* which, "merges magical realism with black humor . . . So different is this gothic novel from Updike's realistic fiction that it seemed a joke to some when it appeared, especially given that Updike is well known for puckish play" ("Critical" 95–6). Similar analysis reveals that many critics—particularly the professional newspaper and magazine book reviewers—have almost completely misjudged the author, or at least fomented a picture of his work that is only partially true.

Rather than the mainstream idea that Updike writes fiction narrow in scope and focusing primarily on suburban topics, a deeper examination shows the expansiveness of his fictional universe and its relation to the wider world. For example, *Toward the End of Time* hypothesizes a new world in the post-apocalyptic United States after a devastating nuclear war with China. While this scenario seems somewhat plausible today, based on the China's incredible economic boom and impressive military might, or at least compelling science fiction, Updike's use of this theme in 1997 reveals his grasp of global geopolitics. While the book is hyper-focused on the daily life of Ben Turnbull, a 66-year-old retired investment analyst, the setting in post-apocalyptic America and the consequences of a war with China enable Updike to place one family within a much broader, more dynamic environment. Throughout the novel, Updike zeroes in on Turnbull's life, but presents the outside world as ominous and chaotic, which keeps the book moving at two different speeds, the deliberateness of its main character's daily rhythms and the strange new nation struggling to regain its footing.

Terrorist, too, surveys life in the post-9/11 United States and correctly anticipates the rise of the so-called *homegrown* terrorist. While Updike had a kind of crystal ball out in thinking through the novel's primary plot, he also wrote the book as a thriller, certainly pushing boundaries, since *Terrorist* came out in 2006, when Updike turned 74 years old. One of the strongest aspects of the novel is the way the author captured the deterioration of American culture based on its commitment to and obsession with consumerism.

This chapter attempts to undo the decades of labeling Updike suffered. Without undermining his ability to speak to the everyday grace of Middle America, I hope to demonstrate that Updike did much more than serve as a mouthpiece for that segment of society, more than just a witty, lucid explainer of the middle class to middle-class book buyers and readers. As a matter of fact, what I plan to show is that we can magnify Updike's place among contemporary literary greats by underscoring his experimental works and expanding the way critics, scholars, and other observers interpret his novels.

Certainly, those who study Updike have thought and written about this topic, yet among the uninitiated, it would help if they understood that Updike wrote high-quality fiction outside the Rabbit books. Furthermore, while it might seem sacrilegious among some readers to claim, many Updike scholars and commentators judge his experimental fiction his best and most enjoyable work, even in direct competition with the Rabbit tetralogy.

Voice and Tone

One can never escape style when considering Updike's work, whether as a novelist, poet, or essayist. In Updike's novels, his voice is to a large extent an additional character. Readers expect an Updikean treatment of the subject, written in that familiar, yet unique, style. The use of voice through literary device allows him to set the tone of the book, driving the aura the reader basically feels as the story progresses, similar to the way a film director uses lighting and shadow to project or heighten a scene or, for that matter, an entire motion picture.

What many readers admire about Updike's commitment to style is his willingness to experiment and adapt through voice and literary technique. While most artists work to find a style and then work to hone it, Updike willingly tests various techniques and different character perspectives. Thinking about his range, one realizes that this is not a common method. Perhaps it is akin to a professional golfer like Tiger Woods seemingly constantly reinventing his swing to adapt to improved technology and physical changes or an older athlete adding new twists to his or her bag of tricks to prolong a career, like Michael Jordan's fadeaway jump shot that he added when the spring in his legs dipped slightly. There are huge risks for athletes when they make these wholesale changes, which are replicated by those who pursue other artistic endeavors. Updike could have taken a more conservative route, but his integrity and intellectual curiosity compelled him to experiment, whether interviewing himself via invented characters or trying to give voice to those that observers might feel exist outside his range.

In *Rabbit, Run*, for example, Updike intentionally used the present tense to keep his hand on the throttle. The book dashes ahead at full sprint when Updike commands, while lulling to a crawl at other points, all driven by the author's voice. Here is Rabbit, in flight away from home, racing for freedom: "The land grows wilder. The road evades great lakes and tunnels through pines. In the top of the windshield the telephone wires continually whip the stars" (35). The present tense gives Updike the ability to control the pace of *Rabbit, Run*, often mimicking the title and sprinting off into the unknown. This example is not complex writing, but Updike adds layers of speed and precision to the passage by showing the reader what Rabbit sees outside the car windows on desolate roads, with only lonely headlights, the stars, and moon to brighten the scene.

For further evidence of Updike using voice to dictate the pacing of a novel, one simply needs to examine the languorous tone of the next two novels: *The Centaur* (1963) and *Of the Farm* (1965). Both books are meditations, thus they evolve slowly. The former, winner of the National Book Award in 1964, is Updike's fictional exploration of his father's life using mythological underpinnings to consider life in small-town Pennsylvania. *Of the Farm*, on the other hand, is set in the present, almost completely on an aging widow's farm. The novel examines the relationship between a mother and a son, and the protagonist's new (second) wife and stepson. Although Updike explores universal themes in these works, the tone is reflective and analytical, often emotional, but in a detached voice. Clearly, Updike intends this languid pace because it reflects the subject matter.

Arguably Updike's most experimental novel, *The Coup* (1978), is literally on the other side of the world compared with *Of the Farm*. The book's creation of an imaginary African nation (Kush) and its ousted dictator (Colonel Hakim Félix Ellelloû) demonstrates Updike's ability to work completely in a fictional world. According to scholar Donald J. Greiner, "Updike has gone beyond looking around him to imagining the idiosyncrasies of his created worlds. The result . . . is a sophisticated comedy of language and disguise" (*Novels* 29).

While *The Coup* received widespread praise, Greiner also points to the criticism the book faced, which centered on reviewers not appreciating his creation of an African main character or their thinking that a white American could not claim to speak for a black man or nation. Interestingly, the criticism reads similarly to the kind Updike faced as reviewers took *Terrorist* to task nearly three decades later. At the time, five years after the 9/11 attacks, critics chastised Updike for attempting to speak for a Muslim American teenage high school student contemplating a terroristic bombing. In each case, the critics seem to have completely misread the novels in question and faulted Updike for having the audacity to attempt it, rather than think about either novel's deeper significance.

Unlike Updike's previous novels, *Terrorist* is a literary thriller, which for Updike was about as experimental as could be. Updike turns the traditional thriller on its head, though, infusing it with a style and layer of sophistication not usually associated with the genre. Not as taut a page-turner or as strictly plot-driven as best-selling authors like John Grisham or James Patterson, I argue that Updike has broader aspirations in *Terrorist*, primarily to outline the new America that emerges post-9/11. This emphasis distinguishes him from other thriller writers, who seem to be most interested in telling a story in a dramatic fashion, with little concern with being considered literary. Although conforming in some ways to the thriller genre, Updike still dictates tone through voice and technique.

One feels the tone of the novel established most clearly in the way Updike creates Ahmad's nuanced personality. The author portrays the dualities within Ahmad through the use of the character's internal thoughts and in conversations. As a result, the reader is presented with the angry, strident side of the teen when he thinks: "These devils seek to take away my God" (3). However, at the end of the same monologue that flips back and forth between the boy and the unnamed narrator, Updike infuses Ahmad with seedlings of doubt that will play a significant role later in the book. The narrator intones, "The deaths of insects and worms, their bodies so quickly absorbed by earth and weeds and road tar, devilishly strive to tell Ahmad that his own death will be just as small and final" (5).

New York Times book critic Michiko Kakutani blasts Updike for doing a "lousy job of showing us why Ahmad is willing to die and kill for jihad," but Updike vividly depicts the anger and uncertainty festering within the teen (E1). When his female friend and love interest Joryleen questions whether God's existence and the possibility that no afterlife exists, Ahmad feels physically ill, explaining, "If none of it is true . . . then the world is too terrible to cherish, and I would not regret leaving it" (72). Interestingly, this discussion takes place in the midst of Ahmad's doubt. He yearns for Joryleen sexually, despite his religious training, which advocates purity. In the passage, the boy is proud of his height and stands above the "short, ripe girl," catching glimpses of the "tops of her breasts . . . still glazed with the excitement and exertion of her singing" (67). With no one to honestly help Ahmad understand the warring factions of faith and doubt he clenches in his heart, the teen is listless and uncertain. No wonder, then, that he falls in succession to a series of father figures, who all place their own needs above his. Ahmad grapples with his transformation to manhood, but does not have the wisdom to see way each father figure manipulates him.

I see Ahmad as an individual in the midst of crisis. When people enter these moments, otherwise senseless events can result, such as the real-life tragedies of the Columbine shootings or the almost daily suicide bombing incidents that take place in Iraq and Afghanistan. Updike admits as much in a June 2006 interview with *BookPage,* saying, "I thought it was important to show how much Ahmad needed to make his own philosophy, as it were, because the environment wasn't coming up with any" ("Interview"). Later, in the same article, Updike directly references how religious zealotry can evolve, explaining:

> I tried to understand him and to dramatize his world. Besides it's not just young Muslims who are killing themselves. We have all these American high school students, steeped in Protestantism and Judaism, who bring guns to school and shoot up the cafeteria knowing they're going to die at the end of this rush. There are a lot of teenagers who are going to take big chances. ("Interview")

Kakutani's criticism of the character, particularly in comparing Updike's vision of a religious fanatic with the works by Joseph Conrad, Henry James, Fyodor Dostoevsky, and Don DeLillo, sounds more like a case of complaining because the character is not what she expected or wished, rather than what Updike created.

At the heart of Updike's creation of an American homegrown terrorist is the question regarding how the young man arrives at the decision to accept the role. In looking for the answer, one cannot discount the mental anguish Ahmad experiences, which Updike ties to the young man's intense faith, burgeoning sexuality, and longing for a father figure.

The reader glimpses this turmoil inside Ahmad in an early scene in which the two teens are talking outside Joryleen's church. She is a member of the choir, but does not think deeply about (or even to show much interest in) religion. Ahmad, however, is overwhelmed by the billowing sermon delivered in a frenzy by the church's black pastor. Then, he longs for Joryleen as she sings, even though he is unable to admit this to himself. Afterward, standing there with her, the teenager is overcome with a toxic mix of strident faith, fear, and sexual repression. Unable to comprehend all these juices churning in him, Ahmad lashes out at Joryleen as the meeting ends, telling her: "You have a good heart, Joryleen, but you're heading straight for Hell, the lazy way you think" (73). In this pivotal scene, the voice of *Terrorist* (Ahmad's mix of faith and doubt) is cast through the teen, as he imagines a "world too terrible to cherish" (72), then casts out the one person who has shown an interest in him. Ahmad cannot control himself and Joryleen is the recipient of his pent-up hostility. At this point, the boy must strike. He continues to cast about, up until the time he decides not to go through with the explosion. In this way, Updike shows Ahmad undergoing a kind of maturation process, breaking from following the direction of others to critically analyzing the situations around him and making up his own mind.

Updike's Thriller

From a symbolic interactionist viewpoint, Updike's use of external stimuli drawn from traveling and lecturing around the globe influenced what he wrote. As a result of purposely expanding the scope of topics beyond the American middle class, the author produced a collection of experimental novels, from *The Coup* to *Toward the End of Time* and *Terrorist*.

Many reviewers, including Kakutani and the late Christopher Hitchens, briefly mentioned *The Coup* when reviewing *Terrorist*, but made little effort to explain why they enjoyed the former and not the latter (which is ironic, given that many reviewers of *The Coup* at the time of its publication criticized Updike for attempting to speak as an African dictator). Ironically, for Kakutani and Hitchens, Updike's creation of a character as a failed African dictator seemed more plausible and believable to reviewers in contrast to the American-born Ahmad in *Terrorist*.

The salient point, however, is that Updike deliberately took the path away from the typical subject matter, thus one can infer that he did so as a result of wide-ranging engagement with world literature and his travels as both a tourist and a literary celebrity. For example, he explains his thinking about the science fiction novel *Toward the End of Time,* saying that "was a deliberately experimental book, although I hope it wasn't an irresponsible one. One of my thoughts was, I had composed a good deal of consistent fiction and I wanted to take a little holiday from consistency" (Reilly 230). What one yearns for is a more detailed explanation or map of why Updike chose this path away from "consistent."

Since we do not have access to this information, perhaps an symbolic interaction perspective provides some rationale. One thought is to look at how life histories (or, perhaps, a writer's experiences) play a role in producing fiction. Michal M. McCall and Judith Wittner offer insight into this brand of storytelling, in which one could arguably place much of Updike's fiction, saying that life stories enable people to "share their experiential solutions to common problems, and thus, create culture: shared understandings of their common situations and agreed-upon ways of acting in them" ("Good News" 59). As a result, one concludes that Updike's deliberate move away from what he labeled "consistent fiction" is a focused attempt at creating tools for readers (and himself) to interpret culture.

In this light, storytelling then becomes a collective activity that helps society interpret events. According to literary critic Barbara Herrnstein Smith:

> [E]very telling is produced and experienced under certain social conditions and constraints and that it always involves two parties, an audience as well as a narrator . . . [and] as in any other social transaction, each party must be individually motivated to participate in it: in other words, that each party must have some interest in telling or listening to that narrative. (quoted in McCall and Wittner 84)

Under these conditions, an author takes calculated risks in expanding his catalog. Updike faces a multitude of concerns as he ventures away from his typical fare, from the conscious decision to make that move to the use of text to create culture for readers. The authoritative voice of the novelist, then, accepts new vigor from an interactionist point of view, since the writer's product is designed to be read and digested.

Symbolic interactionism as a tool for literary analysis can be seen as a powerful means of supporting literature's hope to serve the broader culture. For example, is it possible to look at war the same after one has read Hemingway's *For Whom the Bell Tolls* or Norman Mailer's

The Naked and the Dead, or, for that matter, to conceive of the inner workings of a terrorist the same way after Updike's *Terrorist* or Don DeLillo's *Falling Man,* another post-9/11 novel by one of the nation's literary titans?

The literary techniques Updike employs provide evidence regarding his specific style and how those devices enable the writer to achieve his aspirations. I argue that interrogating Updike's use of phrases, styles, and editorial commentary within the text reveals *Terrorist* as an important work in Updike's catalog and certainly one underappreciated by many scholars and general critics to date. From my perspective, the novel reveals a writer in the midst of transformation, as important external forces—such as the 9/11 attacks and ensuing warfare—compel him to reflect major societal changes in his fiction.

What I find essential in *Terrorist* is that Updike uses literary technique to help solidify his worldview. For example, Jack's wife Beth initially seems like a weak, mousy character teetering on major depression. She is 100 pounds overweight, unhappy, unhealthy, and simply taking up space.

Closer inspection, however, brings to light a different perception. As a device in expounding a specific ideology, Updike creates a character that the unnamed narrator and Jack see as frivolous. By extension, the reader is guided to feel that same way. As a result, an aura of ridicule surrounds what she says and thinks. Updike uses this as a setup to critique a number of popular culture topics, including Oprah Winfrey, psychiatry, and the color-coded threat levels issued by the Department of Homeland Security.

When Jack tells Beth that his moodiness is driven by lack of sleep, even though it is actually her fatness that disheartens him, she explains, "That's a sign of depression, they were saying on television . . . Oprah had a woman on who's written a book" (31). Jack's negative reaction and conclusion that he has fended her off imply that the reader should not take her ideas seriously.

When Beth next turns to confidential information she learned about the threat level in their Northern New Jersey region from her sister at the Department of Homeland Security, actually making Jack promise not to tell anyone, he gets sarcastic in an attempt to shut her up. "Bring 'em on," he jokes, "I was thinking, looking out the window, this whole neighborhood could do with a good bomb" (32). In other words, anything that Beth finds important, the reader is steered to consider absurd, even if there is truth in what she has to say.

Witches and Magical Realism

Updike's last two novels—*Terrorist* and *The Widows of Eastwick*—provide a fascinating overview of the author's late career. *Terrorist*, however, is a stand-alone novel, while *Widows* is a sequel. Both books fit into the subcategory of experimental fiction, the former the author's move to a different genre, while the second contains magical realism and witchcraft as plot points. As such, an interesting way to investigate the two is by exploring them as the writer's last of each type. We have examined *Terrorist* in detail in this chapter and at other points in the book, so now it is time to consider *The Widows of Eastwick* and its dastardly coven.

Updike returned to the three suburban witches—Alexandra, Sukie, and Jane—after almost a quarter century after the first novel. In the ensuing lifetime away from one another, the women focus on reestablishing themselves as individuals and in their new lives within marriages. They are drawn back to one another, though, after all three of their husbands die in short order. This perspective enables Updike to do several things at once, most notably examine the women within the confines of marriage and modern society, contrast their current widowhood with nostalgic visions of the past, and reveal the how aging Americans navigate life.

In other words, what Updike does in *Widows* is marry magical realism and Middle America, using each to provide context and nuance for the other. The result is that the reader is never exactly sure whether the women have true power and a link to the occult or if much of their magic is mythical or a product of their imaginations. There is a duality at every turn, which Updike mines for great consequence. For example, the unseen narrator informs the reader at the start of the novel that the husbands were "concocted" by the "Godforsaken women" and that their deaths were linked by the tie to evil: "Wicked methods make weak products. Satan counterfeits Creation, yes, but with inferior goods" (3). The reader, however, cannot be sure that their deaths or, as a matter of fact, their entrance into the women's lives did not take place coincidentally. Wishing for a mate and then having someone appear later does not mean the wish came true . . . or does it?

Alexandra, the spiritual leader of the coven, not only seems the most realistic in her outlook and actions, but is also the most committed to the idea of witchcraft and its dark magic. Updike makes her character the most down-to-earth of the three, allowing the reader to picture her as the most "typical" of the witches: modest finances, American West/naturalist spirituality, "broadest in body," and with family challenges that mirror the here and now (3).

As a result, Alexandra can be simultaneously bothered by widowhood travel with its "undeniable risk of flight in a time of rising fuel costs, airline bankruptcy, suicidal terrorists" and her past life committed to "a half-baked suburban variety of witchcraft" (3, 6). She mourns her conjured husband, who she supposedly fashioned out of a pinch of Western dirt. At the same time, though he created replicas of her with his clay pottery, "[Jim's] masculine hands shaped blobs upward into graceful vessels with slender waists and swelling bottoms" (5). The loss of domestic routine, companionship, and one's life partner (even if it is a second or subsequent marriage) is at the heart of Alexandra's plight. She mourns losing him much more than she yearns for the reconvened coven.

There are many similar themes between the linked novels. In the earlier book, Vietnam and its consequences served as an overarching theme. Scholar D. Quentin Miller explains that in *Witches*, Updike "is resurrecting Vietnam-era demons in order to respond to the Reagan-era sense that the Cold War has reverted back to its early configurations" (*Cold War* 102). Novelist and reviewer Diane Johnson sees the Vietnam War as the novel's central concern, saying, "[T]he troubled male world of war and crime casts its more important shadow over the limited, domestic self-interest of the women witches" ("Warlock"). Some 25 years later, however, war still ravages the pristine idea of the United States, but the enemy this time is wholly different than the Cold War Soviet Union (which no longer even exists, since the nation has reverted to the official "Russia" moniker). In its place, the United States battles a globalized, nationless enemy in the form of terrorism. The ideology is given a face as the George W. Bush administration links terrorism with Iraq.

Therefore, when Alexandra tours the Canadian Rocky Mountains, she criticizes Manifest Destiny for solidifying a philosophy that necessitates war. American history, to her, is "boy soldiers [that] lost limbs and died." She thinks, "The daily death-tolls from Iraq were worth escaping" (8). This thinking links the two novels, since the potential for terrorism merges the early 1980s with the post-9/11 world of the 2000s. The homegrown terrorism of *Witches* is built on anti-Vietnam activism, which causes Reverend Ed Parsley (Sukie's lover) to join an underground group and eventually die in a bomb-making fiasco. As Miller indicates, there is even more at the heart of the earlier novel, which Updike then links in *Widows*. In *Witches*, Miller explains, "Also implicit in both [homegrown and global terror] is a critique of American foreign policy as being motivated entirely by money" (*Cold War* 103). The continuation of marauding foreign policy is a major theme in the earlier work, but serves a lesser role in the latter, but to be fair, hangs over the book nonetheless.

When the women return to Eastwick, the novel moves into darker areas of revenge, murder, and death, yet also includes the opposite with tales of conception, rejuvenation, and the innocence of youth. Whether witchcraft can be credited or blamed for any of this, Updike walks the reader through life's changes as age and entropy take a more prominent role in people's lives. Alexandra, Jane, and Sukie cannot turn back the hands of time, or even reunite the coven to save one of their own. As Jane complains about the mysterious pains that radiate through her chest, the narrator intones, "We all have ends. The heart beats time. Time beats us" (197).

Rather than fixate on the unfixable past, Updike seems to be saying, one should create a legacy through family. As opposed to Updike's credo at the opening of *Due Considerations*: "Bills come due; dues must be paid" (xvii), the idea at the heart of *Widows* is that life's sorrow is enough payment and one must counter that pain through "the daily happiness of a real life resumed" (307). Like a heartbeat, time does not stop, but even as one ages toward the unknown, there is life left in the offing.

***

In *Updike: America's Man of Letters*, Pritchard chronicles Updike's work through the new millennium and analyzes the novels that move beyond realist perspectives, which he labels "extravagant fictions." What Pritchard so ably demonstrates is that Updike took a decidedly different turn beginning with *The Coup*: "a writer who after twenty years of fiction might have been content to rest on realist laurels. Instead he came across as dazzler and showman, as Nabokovian illusionist, in a more radical way than he had hitherto demonstrated" (195).

What I would add to Pritchard's overview is that Updike's so-called realist work often took on an experimental frame that forces us to shift our understanding away from the overused albatross: chronicler of suburban America. There are deliberate topics that the author chose to write about and in a specific way that necessitates our reinterpretation of his catalog. Scholar John N. Duvall is even more direct, claiming, "[M]uch of Updike's fiction since *A Month of Sundays* (1975) reveals a novelist who, if not exactly postmodernist, has read a number of key poststructuralist texts that inform postmodern poetics and has experimented with postmodern narrative strategies" (162).

Updike conveys a sense of the mix of earthly and heavenly, along with a possible dose of reality, in a piece written for the Franklin Library's First Edition Society printing of *Witches*, explaining the idea behind the novel: "I have tried here, in my own style, to give gossip a body and to conjure up human voices as they hungrily feed on the lives of others. The appetite is not trivial; we write and read novels to satisfy it" (*Odd Jobs* 856). As always, there is a central idea in Updike's novels. However, he is playful and experimental in how he transmits the material. Certainly, it is a deliberate choice to move away from so-called straightforward, realistic fiction. To the reader's delight, Updike is willing to make that change. That he does it so well is a further tribute to his expanse of talent and commitment to craft.

CHAPTER 11

Updike's Audience

> Meanwhile the books multiply . . . Somewhere in their several million pondered, proofread, printed words I must have done my best, sung my song, had my say. But my panicked awareness . . . is of all that *isn't* in them—almost everything, it suddenly seems. *Worlds* are not in them. In the face of this vacuity arises the terrible itch to—what else?—write another book, a book that, like one more ingredient sprinkled into a problematic batter, will make the whole thing rise . . . Squinting, I can almost see the jacket, and make out the title page, in thirty-six-point Perpetua.
>
> —John Updike, from the 1997 essay "Me and My Books"

Sitting alone, staring at a blank computer screen, and eager for words to pour out, a writer might feel far removed from his audience. Regardless of pedigree, creative spark, publication history, or approaching deadline, the writer begins in isolation. Even if one still employs pad and pencil or scribbles down notes and furiously creates detailed outlines, writers here share a link to a voice inside yearning for production. Novelist E. L. Doctorow examines this idea, explaining, "the work itself is hard and slow and the writer's illumination becomes a taskmaster, a ruling discipline, jealously guarding the mind from all other and necessarily errant private excitements . . . You live enslaved in the piece's language, its diction, its universe of imagery, and there is no way out except through the last sentence" (*Creationists* x). The act of writing itself is painful and taxing, exacting both an emotional and physical toll. One might suggest that it is akin to a daily process of opening a wound just a little to let the blood flow.

The track record of famous authors who have dealt with these demons by wreaking havoc upon themselves reveals the potential depths of this anguish. Updike acknowledged the toll writing and celebrity takes, explaining in a 1975 interview at the height of his own fame comparing himself with a boyhood idol, "Hemingway was a writer who was truly . . . destroyed by his own persona and his own huge name, as well as by his own private lust for alcoholic fun" (Plath, *Conversations* 81). Writers dream of publication, but anyone interested in how writers create must wonder why they push themselves like this, often with the odds stacked so clearly against getting in print. Yet is there a writer without an audience?

When observed from this viewpoint, writing looks like an entirely isolated enterprise. The process, however, hinges on how potential readers interact with the work. Even if the writer considers herself her own primary audience, there are numerous other readers that must be considered, ranging from friends or others who might give the work a critical eye to a series of editors and marketing professionals that decide to publish or reject. What a writer sets out to do from that solitary moment gains momentum the second he wants to deliver the work to the larger world. Consequently, the awareness of the route to publication must enter the writer's outlook.

This chapter investigates how various audiences, from editors and publishers to general readers and professional critics, examine Updike's work, with specific emphasis on *Terrorist*. By analyzing existing sources from this perspective, I explore what it means for a literary artist and celebrity to also coexist as a working professional. This path moves from research, examining topics, and writing to eventually finding one's way to publication and later review. For Updike, who enjoyed both critical and mass appeal, an investigation into his readers and reception uncovers interesting information about society on a larger scale, including material about changing literary tastes and transforming cultural norms. For this study, the focus on *Terrorist* provides an analysis of Updike's reception as a famous author, which must be taken into consideration when looking at his later career. Since the book is his last stand-alone novel, an exploration of how audiences received, reviewed, and purchased it will deliver an exploration different than at earlier points in his career.

What follows also provides insight on the critical reception of Updike's work as the author moved beyond novels about middle-class Americans and suburban life. I plan to examine clues about how an internationally famous writer struggles with the burden of fame and the prominence of the Rabbit tetralogy within his broad catalog as he attempts to branch out from those earlier novels.

Terrorist is an intriguing case study in examining Updike's body of work. First, in terms of genre, the novel is categorized as a thriller, completely new ground for the author. Related to this notion is Updike's willingness to confront a difficult, topical subject, in a genre that demands attention to suspense and plotting perhaps more than Updike's traditional strengths in character motivations and development. Addressing the real world in seemingly real time necessitates that Updike elevate these techniques, which could be argued as drawing away from his natural style. Without doubt, this transformation influenced the thinking of those who reviewed the novel.

At the same time, it stands to reason that Updike realized these points about *Terrorist*, due to his comprehensive attentiveness to all aspects of the publishing business. Maybe he found motivation in achieving a spot on *The New York Times* Best Seller list toward the end of his career, since most of his work did not appear there. In fact, his most recent book to make it on the list had been an edited anthology of short stories, *The Best American Short Stories of the Century*, edited with Katrina Kenison some seven years earlier. The fact that the author agreed to an extensive marketing campaign for *Terrorist* indicates that he had best seller aspirations for the book.

This chapter asks readers to engage with Updike and the various audiences that intersect with the publication of a novel. I begin with his relationship with acquisition and general editors, publishing staffers, and others who are the first people outside the author himself to engage with the manuscript. Next, the chapter considers how Knopf's marketing department chose to publicize *Terrorist*. This analysis is often an overlooked aspect of the publishing industry, but critical in understanding how Updike and Knopf executives approached the book.

Naturally, considering that these first two parts revolve around getting the book into the hands of readers, the last two sections engage the post-publication reaction. The examination first views the public response to *Terrorist*. Then, attention is directed to the professional critics. Given the stakes of a novel like this one, which the publisher expects to sell well, the critical reaction is an important part of the picture. In many cases, these journalistic pieces also set a tone for a novel's initial scholarly reputation.

Updike and Editors

As a freelance writer, even one famous, celebrated, and hardworking, Updike remained mindful of the marketplace. He approached the craft as a profession, which necessitated nurturing relationships with editors, particularly at *The New Yorker*. The magazine sustained his early career and then enabled him to flourish as a freelance critic and essayist throughout the rest of his life. Outlining his thoughts about writing and product, Updike says, "I think you set up shop as a storyteller, a story maker, a story seller, and it becomes your product, something you're going to live by, like shoes" (Schiff, "Conversation" 430). He set an early goal of publishing six stories a year in *The New Yorker*, which he calculated would enable him to support his growing family in small-town Ipswich, Massachusetts. The idea of publishing half a dozen stories a year in one magazine is probably incomprehensible to contemporary writers since today's magazines simply do not provide that kind of space to fiction. For example, a single short story in *The New Yorker* today can launch a writer's career or solidify her standing among the current crop of greats. Although Updike made the decision to quit his job as a staff writer for the magazine and move from New York City to a suburban home in the late 1950s, he remained keenly aware of who purchased his "shoes."

Over his long career, Updike left few topics unturned regarding the publication process. However, one must make a conscious decision to accept, accept with reservation, or decline what he said, since he wore several guises in these exchanges, including professional writer, literary celebrity, and salesman. From a symbolic interactionism view, the interview process itself seems suspect. Such exchanges certainly contain elements of performance, which Updike acknowledges. Not only is he facing a specific interviewer, but also he understands that a potentially broad audience also exists who will read, watch, or otherwise ingest the content he delivers. In that personal exchange with the interviewer, Updike's thoughts about a book or its characters might be pulled directly from his memory, but there is an exchange taking place with the other individual that is forcing the ideas to evolve.

Looking back on his early experiences with *The New Yorker*, for example, reveals a writer keenly aware of the predilections of his editor. In an interview with literary scholar James A. Schiff, Updike recalls, "There were many things he [editor Harold Ross] did not think should be in the magazine; he saw the magazine as entering a middle-class home, and he wanted something that the children of the household would not be threatened by" ("Conversation" 433). In response, Updike wrote short stories that fit Ross's expectations, sending racier pieces to other venues and editors that did not carry these same restrictions, such as *Harper's* or *Playboy*.

For a researcher, investigating how a contemporary author conducts business with editors is a difficult task. Often these interactions only surface long after a writer dies or in an editor's later memoir. Legendary Scribner's editor Maxwell Perkins, for example, provided new insight into his dealings with Ernest Hemingway and F. Scott Fitzgerald in his memoir. Today, though, most book and magazine editors do not hold the celebrity status they once did. Given the consolidation taking place in the modern publishing industry and revolving corporate ownership of most houses, it is difficult to imagine this difficulty improving for future scholars.

Furthermore, the Information Age has diminished the central role of a writer's archive or papers, which scholars have used for generations. For example, depending on the working relationship between the author and editor, records were probably erased—simply deleted from an e-mail inbox or voice mail system. In Updike's case, he remained a letter writer, though many of these were merely brief notes, but these missives and others will still provide valuable insight into his editing and revision processes.

Updike's recent death and the subsequent outpouring of recollections from friends, family, and publishing associations, however, provides unique insight into how the author and his editors interacted. According to Sonny Mehta, publisher of Alfred A. Knopf, Updike:

> [C]ared about the process, about the mechanics involved in making a book. He paid as much attention to those details as he did to his writing. He was an author with the heart of a publisher and a frequent visitor to our offices. He cared about the weight of paper, the inking on the page. He cared about the size of the trim, the trim of the book, the color of the top stain, he cared about fonts, and he cared about the images on a jacket. ("Tribute")

As Mehta indicates, Updike clearly immersed himself in the tiny details of bookmaking because he correlated them with the conduct of a professional writer and the actions of an artisan.

Furthermore, since he rarely accepted advances on his novels—the lifeblood of the writing life for many fiction authors—the seemingly minute aspects of the industry took on added meaning. Inspecting the "shoe" as it transformed from manuscript to printed book must have developed into a natural step in Updike's creative process.

In "Me and My Books," a 1997 essay published in *The New Yorker,* Updike addresses his love of the book production process, explaining, "fussing with the type, the sample pages, the running heads, the dust jacket, the flap copy, the cover cloth—has perhaps been dearer to me than the writing process." Whereas one would imagine a writer most closely allied to writing and revision, for Updike, the final published product "hangs as a shining mirage luring me through many a gray writing day" (*More Matter* 759). Still, like today's authors obsessed with Amazon rankings and Googling themselves, Updike admits searching for his own books in small-town libraries, fascinated with the ones that show the most wear and tear from repeated readings (as Fitzgerald did in Hollywood the late 1930s to uncover whether or not he was still relevant). Updike recognizes the strong tie between writing and publishing, hazily switching sides over which aspect is most dear to him, but remains mindful of the ultimate goal of attracting readers.

In attempting to interrogate the relationship between Updike and his various magazine and book editors, one would be remiss in not addressing the role the writer's persona played, because Updike is almost universally praised for his kindness and humility by those who knew him well and others he met in passing. This kind of analysis is perhaps the most difficult to undertake, however, since I did not know Updike personally, and many of the recent accounts have been laudatory, delivered after his death in celebration of his career. So I will piece together some viewpoints here, understanding that it is done to hone in on some specific characteristics Updike employed with his editorial peers not to assess his personality or drudge up any controversial topics.

Foremost in Updike's repertoire was his humor, much of it self-deprecating. For example, addressing a large group at a sponsored lecture series in June 2009, the author addressed the common myth that he could sneeze and *The New Yorker* would publish it, saying, "I'm still very rejectable (laughter) and still very grateful when I can get something into the magazine" ("Bartos Forum"). This humility, which cannot be assessed as real or contrived, worked to establish a persona the author found comfortable. Similarly, a 2001 panel appearance with a small group of English literature scholars showed Updike using laughter as a way to charm the audience. Discussing a relatively obscure Updike short story, the author himself misquoted the title, while the academics all knew it and chanted the title in unison. Rather than embarrassment, the author handled the exchange breezily, saying, "That's right, I have all of these Updike experts here. It makes me feel relatively ill informed" (Schiff, *Cincinnati* 55). Being on the ball with a quick quip or humorous remark served Updike well in creating his public persona.

From a symbolic interactionist perspective, Updike's internalized self met with external forces (like a live audience) to transform into a version of Updike as speaker that he found comfortable and fit into the audience's mental image of *author*. Social interactionists view this phenomenon as the *me*, or socialized self, that is the source of human freedom. Updike up on stage is conducting "mind activity," and thus able to "analyze situations and direct himself . . . to perform a certain way in a situation." The exchange process with the audience causes everyone involved to "reanalyze situations, to recall past and construct future as action unfolds." Through the words flowing between Updike and his audience, new ideas are generated and fresh synthesis developed. The speech itself and the audience's questions are, according to scholar Joel Charon, "new creative efforts by symbol users, synthesizing and analyzing in unique ways." Furthermore, he explains, "Humans are not sometimes creative; they are creative in *all* situations" (191). Updike's constant transformation, particularly on stage, includes adopting guises that make the role easier for him to fulfill, particularly as a lifelong stutterer and suffering off and on from the skin condition psoriasis.

One sees how Updike's humor worked to his advantage when listening to David Remnick of *The New Yorker* tell stories about Updike's interaction with editors at the magazine. Writing to Editor Henry Finder about his new computer, Updike explained, "I finally found a typeface on this dratted machine that I like. Easy to read on the screen and not too bad when printed out. It's called Lucida Bright, which sounds to me like an Evelyn Waugh heroine." At other times, Remnick recalls Updike adopting a weary, yet comical, voice. After reviewing Robert Alter's translation of *The Five Books of Moses,* Updike wrote, "Oy vey, as Moses said to Zipporah, what an assignment!" ("Tribute"). The wit and urbanity in such notes certainly endeared the author to the receiver.

Given the task of assigning a review essay, would any editor who could call on Updike not give him the assignment, particularly given the care he demonstrated when assessing each piece? According to Remnick, even at a point in which Updike no longer needed *The New Yorker,* he continued to accept nearly every assignment given to him, regardless of the topic. Maybe gratitude is the simple answer. Perhaps Updike continued to publish in the magazine because it provided a stage early in his career that launched him to fame. Likewise, one assumes that enduring Knopf's cross-platform marketing campaign for *Terrorist* came down to Updike realizing that he could still give back to his longtime publisher.

Judith Jones, Updike's editor at Knopf for almost 50 years, echoes many of the statements made by his magazine editors, but adds to the picture by revealing the author's total participation in the bookmaking business. With Updike rarely taking an advance on his books, he had a certain freedom that most authors do not hold. He did not like to talk about his current projects, according to Jones. The day a manuscript appeared, she opened it as if it were a present. But it was a gift with instructions on how to proceed: "the package would arrive, and we'd open it. It was complete with an image for the jacket, a sketch of how it should be designed, instructions to Peter Andersen about the type and once more we were plunged into the fun of making a book" ("Tribute").

For many writers, the cat-and-mouse game between copyeditors, editors, and the writer nearly ruin the thrill of publishing. However, Jones found working with Updike exhilarating:

> To me, it was always a treat to go through his first pass, his second pass, sometimes even a third pass, and see all the refinements he felt compelled to make, sometimes to sharpen what he called his 'regrettable phrasing,' sometimes to justify the line, and occasionally, because he got carried away with his own words, I was even asked to comment and tell him if I thought he had gone too far. ("Tribute")

Examining the relationship between Updike and his editors, one must at least question the consequences of an editor receiving the familiar letter from Massachusetts with Updike's smudged print in the upper left-hand corner. Certainly, if one accepts the premise that editors who work at *The New Yorker* are lovers (or at least admirers) of the written word, then it must have been a treat to receive a letter or phone call from Updike the literary celebrity. His longtime editors, such as Roger Angell, essentially grew up with him, but newer members of the Updike team quite possibly would have studied his work in college or read it for pleasure. Receiving a letter from Updike for a lover of words, then, is akin to getting a signed baseball from Willie Mays or an autographed photo of Marilyn Monroe.

Clearly, Updike relished working with editors. His graciousness played a part, revealing him as a thoughtful, courteous writer, who did not demand and bully, even though he could have acted that way as his fame grew. That Updike conducted himself without an agent and did not count on advance money to finance his work speaks volumes about his standing as one of the last literary greats.

Updike's Public/Public's Updike

Whether Updike accepted the label "public intellectual" or not, he undoubtedly played the role. There are conflicting reports of how he felt about his early and enduring fame. However, there certainly seems to be an aspect of the interplay that he understood to be part of the exchange between writer and his audience. Being out there in the public sphere, whether that meant writing literary criticism for *The New Yorker,* appearing on television talk shows, or speaking at a university lecture series, meant that people had ample opportunity to create an image or public persona of him that fit their impression of what it meant to be a *writer*. For some individuals, Updike and his public image may have served as their ideal vision of a writer.

More importantly, for a literary figure of Updike's stature, an additional expectation develops. According to James Phelan, the "lines between author, reader, and text become blurred . . . rhetoric is the synergy occurring between authorial agency, textual phenomena, and reader response" (xii). The reading public, and certainly the author's devoted following, carves out of its collective consciousness what to expect from an Updikean piece. One imagines in this sense that the actual Updike the writer dissolves or disappears as the reader interacts with what they deem Updikean.

For his fictional works, readers anticipate (or possibly require) a similar voice and feel in each subsequent novel or short story because they sense in it something that they can relate to consciously or subconsciously. "Most readers," scholar Janice Radway explains, "willfully engage texts from their own ground, wandering about within them sometimes aimlessly, sometimes hell-bent on a purpose. They raid them, remake them, perform them . . . they write them anew" (339). In other words, readers return to authors that provide them with a setting, situation, or characters that allow them to adapt themselves to. As such, the old adage "diving into a book" makes perfect sense. In addition, though, the reader is also diving into the author.

Updike's boyhood dream of writing for *The New Yorker* provided him an intellectual home. From the glossy pages of the magazine, countless readers poured over his work, whether fiction or nonfiction, expanding his readership far beyond most of his peers. According to David Remnick, "Anyone associated with the magazine has to admit that John was *The New Yorker*. He was the magazine. He enlarged it, he graced it, he gave it intellectual ambition and a particularly shimmery American tone. He gave it a horizon, just out of site ("Tribute"). Many of life's certainties are not eagerly anticipated, but readers of *The New Yorker* could count on Updike's appearance in its pages almost like clockwork. The strong link between the literary sensibility of the magazine and Updike as its champion gave readers a way to approach the magazine and his work as an author.

Concurrently, Updike's conception of the "ideal reader" of *The New Yorker* played a part in how he wrote, particularly in the early years of his career when he counted on the magazine as his primary means of supporting his family. According to literary theorist Walter J. Ong:

> [T]he writer must construct in his imagination, clearly or vaguely, an audience cast in some sort of role—entertainment seekers, reflective sharers of experience . . . [and] the audience must correspondingly fictionalize itself. A reader has to play the role in which the author has cast him, which seldom coincides with his role in the rest of actual life. (12)

The New Yorker represented a comfort zone for Updike. He knew the magazine so well, pouring over the pictures and text as a young teenager and devouring it as he grew up, that he may have known the typical magazine reader better than the editors running the publication. Still, Updike could not be certain his fictionalized reader equated to the magazine's actual subscribers.

At least early in his career, Updike imagined his ideal reader, "pampered and urban, needing a wholesome small-town change from his then-customary diet of Westchester-adultery stories . . . a body of my fellow Americans to whom these modest doings in Pennsylvania would be news" (*Odd Jobs* 135). Updike's ideal reader found interest in a vision of the real United States, but he allowed for differences of what Middle America meant for different people. He explains, "From *Rabbit, Run* on, I have often been accused of painting a bleak picture of American reality. But I must say that when I'm drawing that picture, I rarely feel I'm portraying something especially bleak" (Reilly 239).

Although not a central cog in scholar Mark McGurl's postwar creative writing "program era," in that he did not teach creative writing or derive his primary income from a college or university, Updike still benefited from the rise of creative writing in American institutions of higher education. As greater numbers of colleges implemented creative writing programs at the undergraduate and graduate level and students flocked to fill vacant seats, Updike held the increasingly sacred title—*author*—a position these writing students aspired to attain. He and a handful of others who stood at the top of writing's Mount Olympus served as heroes or inspirations for those attempting the climb.

More importantly, however, as McGurl explains, "the largest number of serious readers in the postwar period . . . have been produced through the agency of the school, where millions of students were first introduced to the refined pleasures of the literary and convinced . . . of its worth as a mode of experience" (64). Out of these "millions," certainly, came the majority of Updike's most devoted followers. Who better than an audience trained to recognize beautiful writing to shimmer with anticipation at the arrival of each new Updike tome? The creation of this ready-made audience of potential book buyers is the real benefit of the postwar creative writing movement.

In contrast to Updike's traditional path, writer Michael Chabon stands as the program era's version of Updike. After graduating from the University of Pittsburgh, Chabon entered the Master's of Fine Arts creative writing graduate program at the University of California at Irvine. Also a stylist, whose early work is noted for its delicately crafted sentences, Chabon scored the then-record highest advance payment ever given for a first novel for *Mysteries of Pittsburgh* (1988). In 2001, he won the Pulitzer Prize for *The Amazing Adventures of Kavalier & Clay*.

Like Updike, Chabon does not rely on teaching to support himself and his family, though he has held visiting writer posts, lectured at universities, and spoken at writer retreats and conferences. Given the transformation of popular culture to a predominantly television and movie era, Chabon has work optioned by film production companies and worked as a screenplay writer. The former includes the critically acclaimed *Wonder Boys* (1995), while Chabon also wrote for the blockbuster film *Spider-Man 2,* which grossed more than $783 million worldwide. Chabon's more recent works have been quirkier, ranging from young adult novels to hard-boiled detective pieces and science fiction.

Perhaps for Updike, the commitment to the full sweep of the institutionalization of creative writing programs smacked too much of rigidity or bureaucracy. Maybe he did not want to face the criticism that his good friend Joyce Carol Oates confronted for simply writing too much. As McGurl relates, Oates's prodigious output, what he labels "maximalism," drew fire, indicating to some reviewers that she "doesn't write books now, the books write her" (quoted in McGurl 298). Although not a formal component of the system, Updike prospered in it. Teaching the love of writing (and by extension, reading) to eager undergraduate and graduate students created an audience for his work, whether art and literary criticism in *The New Yorker* or his most recent novel.

Interrogating 9/11 and Selling Terror

The publishing industry lags behind its mass media brethren in using all the available marketing tools at its disposal to turn books into events. Even the splashiest marketing campaign for a novel pales in comparison with the release of a film, music CD, or iTunes single. For example, while a coup for a book launch might be an author appearance on NPR, advertisements for movies are shown nationwide for weeks prior to release. Sticking to its early twentieth-century model for selling books, basically publishing them with little coordinated thought about how to get the thing in the hands of a reader who is ready or eager to buy it, keeps the industry at a perpetual disadvantage versus other popular culture channels.

Given the relatively ramshackle state of book marketing, publishing houses fall back on the few outdated modes of generating buzz they have used for generations, such as author appearances and book signings. For authors who have not yet established a following, these events are fraught with fears of reading to empty rooms and traveling hundreds or thousands of miles to a signing only to have a handful of people attend. Regardless of how dreadful and hit-or-miss these efforts are, they are viewed as a kind of rite of passage for writers the publisher believes might sell. On the other hand, one expects that mass-market writers will support their books via these channels, since their books are more important than literary ones in driving the bottom line.

Given the odd configuration of celebrity in modern bookselling, it is strange when a famous literary author like Updike goes on tour to launch a new novel. For one segment of the audience, he is a central figure in modern American letters. Others, however, will have little knowledge of him in the swell of more popular and famous mass-market authors. Scholar Loren Glass comments on this duality regarding the idea of celebrity in the modern bookselling marketplace, explaining, "Celebrity, of course, remains a crucial ingredient in the marketing of books, but like publishing itself, it has become almost entirely absorbed into the protocols of the general field of cultural production" (199). In this marketplace, publishers elevate certain books they decide "have legs," at the expense of nearly every other title in their catalog. As Glass correctly indicates, it is the consolidation of the publishing industry from family-owned firms to multinational conglomerates that leads to a publisher primarily pushing mass-market titles and authors. As a result, Glass sees the end of the literary celebrity in the image of Hemingway or Kerouac, simply because the culture industry no longer has room for nurturing careers nor building fame slowly.

In promoting *Terrorist*, one sees that Knopf hoped to capitalize on Updike's position as a historically significant literary figure, while at the same time, calling attention to his ability to address contemporary challenges in the post-9/11 era. The book jacket itself, a part of the publishing process Updike reveled in, is telling. While one's eyes might be drawn first to the shadowy figure at occupying the center of the image, it is Updike's name across the top of the cover that is most striking, significantly larger than the title and dwarfing the subtitle "A Novel" in the lower right-hand corner. In accentuating the author's name, rather than the title or status as a novel, adheres to a trend used to sell mass-market books—using the author's name as the primary means of selling the book. One often sees marketing ploy used to promote books by authors such as Stephen King, Dan Brown, and James Patterson.

The publisher's decision regarding the sales potential of *Terrorist* is also evidenced in the difference between its cover and that of Updike's recent previous novels, including *Villages*, released two years earlier. The blue-gray cover for the *Villages* hardback placed the title at the top of the page in a reddish font. Updike's name is in the same color, though not as boldly as the title. The central image is the painting *The Turkish Bath* (1862) by Jean Auguste Dominique Ingres containing a provocative display of a dozen or so naked women, in a neoclassical vision of a Harem scene. In 2002's *Seek My Face*, the hardback cover features a close-up of a featureless face. Updike's name is across the forehead of the face in a font larger than the title of the novel, but the black lettering relegates it to secondary position. By contrast, the white lettering of the title stands out.

The decision to use renowned book jacket designer Chip Kidd, who had produced other Updike covers, such as *Memories of the Ford Administration*, to create the *Terrorist* cover separated the novel from Updike's stylish earlier ones. According to Kidd, he and the author worked closely on the design, with Updike finding the image and Kidd discovering a way to best employ it. "It's tough to do something fresh with the word terrorist because we're so inundated with it," Kidd says. "On the cover there's this initial shadowy figure, but when you turn it upside down it's just a guy's reflection on a rainy street" (Yurchyshyn "How"). The stark white font used for the title and Updike's name grew out of the author's initial idea to present the image as a newspaper headline.

Central to Knopf's marketing, *Terrorist* was Updike himself taking a commanding role in selling the novel. While some factions of the book-buying public might not find Updike's promotional efforts appealing, his willingness to hit the road caught the attention of *The Wall Street Journal*. Reporter Jeffrey A. Trachtenberg noted:

The author, who has rarely promoted his previous books, is making TV appearances and touring several cities at the request of his publisher. It is the first time he's been on the road in 16 years. Carole Horne, the head buyer at the Harvard Book Store in Cambridge, Mass., says she ordered 700 copies of *Terrorist* in advance of a reading Mr. Updike is giving at the store on June 29. ("Updike's")

While Trachtenberg overstates Updike's lack of a role in selling his previous books, the *Terrorist* marketing campaign hinged on Updike's ability to use his fame as a means of attracting attention, such as answering questions about earlier works that he had dealt with many times in the past, while at the same time enthusiastically promoting the new novel and fielding those questions with equal aplomb.

Rather than wait and see if Updike's book sold based on the topicality of its subject matter, or even his intense fame, Knopf approached the novel as it would be a mass-market seller. The publisher sent out approximately 2,500 advanced reader copies (ARCs) to individuals who might play a role in selling it, from distributors and bookstore personnel to journalists and media people. By distributing ARCs, Knopf took a gamble that popular interest would overwhelm or at least balance out any potentially negative reviews that might appear. "It was about getting them to read Updike, whom they may not have read in some time," explains Paul Bogaards, a Knopf spokesman (quoted in Trachtenberg "Updike's"). The move also showed Knopf's willingness to prove that Updike remained a relevant novelist, confronting challenges facing the nation in the twenty-first century.

From a researcher's perspective, it is impossible to ignore the strictly financial rationale for Knopf and Updike to take every possible step in marketing *Terrorist*. In modern publishing, the houses rely almost exclusively on mass-market sales to drive revenues. In other words, the potential profit from three or four James Patterson novels annually enables almost every other work to break even or lose money. Since Updike did not rely on large advances against royalties, Knopf had little to lose in designing a broad marketing campaign for the novel. More importantly, if *Terrorist* developed into a hit, it would unexpectedly stand as a revenue-generator for that fiscal year.

For Updike, the consummate freelance writer, the one who rarely (if ever) turned down an assignment, the opportunity to hit the best seller lists one more time at the end of his career probably stirred his thinking. Updike told Trachtenberg that "he decided to do a promotional tour because Knopf told him it would help sell books." Moreover, using an appropriate sports metaphor, Updike explained, "It's something I discovered I can do . . . like Muhammad Ali, who towards the end of his career discovered he could take a punch. I can take the punch of a book tour . . . and I might be on the mat before you know it" (quoted in "Updike's"). There is an air of bravado in Updike comparing himself with the former heavyweight champion of the world. However, given his celebrity status and past accomplishments, the writer certainly shared similarities with the boxer as he faced down the end of his career. Updike also stood keenly aware of his dwindling time on the national stage. He explained to journalist John Freeman, "I felt while I was writing that this book had potential for selling a little better than the others. But my college education leads me to distrust any book that sells well" (A2). The quip at the end of this passage demonstrates Updike's routine self-deprecation, but the prospect of leaving the literary world with another big seller had meaning for him.

The wish to achieve another best seller, combined with Knopf's desire to build a high-profile marketing campaign around *Terrorist*, led Updike to hit the publicity trail. The 74-year-old author spent two weeks touring the country, primarily granting interviews and appearing at lectures. After returning from the trip, Updike sat for a day filled with interviews in the publisher's New York City offices. Each interviewer came in to speak to him in 30-minute timeslots. Interestingly, this style of interviewing grew out of Hollywood press junkets in which film stars endure a barrage of interviews just prior to the release of the film from a central location. Like satellite radio and television tours, the method enables a broad swath of reporters to receive access, thus satisfying their audiences without requiring the celebrity to travel extensively or the outlets ponying up the funds to send reporters out following the celebrity. Using this style of interview for Updike's new novel suggests the height of his celebrity status and the widespread interest in his work.

The ensuing media blitz surrounding *Terrorist* produced at least 975 newspaper articles, reviews, interviews, or radio appearances globally. Despite this number of searchable returns, the actual number of media impressions (potentially geometrically larger) through blog hits and Web articles is impossible to calculate. At this time, general search engines, such as Google and more specialized private databases do not have the capability of finding all this information. However, the tools that are available indicate *Terrorist* received enormous review and commentary both online and in traditional media outlets.

According to Trachtenberg, the marketing push resulted in Updike's biggest seller in decades, despite a number of negative reviews: "The book was No. 18 on Amazon.com on Sunday and debuted last Friday on *The Wall Street Journal* list at No. 6. Since its publication June 6, Mr. Updike's publisher . . . has gone to press six times and has increased the number of books in print to 118,000 from 60,000" ("Updike's"). By contrast, the author's recent previous novels ran in the 30,000 to 40,000 range, vastly more than most novelists sell, but nowhere near the major best seller lists. A week later, *Terrorist* entered the *New York Times* Best Seller list at number eight (see Table 2.1 for more information on Updike's book sales throughout his career).

Reception of *Terrorist*

Updike may be the most open literary writer in America when it comes to discussing his critics and reviews. Perhaps his role as a book reviewer and essayist increased his awareness of how authors are stacked up against one another, or maybe it occurred once he occupied the more rarefied air of Pulitzer Prize and National Book Award winner. Regardless of the origin, Updike knew that reviewers, scholars, and critics kept score. As a result, he took pains to discuss who might have authority when examining an author's output, explaining:

> You know, it's a strange experience talking about your own books, especially since an author is by no means the last authority about what he has written. I wind up talking about Updike's book according to Updike, but there is always the very real possibility that there is a good deal in the book which you, the author, don't understand. A more reliable memory involves what you were trying to do. (Reilly 240)

Like presidents who attempt to create the foundation for the way historians will interpret or assess their presidencies, Updike worked diligently to set the tone for his place in literary history. Many of Updike's Henry Bech stories, collected as *The Complete Henry Bech* (2001), for example, are amusing revenge stories in which a decidedly evil New York City writer exacts revenge on his critics.

It is no secret that Updike's 1989 memoir *Self-Consciousness* grew out of an attempt to get the details out before a potential biographer might. A decade later, he spoke about literary biography (published in 1999 in *The New York Review of Books*) in honor of the 200th volume produced by the *Dictionary of Literary Biography,* actually calling into question the sensationalist aspects of many of these tomes. Instead, he preferred biography that opened new inroads into re-examining a writer's work. Updike did not hide his disgust at the thought of a biographer: "disturbing my children, quizzing my ex-wife, bugging my present wife, seeking for Judases among my friends . . . and quoting *in extenso* bad reviews I would rather see consigned to oblivion" (*Due Considerations* 10–11).

Although only mentioning reviews in passing, this statement reveals a great deal about Updike's thoughts on the subject. What one sees in his writing is a conscientious decision to see bad reviews as settling into oblivion. At other times, the author talked about how books that received only fair reviews at publication later morphed into being considered his finest works after reassessment by academic critics, particularly *The Centaur*. In another well-known case, scholar Harold Bloom loudly proclaimed *The Witches of Eastwick* Updike's greatest novel, while curtly dismissing the rest, including *Rabbit, Run*. Updike later told an interviewer, "I was pleased Bloom liked the book, but at the price of all the others, it was a kind of heavy price to pay" (Plath 261). The author understood the permanency of critical viewpoints from the perspective of a writer and as a venerable book critic himself.

Updike certainly held a roller-coaster relationship with both professional and academic critics, which may have sparked his pragmatic thoughts about reviews. On the other hand, discussing reviews so openly might have also been a way to begin his own agenda-setting when it came time for critics and scholars to analyze his catalog.

Returning to *Terrorist*, Updike's tireless marketing work and Knopf's willingness to invest resources into the promotional campaign vaulted the novel to best seller status shortly after its release in mid-2006. The publisher pushed the book similarly to how it would a mass-market name writer and the results followed. While many mass-market thrillers sell well, most do not get reviewed in mainstream publications. By contrast, capitalizing on Updike's celebrity and the new ground he covered in penning a thriller, *Terrorist* received reviews in magazines and newspaper across the United States and abroad. Taken as a whole, though, the reviews were decidedly mixed, at best.

Unlike many other post-9/11 novels, such as Don DeLillo's *Falling Man*, *Terrorist* does not draw on the immediate aftermath of the attacks. For example, DeLillo's book literally begins with a main character emerging—soot-covered and dazed—from the World Trade Center. Updike's novel is set at least one year after September 11 and possibly several years in the future, though the character's vivid memories of that day and the popular culture references place the timeline within the near future.

Why would Updike skew so far from the safety of suburbia to write a novel that deliberately creates a sympathetic portrayal of a would-be terrorist in the post-9/11 United States? Surely, if one looks back on the reasons Updike says he writes, then the conclusion is that he purposely meant to make a statement about the country and its people in the early twentieth century. In this light, I see *Terrorist* as his warning shot directed at readers who might then act upon the shoddy, flabby, yet wonderful, America he unveils. Scholar Molly Abel Travis explains, "Texts do not perfectly reproduce ideology, for language is not univocal, centered, and fixed. Resistance to ideology is inherent in every ideological stance" (5). Updike, then, is delivering his worldview, but doing so in hopes that the reader as agent will react.

Updike imagined this exchange in a futuristic, farcical essay, reprinted in *More Matter,* between a writer and Martian, explaining American fiction to alien life forms. In the piece, Updike calls the "distinction" between readers and writers "entirely illusory." He explains, "The writer is a reader, reading what he writes as he goes along, watching the text create itself, and the reader as he reads creates the story in terms of scenery he can imagine, faces he can see—it's the story of his life!" (65). Updike then expounds on the positive outcomes of fiction, making the world more sympathetic and exulted, while at the same time reducing cruelty, xenophobia, and paranoia. The dance, in his mind, is between writer as writer and reader and reader as interpreter and inflator.

In examining the professional reception of *Terrorist,* one is drawn to the old adage "any publicity is good publicity." The novel stands as one of the most successful of his late career from a sales standpoint, yet reviewers wrote negative (often scathing) invectives that collectively called into question just about every single aspect of the book. Even those who viewed *Terrorist* favorably did so with reservations, sometimes out of reverence or respect for Updike's past glories. Two thoughts that might account for abuse are that perhaps the marketing campaign somehow sullied the author in the mind of critics and journalists, thereby predisposing the novel to poor reviews by serious reviewers who grew tired of hearing and seeing Updike plugging it. Second, given that the book is clearly a thriller, maybe reviewers thought they could be harsher, since it was not the author's typical literary fiction. In other words, in addition to taking shots at Updike, they also rebuked the thriller genre at Updike's expense. The sensationalist aspects of contemporary journalism might have also played a role in the reviews. The old adage, "it bleeds, it leads" is used sarcastically, but has merit in an era that focuses on celebrity news and turmoil. A reviewer beating up on Updike creates an atmosphere that draws additional readers and viewers.

Reviews

Despite how he might have felt internally about the growing list of negative reviews for *Terrorist,* Updike approached them with his typical graciousness and self-deprecating manner. Speaking in front of a packed house at the New York Public Library, he joked, "I've been on tour with this book for two weeks and met a lot of people and faced some audiences and mostly what I get is flattery and 'how nice' and 'loved your stuff' and all this so you begin to think that you're a pretty swell fellow . . . and Michiko Kakutani brings you back to reality in a very healthy way" ("Bartos Forum"). Kakutani is arguably the most widely read book reviewer in the United States as lead critic for *The New York Times,* so her scathing review of *Terrorist* made waves in literary circles and set a tone for the general impression of the novel. Despite several other more balanced reviews to appear in the paper's pages, as well as an interview with Updike about the book, once Kakutani came out swinging, she provided the rest of the reviewer community with a license for brutality.

Asked specifically about Kakutani, Updike quipped:

> "Michiko Kakutani and I have danced many a round together and her reviews of me seem petulant . . . she gets on a subject, a point of the book, one tiny point of the book, and won't let it go. And she is censorious . . . I never feel in her much of an effort to say, "Well, that's true, but this is good about the book, or this book does that." I don't feel this so keenly when she reviews other authors. ("Bartos Forum")

Listening to the taped remarks, one hears the joking tone in Updike's voice in answering the question about the reviewer and the audience's uproarious laughter. In his dance metaphor and the use of the word "petulant," though, one senses not only that the author purposely calls her out for her unreasonableness, but also that he expects nothing less. Petulant smacks of wording a parent might use to describe an ill-behaved child, so there is a tone of fatherliness in Updike's usage, perhaps since her style appears to him a violation of his own rules regarding how one should compose book reviews.

In contrast to the prevailing negativity represented by Kakutani, writer Bryan Appleyard, reviewing for *The Sunday Times* (London) hailed the "public enthusiasm" for the novel that showed its staying power "beyond the terms of critical discourse." For him, Updike stepped into a much-needed gap for Americans "seeking authoritative voice to tell them what is going on." By purchasing the novel, the book-buying public sent a message about its own desires, according to Appleyard ("Our Eye").

Writer John Irving noted how the terrorism culture that developed in the United States and globally after 9/11 played a central role in how professional critics reviewed the book, explaining:

> His novel *Terrorist* was criticized by the sudden abundance of terror experts; Updike didn't get this right, or he didn't correctly understand this element, or—whatever. I thought the novel was an amazingly quick study, and an insightful one. I cared about the characters—something many intellectuals who write fiction don't get at all. ("Dear John")

Table 11.1 presents a sampling of American newspaper reviews of *Terrorist* by publication date and highlights some key thoughts contained in the review that encapsulates the reviewer's thoughts regarding the novel. Although this group of reviews is by no means exhaustive, it encompasses many of the most admired and widely read book reviews in the country. Given the relative difficulty of tracking Web-based information, even from just over three years ago, I decided to stick to print-based sources. At this date, it would be impossible to accurately track the number of blogs and other Internet sources that commented on or reviewed the novel. Given the geometric growth of blogging and other social media websites over the last three years, one should assume that these channels helped Updike sell the book.

This sampling of 12 newspaper reviews reveals the disappointment in that reviewer community regarding *Terrorist* and supports the generally held belief that the novel received mixed reviews. From an audience and reception point of view, however, the table amplifies the disconnect between reviewers and book buyers. Despite what would certainly be considered crushing reviews, particularly by Kakutani and Christopher Hitchens in *The Atlantic*, the novel debuted in the top 10 on *The New York Times* Best Seller list, as well as many additional local lists. Clearly, the segment of the population that reads continued its fascination with terrorism, even five years after the attacks on New York City and Washington DC.

Table 11.1   A Sampling of the U.S. Newspapers with *Terrorist* Review Date and Key Remarks

Newspaper	Review date	Key phrase(s)
The Washington Times	June 4, 2006	"tackles the biggest subject of our age yet manages to feel insubstantial . . . don't confuse insubstantial with uninteresting"; "a page-turner, a treatise on unqualified hatred embodied by a lanky high school student"; "exquisitely detailed descriptive passages . . . eerie ability to capture a mood or moment in just a few phrases"; "subject matter strays far afield from his usual méticr"; "adept at capturing Islamic radicalism's allure"
The Washington Post	June 4, 2006	"Nothing plausible about the characters of this book"; "their harangues are always delivered in a slightly satirical key, as if none of it really mattered"
The Boston Globe	June 4, 2006	"Emotionally daring . . . gripping in its insight . . . also uneven: sometimes dull . . . a couple of ludicrous plot developments that rob the novel of its ultimate punch"; "some-times wrenching in its authenticity"; "riveting plot"; "usual grace with form and content"
The New York Daily News	June 4, 2006	"The book itself fails in its own higher purpose, trying to explain on a micro level how homegrown rage is nurtured. The good news is that Updike's comfy genius still stands"; "Updike has too much humanity to really grasp the ugliness . . . ultimately suffers not because it doesn't feel real, but because it really feels"
St. Petersburg Times	June 4, 2006	"*Terrorist* fails because Updike doesn't know Ahmad Mulloy"; "book never achieves anything deeper than a rhetorical truth"
The Philadelphia Inquirer	June 4, 2006	"moves beyond stereotypes of the fatherless and brotherless to a meditation on the mysteries and terrors of alienation and faith"; "not without flaws . . . plot turns on clunky contrivances and coincidences"; "burrows beneath the surfaces of American popular culture, which Updike traverses so well, to truths worth remembering"

(continued)

168 John Updike

Table 11.1 (continued)

Newspaper	Review date	Key phrase(s)
USA Today	June 5, 2006	"most adventurous and accessible novel in decades . . . summer's most rewarding book"
The Los Angeles Times	June 5, 2006	"Feels flat-out rigged . . . indulges in some gratuitous button-pushing"; "collection of grotesques"; "contrived plot"; "an interesting, if failed, thought experiment"; "saturated in paint-by-numbers angst"
The New York Times	June 6, 2006	"completely unbelievable individual: more robot than human . . . cliché . . . one-dimensional"; "cartoonish stick figure"; "lousy job"; "maladroit novel . . . dubious"
The Wall Street Journal	June 9, 2006	"A high-brow novelist trying to write below his pay grade"; "uncongenial to his talent"; "It all falls flat . . . squandered by the hopeless plot"
The Christian Science Monitor	June 13, 2006	"results aren't always impressive"; "Updike never really seems to inhabit Ahmad"; "All the Muslim characters . . . in the terrorism business"
The San Francisco Chronicle	June 18, 2006	"timely novel with a queasily plausible plot"; "wholly without credibility"; "Ahmad sounds [like] a wooden actor with a bad accent"; "Updike has lost, or perhaps abandoned his gift for characterization"

More important, however, is that Updike overcame negative reviews by committing to a tireless marketing effort. Also it would be naive to dismiss the author's standing as one of the nation's most acclaimed writers and the role that played in pushing sales.

Table 11.2 presents a sampling of magazine reviews of *Terrorist* by publication date and highlights key ideas contained in the review that encapsulate the reviewer's opinion of the novel. Although the magazine reviewers generally had more space to discuss the novel in comparison with the limited word counts in most newspapers, as a whole, the longer reviews were about equally mixed.

Most of the 10 publications listed earlier are glossy, consumer-oriented magazines. *Library Journal,* however, is included based on

Table 11.2 A Sampling of the U.S. Magazines with *Terrorist* Review Date and Key Remarks

Magazine	Review date	Key phrase(s)
Library Journal	May 15, 2006	"Updike captures brilliantly the coercive tactics of the organization and the young boy's uncertainties"; "falters in his portrait by depicting Ahmad as a 'typical American teenager' "; "All libraries will want to order this"
New York Magazine	May 28, 2006	"latest in a long line of Updike boys failing their way to manhood"; "Ahmad wants to be used . . . a luminous jerk . . . a romantic egoist"; "characters in *Terrorist* may be sketchy . . . action perfunctory . . . stereotyping wearisome, but Ahmad stirs up sediment in us . . . we are made more complicated"; "Unlike every other novelist . . . Updike isn't writing from the victim's point of view"
Atlantic Monthly	June 2006	"Given some admittedly stiff competition, Updike has produced one of the worst pieces of writing from any grown-up source since the events he has so unwisely tried to draw upon"
Newsweek	June 5, 2006	"Make[s] you wonder if terrorists, like all monomaniacs who dread complexity and ambiguity, aren't basically boring people"; "Lame-brained, improbable"
The New York Times Book Review	June 18, 2006	"One of the most interesting things . . . is its convergence of imagined views about the way this country is and the way it appears"; "Its tensions are well calibrated and the points of view clearly and at times ironically presented"; "Seems meant as a fable . . . history, in disposing of empires, admits of no innocents and spares no one"
Harper's	July 2006	"The portrait is troubling . . . seems to us something of a monster"; "The story line . . . contains few surprises"; "predictable and unremitting . . . formulas . . . one struggles in vain to take them seriously"; "Updike provides fixed positions and a vaguely plausible outline . . . no instinct for the stir of controversy"; "too much the prisoner of fact . . . too inhibited by his sense that things are as they are"

(continued)

Table 11.2 *(continued)*

Magazine	Review date	Key phrase(s)
The New Republic	July 3, 2006	"Even Updike's attempts to forgo his own lyricism and make Ahmad sound stumblingly prosaic do not really convince"; "Merely the generalized fluid of God-plus-sex that has run throughout all his novels"
The Nation	July 10, 2006	"Lifted from the headlines like an episode of *Law & Order*"; "plot moves along with the slack predictability of a screenplay"; "real trouble lies with Ahmad, whose piety quite literally defies belief"; "all information, and it withholds from the reader the critical contribution fiction might make to our understanding: what it feels like to murder for God"
The New York Review of Books	July 13, 2006	"burning-fuse plot makes this the most mechanically compelling novel that Updike has yet written"; "Ahmad Mulloy, a teenage John Updike with a prayer mat, who cannot help but love the America whose enemy he must become"; "Updike shrinks from giving any real credence to the ideology that drives his plot . . . the book becomes a temporarily enthralling, but ultimately empty, shaggy dog story"
National Review	Sept. 25, 2006	"bold literary effort to come to terms with the post-9/11 world"; "atmosphere he creates is incandescent"; "manages to make a terrorist . . . a sympathetic subject"

its status as a trade magazine for librarians, a key audience for getting books into the hands of general readers. According to a search of the WorldCat database of libraries worldwide, the hardback, English-language edition of *Terrorist* is held in more than 3,000 collections. In comparison, the hardback, English-language edition of *Twelve Sharp* by Janet Evanovich, one of the number one novels on *The New York Times* list while *Terrorist* was in the top 10 is carried by slightly more than 3,500 libraries worldwide.

Examining the newspaper and magazine reviews to gauge how this particular audience interpreted *Terrorist*, two recurring themes emerge. First, the professional critics view Updike's prose style both strengthening and weakening the novel, as if the beauty of the observational writing diminishes from the jihadist anger Ahmad should profess. Second, many of the reviewers took Updike to task for not writing the book they wanted to read, rather than the book he authored. For example, writer Jonathan Raban, reviewing the novel in *The New York Review of Books*, explained:

> If only the novelist had spent more time dreaming himself into the paranoid and angry world of [Sayyid] Qutb and his followers, and given Ahmad Mulloy sufficient intellectual and emotional wherewithal to justify his adherence to the crooked path of righteous violence, *Terrorist* might have stood among Updike's best work. As it is, it conducts an energetic, entertaining, but disappointingly unconsummated flirtation with its important subject. (10)

This brand of criticism is common among professional reviewers, although it violates Updike's own rules for reviewing. In the nonfiction collection *Picked-Up Pieces*, he outlined his thoughts after being on the receiving end of negative criticism. First on his list: "Try to understand what the author wished to do, and do not blame him for not achieving what he did not attempt" (14). The Raban review quoted earlier falls into this category, as do several others. There are hints of this criticism in the infamous Kakutani review as well.

CHAPTER 12

Racing toward the Apocalypse: Updike's New America

[T]he theme of terrorism was there, and I had my sense of participating in it vicariously, and I thought it would be a service to the state of the nation and the world of fiction if I tried to dramatize a young man, a young devout self-converted Muslim living in Northern New Jersey, in a not-very-promising metropolis city, and tried to dramatize him from within and show how he was slowly involved in a terrorist plot.
—From a 2006 interview with John Updike

Here is an argument for serendipity: John Updike, a resident of Beverly Farms, Massachusetts, who normally spends his mornings in virtual seclusion, writing, happens to be less than a mile away from the World Trade Center on September 11, 2001. Rather than watching from home or seeing clips played over and over again on subsequent news broadcasts like the vast majority of American citizens, fate somehow intervened, resulting in Updike watching the Twin Towers fall from a tenth floor vantage point, on what he deemed an otherwise mundane trip "visiting some kin" in Brooklyn Heights (*Due Considerations* 117). Consequently, one of America's greatest living writers just happens to witness firsthand the defining moment of the twenty-first century. It comes as no surprise, then, that *The New Yorker* published Updike's observance and response to the terrorist acts in its September 24, 2001, issue, its first to appear after 9/11.

Given Updike's prolific work as a journalist and critic, one presumes that his thoughts on the terrorist attacks would have been printed whether or not he actually saw the destruction, but his on-the-scene reporting gave his words added consequence. Updike's description of the horror and personal response provided readers with an additional tool to process the events. He captured the heartache Americans felt at the moment, explaining, "We knew we had just witnessed many deaths; we clung to each other as if we ourselves were falling" (*Due Considerations* 117). Updike also summarized the immediate post-9/11 mood, saying, "The nightmare is still on. The bodies are beneath the rubble, the last-minute phone calls—remarkably calm and long, many of them—are still being reported, the sound of an airplane overhead still bears an unfamiliar menace, the thought of boarding an airplane with our old blasé blitheness keeps receding into the past" (*Due Considerations* 117–18). Here, the nation's preeminent "man of letters" plays an important role in helping people mentally and emotionally process the terrorist attacks.

The power of Updike's nonfiction essay based on his firsthand account of 9/11 is revealed in two ways; first, when the author died on January 27, 2009, many of the obituaries that appeared worldwide included the piece in their overviews of his life and work, despite an oeuvre that includes basically a book a year published from 1959 to 2009; and second, the short essay led to the creation of *Terrorist*, published five years later.

Comparing Updike's real-life description of 9/11 published in *The New Yorker* and the subsequent use of the theme in *Terrorist* reveals not only similarities, but also distinct differences. In the nonfiction essay, for example, Updike quotes terrorist mastermind Mohamed Atta telling a neighbor that he did not like the United States because "it was too lax . . . I can go anywhere I want to, and they can't stop me" (quoted in *Due Considerations*, 118). Subsequently, in the post-9/11 world of *Terrorist*, Americans trade their physical freedom for freedom to pursue consumerism. Jack surmises that "America is paved solid with fat and tar," which keeps people bloated and satisfied, but allows "religious fanatics and computer geeks" free reign (27). In this instance, it seems as if Updike's initial thoughts and reactions to the real-life terrorist attacks in New York City inform his later novelistic storytelling.

From the symbolic interaction perspective, Updike's use of real-life events to fuel his storytelling efforts exemplifies the complicated nature that exists between self, events and issues, and experiences. Terrorism is a subject created according to cultural understandings (and possibly prior to 9/11, misunderstandings) of the term, yet Updike also interprets the idea based on his lived experience and the social interactions with himself and others. Making matters more complex, the author's perception of terrorism and its consequences are filled with a lifetime of cultural representations, drawn from film, television, books, and journalistic accounts of terroristic acts. Interestingly, the characters in the novel confront the same interactionist issues. Although the fictional world of New Prospect, New Jersey, is imaginary, characters in that world face a quasi-realistic framework in which 9/11 occurred and presents ramifications.

In *Terrorist,* for example, Ahmad's Lebanese American boss Charlie Chehab draws parallels between modern jihadists and the revolutionary forces led by George Washington. Charlie's underlying assumptions about both groups are drawn primarily from cultural representations, though he does in fact have firsthand experience with would-be terrorists. The idea of George Washington as hero of the Revolutionary War also holds its own meaning. Sociologist C. Wright Mills explains how the cultural machine is used to create self, calling it "the lens of mankind though which men see . . . interpret and report what they see . . . it is the semiorganized source of their very identities" (406). Charlie's heroic stance—tying jihadists and anti-American Muslims to the preeminent founding father—enables him to manipulate Ahmad based on their shared cultural representation of George Washington as the father of the nation and its foremost patriot.

If written prior to the terrorist attacks on the United States, *Terrorist* might have merely served as another example of an Updike fictional departure or, in the minds of some critics, a deviation—similar to earlier works in which the renowned chronicler of the suburban United States explored a global topic. Given such a scenario, readers may have scratched their heads and wondered why Updike would produce a thriller with political overtones at this seemingly late stage in his career. Certainly, critics would have noted the striking deviation from the content of the Rabbit series, perhaps comparing it with other significant Updike experimental works, such as *The Coup* or *A Month of Sundays.*

As interesting as questions about the novel are if the attacks on the United States did not occur, one cannot analyze *Terrorist* outside the context of 9/11. The work is a product not only of the events Updike witnessed that day in Brooklyn Heights, but also that derived from what pundits deemed "the post-9/11 world," a new cultural environment fundamentally different than had existed before. In an interview appearing in *Book* magazine, Updike discussed his rationale for writing the novel, saying:

> And as a novel like *The Coup* shows, I'm interested in Islam as a more fiery and absolutist and, some would say, fanatical brand of theistic faith. So it was not just my happening to have been there

but my sensation that I was qualified to speak about why young men are willing to become suicide bombers. I can kind of understand it, and I'm not sure too many Americans can. ("Interview")

Immediately after September 11, the nation turned more patriotic, lauding the heroic efforts of firefighters and police officers in New York City and around the country. President George W. Bush also garnered nearly universal support for military efforts, including the October 2001 military invasion of Afghanistan and other efforts to destroy Al Qaeda, the terrorist cell network headed by Osama bin Laden.

The Bush administration also launched a series of domestic security programs to counter potential future terrorist threats. The president authorized the creation of the Department of Homeland Security to coordinate protection efforts at home, naming former Pennsylvania Governor Tom Ridge as its first director. Homeland Security later initiated a national alert system indicating various national threat levels, ranging from red (severe risk) to green (low risk). Bush also worked with members of Congress to pass the USA Patriot Act (2001), which granted federal authorities broad powers to sniff out and counter potential security threats.

On the cultural front, commentators argued that 9/11 would fundamentally change the nation's viewing, reading, and media habits. In response, many radio stations dropped songs with lyrics that might be considered offensive, and movie and television studios censored themselves. For example, producers of the $85 million Arnold Schwarzenegger blockbuster *Collateral Damage* cut scenes related to plane hijacking and pushed its release date back to 2002. Meanwhile, executives in charge of the hit HBO television series *The Sopranos* deleted scenes of the World Trade Center Twin Towers from the program's opening credits. Although Updike is noted for the role nostalgia plays in his work, *Terrorist* focuses on what remained in the wake of September 11.

This chapter uses *Terrorist* as a way of questioning the common misperceptions regarding the scale and scope of Updike's fiction. I argue that the novel, which catapulted Updike onto various best seller lists, became a main selection of the Book-of-the-Month Club and sparked general controversy, but appeared to rather mixed reviews, captures Updike's vision of a new United States and the nation's relationship to the world in the twenty-first century. By examining the novel's content, the chapter recasts Updike. Rather than encased in the mantle of the Rabbit series featuring everyman Harry "Rabbit" Angstrom, in *Terrorist,* one sees Updike shape a new worldview transformed by the terrorist attacks on the United States, which he witnessed firsthand from just a mile away on that fateful day.

Updike's vision of the post-9/11 United States centers on the idea of faith and lack of faith in the modern world. For Updike, consumerism and its consequences replaced religion and people's central belief in the American political and social system, ultimately debasing the foundational ideas that built the nation. Instead of a fervent belief in the American way or American Dream, Jack Levy laments the impulse to purchase "tawdry junk" that fills people's daily lives (20). The lack of faith, passion, or commitment to "the right path," leads to a world "full of nuzzling," according to Ahmad's mentor, Shaikh Rashid, "blind animals in a herd bumping against one another, looking for a scent that will comfort them" (10).

Pieces of Updike's New America

In *Terrorist*, Updike uses a number of literary techniques designed to guide the reader through the complex ideas at the novel's core. This is the type of writing that gained the author widespread acclaim from the earliest days of his career in the 1950s. While commentators often get caught up in examining Updike as a lyrical writer, within the unique style, one finds a strong and distinct worldview. Many journalistic critics, however, overlook the foundational viewpoints and concentrate on his style, as if it is pretty gift-wrapping paper concealing an otherwise empty package. Commenting on this criticism, Updike once noted:

> My first books met the criticism that I wrote all too well but had nothing to say. My own style seemed to me a groping and elemental attempt to approximate the complexity of envisioned phenomena, and it surprised me to have it called luxuriant and self-indulgent; self-indulgent, surely, is exactly what it wasn't—other-indulgent, rather. (quoted in Tanenhaus)

The criticism regarding Updike's perceived style over substance stuck in his gut. From this perspective, *Terrorist* can be read as the author's attempt to answer this ongoing criticism.

Updike's evolving ideas about the United States, the nation's place in the world, and the consequences of this interaction become the driving forces behind the taut thriller. At the heart of the change in Updike's perspective is the wholesale alteration in scope. Contrast, for example, the limited focus of *Rabbit, Run* and its sequels. In *Rabbit, Run,* the main protagonist's actions wreck havoc on his immediate family, perhaps most exemplified by the dehumanizing consequences for Rabbit's wife Janice. She combats her husband's infidelity and desertion with alcohol, resulting in the *accidental* drowning of their newborn daughter. *Rabbit, Run* symbolizes Updike's emphasis on the individual's place within the family and community and the dire results that might take place if one deviates from that standard.

By contrast, the reader finds in *Terrorist* that the primary characters possess broader impulses, though their lives are all intricately interconnected. While they are deeply joined on a personal level, characters such as Ahmad and Charlie also have ties to the larger world outside. For Updike, the emphasis shifts from the axis of the immediate family and consequences on a small part of the community, as in the Rabbit tetralogy, to characters whose lives are intertwined on a micro and macro level. They hold worldly outlooks and view themselves as part of the global village—even if parts of this broader community must stand at odds.

Faith and Authenticity

Ahmad's faith is arguably the central topic in *Terrorist*. Although just 18 years old and a recent high school graduate, he grapples with life-altering ideas and events that are too complex for him to adequately assess. Consequently, some prominent journalistic critics found Ahmad problematic. For example, Michiko Kakutani of *The New York Times* labeled the character a "completely unbelievable individual," "cliché," "static," and a "one-dimensional stereotype" (E1). These misgivings, however, are the product of not assessing what Updike wrote, but instead that the author did not create the kind of character the critic favored. Kakutani herself compares Updike's Ahmad negatively with characters in the works of novelist Don DeLillo and the real-life portraits of the 9/11 hijackers written by *Los Angeles Times* journalist Terry McDermott. I argue, however, that a deeper textual analysis reveals Ahmad as a complex character in the midst of wholesale transformation. In Updike's post-9/11 worldview, everything is entwined.

The primary concern of critics such as Kakutani revolve around what one teen could think, feel, and believe at such a young age. On one hand, while reviewers could argue that many teens fall into a kind of angst-driven mentality when turning 18 years old and graduating from high school, what separates Ahmad is his true outsider status as an American-born Muslim at this specific moment in the nation's history. He is different from other Muslims in the United States, not born into or raised in the faith or taught Arabic as a first language. Also he is not part of the Black Nationalist Muslim movement, which has a modern history as a fringe, but somewhat accepted religious group. Updike uses this context to provide the teen with a depth that asks the reader to think deeply about the consequences of 9/11 and its aftermath on the meaning of the United States.

In a pivotal scene in *Terrorist,* Updike uses this context brilliantly to force the reader to engage with the nation's foundational belief system, in both its institutional and its legal senses and the broader set of ideas that people see at the heart of being American. Returning from a delivery, Charlie and Ahmad drive into a park in Jersey City, New Jersey, where they get a clear view of the Statue of Liberty, with Manhattan jutting out toward them in the near distance. Although it is a beautiful summer day, in their work clothes of overalls, boots, and Ahmad's ever-present black jeans, the two foreign-looking men are viewed apprehensively. Instantly, they "attract suspicious glances from older, Christian tourists" (186). Charlie is disgusted by the "dirty little looks," they receive (187), Updike's nod at how white Americans view Americans of Middle Eastern descent in the post-9/11 world. Ironically, though, Charlie is actually in the middle of an anti-American tirade, basically prodding Ahmad toward agreeing to become a jihadist. The ideas as play on the surface and just below it in this scene typify the deep thinking at the heart of Updike's thriller.

Charlie criticizes not only George W. Bush, but also everyone who works "serving the empire in their way," whether that is a soldier, investment banker, or waitress (187). Charlie asks Ahmad if he would give his life to fight them, though there is confusion regarding whom the term addresses. For Charlie, it seems to be the United States, while Ahmad hesitatingly adds, "If God wills it" (189). Confusion exists because the stakes are not clear at the time and Ahmad does not want to disappoint his older male friend, another in a long line of father figures for the teen.

In the scene, Updike is playing with people's prejudices, but creating an instance where their bigotry is warranted. The author asks the reader to contemplate a world in which seemingly ordinary people might be terrorists. He is also forcing the reader to consider the many ways an American might become anti-American.

Like many central fictional characters, particularly in coming of age tales, Ahmad carries the weight of the world on his shoulders. Although surrounded by others, he is essentially isolated from the outside world. In many respects, the young man is the ultimate outsider. He is uncomfortable in any of the worlds he orbits, from his identity as a student to his place in a fatherless home with a gadfly mother who takes minimal interest in his day-to-day life. Clearly, Ahmad is confused.

As a young Muslim, Ahmad turns to his strict religious training for answers, even though he does not believe that his teacher, Shaikh Rashid, holds God as close to his heart as he does. Consequently, as a result of his beliefs, Ahmad determines that American society is evil. Doubts, however, creep in. The teen is essentially left to himself to deal with the heap of existential angst produced as a result.

Ahmad's outsider status sets him apart from other characters and fuels his commitment to Islam. At school, Ahmad is a bright student, dumbing down in "voke" classes and basically has no friends. Even his primary sport—track—is one that emphasizes individual achievement, despite the team setting in high school track and field competitions. At home, Ahmad and his mother have difficulty communicating, as if the ghost of his father, who abandoned the family, is ever-present.

Updike captures the conflict within Ahmad early in the novel. The reader's first interaction with the character is in what the teen internalizes: "*Devils,*" Ahmad thinks. *These devils seek to take away my God* (3). The objects of Ahmad's disgust ("devils") one finds in the ensuing lines are the individuals who make up the high school community: scantily clad, tattooed girls; strutting, sauntering boys with "dead-eyed" expressions; and teachers who "make a show of teaching virtue," despite their "lack of belief" (3). Given the general mind-set of most high school students, the idea of them actively attempting to take away someone's God is difficult to comprehend. Beginning the novel inside the main character's head, though, allows Updike to reveal the depths of Ahmad's struggle.

Although Ahmad is disgusted with his high school classmates, he directs his fury at Central High's teachers. Like teenagers that have a great deal of energy, but often lack wisdom, Ahmad lashes out at the authority figures nearest to him. Contrasting the way in which he disparages the students and teachers, it becomes clear that while Ahmad loathes the other high school students, he hates the teachers.

The critique of the students is actually somewhat detached, focusing on the way they look or act—"girls sway and sneer and expose their soft bodies"—based on traditional high school caste systems (3). When Ahmad disparages teachers, however, the attack gets personal. Teachers, according to the teenager, are "puffy" with "bad breath" and "unclean." He criticizes them because, "Their lives away from the school are disorderly and wanton and self-indulgent" (3–4). More importantly, though, they push a belief system that is "Godless," not because they believe in what they are saying, rather to "instill virtue and democratic values" supported by the state government and federal officials in Washington, DC (4). The vitriol Ahmad spews at the Central High faculty identifies those he actually believes are taking away his God. He indicts them for not being authentic, in contrast to the students, who merely act a role promulgated through mass popular culture channels and the nation's overwhelming consumer culture. In Ahmad's mind, the teachers should be severely sanctioned because they do not believe in the ideas they teach and at the same time stand as mindless consumers. Both roles carry out the wishes of the nameless, faceless authorities that control the country.

Updike moves quickly from what Ahmad is thinking in the first two paragraphs of the novel to a third person, omniscient narrator in the third. The scene begins from a detached perspective, placing the teen in an urban setting at the start of spring. In contrast to the fiery rhetoric of the opening, Updike quickly switches tone, providing factual details: "Ahmad is eighteen. This is early April; again green sneaks, seed by seed, into the drab city's earthy crevices" (4). There is a journalistic feel to these lines, though lightened by Updike's flourishes of "green sneaks" and "earthy crevices." Butted up against the anger of the earlier paragraphs, these lines serve as a kind of pause, allowing Updike to bring the reader to normality after the vitriol of those viewed as Godless.

The break, however, is short-lived. Updike jumps back inside Ahmad's mind, saying, "He looks down from his new height and thinks . . ." (4). What the boy then thinks is another indication of his confusion ". . . that to the insects unseen in the grass he would be, if they had a consciousness like his, God" (4–5). The move from condemning Central High's faculty for their lack of belief to his own vanity in assuming a God-like pose presents the central fulcrum of Ahmad's dilemma. No one quite measures up on his scale of belief, thus proving that they are inauthentic, yet he himself doubts his own faith. This early passage sets a tone that many critics clearly missed—Ahmad's fervor counterbalancing his youth and immaturity. At times, he seems like the classic male, only child in a single-parent home, forced to grow up quickly as the man of the house, yet still grappling and confused by the added responsibilities of such a title.

Updike reveals the depths of Ahmad's doubt in the same paragraph. As he contemplates his height after growing three inches in the past year, Ahmad thinks that he will not get taller "in this life or the next" (5). However, he cannot help questioning the thought: "*If there is a next,* an inner devil murmurs" (5). Ahmad continues the line of questioning, wondering what evidence proves that there is a next life. Instead of rigidly accepting what he has learned in the Koran, he believes that there must at least be a hell to provide the energy needed to "maintain opulent Eden" (5). Oddly, after his rampage against his teachers, Ahmad uses an idea he could only have learned in school, asking "What of the second law of thermodynamics?" (5). By deliberately introducing the second law into the internal questioning process, Updike shows Ahmad at odds with his religious and secular educations.

What the reader finds in the first several pages of *Terrorist*, I argue, is a central figure wrestling with ideas crucial to his understanding of himself and the broader society. This analysis reveals Ahmad as a character with depth by exploring Updike's use of rhetoric and internal monologue to show contrasting aspects of the teen's thinking.

Consumerism as a New Religion

One of the criticisms leveled against Updike over his long career is that by chronicling the intimate details of the lives of suburban people that he in many respects supports or validates that lifestyle, particularly the cozy *Americanness* of the never-ending quest for more. However, the idea that a writer supports or validates a particular lifestyle because he uses it as a central topic is problematic. Similar to the way critics and scholars misinterpret F. Scott Fitzgerald's interpretation of the rich, thinking of the author as a kind of apologist for the excesses of the American aristocracy, Updike's deep insight into middle-class life hangs like an albatross around his neck. The need for critics to create a sound-bite overview or description of a writer's work says more about the critic's goals and aspirations than it does the novelist's. Commentators who are able to create such pithy overviews can gain additional readers, some level of fame, and, ultimately, more work by doing so. As a result, it makes sense for critics to use this kind of shorthand in their work, despite what a careful reading might reveal.

One of the central criticisms Updike levels against the post-9/11 United States is its emphasis on consumerism. Nearly every character in the novel holds negative opinions of the generally held belief that people need to be constantly buying things. Ahmad and Jack, in particular, launch into tirades condemning foods and other items that make people complacent, lazy, and apathetic. For example, Ahmad tells Joryleen, "All America wants of its citizens, your President has said, is for us to buy—to spend money we cannot afford and thus propel the economy forward for himself and other rich men" (72). When she protests that Bush is not her president, the boy responds that the individual holding the office does not matter, saying, "They all want Americans to be selfish and materialistic, to play their part in consumerism" (72). The exchange points to a major theme in *Terrorist*: how the American focus on consumerism developed into a new kind of religion.

Although Jack with his world-weary demeanor longs for times when consumerism played a less central role in American life—as if that time ever existed—it is Charlie Chehab, the first-generation Lebanese immigrant, who almost lovingly analyzes the national obsession with more. For Updike, Charlie can be seen as a kind of mouthpiece, but possibly an unreliable one, since at the end of the novel, he is identified as a CIA informant who manipulated Ahmad for the good of "the company." Once this plot point is revealed, the reader is left wondering what aspects of Charlie's relationship with Ahmad portray genuine friendship and what could be labeled pure manipulation. Basically, everything Charlie says must come under new scrutiny.

Charlie loves two things: George Washington and television commercials. At one point, he waxes enthusiastically about Levitra ads and the soft-focus camera shots of women tacitly talking about their man's erections. Charlie enjoys TV ads so much that he proclaims that he would be making them if it weren't for the responsibility of keeping the family business running. Ironically, Charlie realizes "it's crap," meant to keep "the masses zombified" and purposely designed to "mess with your heads," but he still wants to jump right in (173). The rest of television, from the evening news to sports programming is completely worthless in Charlie's mind. Instead, he talks about "The new powers that be, the international corporations, [who] want to wash your brains away, period. They want to turn you into machines for consuming—the chicken-coop society" (172). What the reader does not realize until the end of the novel is that Charlie is actually orchestrating his own brainwashing campaign, acting out the traditional good cop role in his own little pro-terrorism commercial. Like the general public that envisions its dreams fulfilled in little pills and vials, Ahmad eagerly soaks up the pabulum, buying into Charlie's thinking, despite his doubts about his meaning and sincerity. While Ahmad references "the Straight Path" (173) and quotes the Koran, Charlie chatters on about Ex-Lax and female sex enhancement drugs (174–75).

Race

In Updike's new, post-9/11 United States, race remains a central challenge. The terrorist attacks and the Bush administration's subsequent "War on Terror" just expanded the list of those who *regular* Americans could either secretly or openly distrust. It is as if the main focus of racism merely shifted for a time. Blacks, Hispanics, and other minorities did not win an ideological victory, rather a short reprieve, as people turned their attention to those of Middle Eastern descent.

While Ahmad is still a high school student, Tylenol Jones (athletic, bully, African American) derogatorily calls him an "Arab" (97–98) four times, meant to goad the boy into a fight. Earlier, Tylenol explained, "Black Muslims I don't diss, but you not black, you not anything but a poor shithead. You no raghead, you a *shit*head" (16). Later, as other students gather in anticipation of a fight, Tylenol then says, "You all [Arabs] faggots, man" (98). The cutthroat world Updike creates in New Prospect holds no hope for any kind of solidarity of the oppressed.

Ahmad's upright standing based on his religious training and neat appearance is often contrasted with the majority of high school students at Central High, primarily "blacks and Latinos, the gang allegiances declared by the blue and red of the belts on their droopy, voluminous drawers and their headbands and skull-fitting do-rags" (97). Updike uses the divergent styles of Ahmad and other students as a way to portray how low people of Middle Eastern descent fell in the post-9/11 United States. Examined objectively, one would assume that Ahmad would be considered attaining a higher social standing that Tylenol, but not in a world that sees anyone who looks Arabic as a potential threat.

For Ahmad, his mixed heritage is also a constant reminder of race. He often juxtaposes himself against his white, Irish American mother, who he views as whorish, stupid, and overly American in her consumerist mentality.

Updike's sense of race seems little changed by September 11, beyond simply heightening suspicion of Arabs and Arab Americans. As a non-practicing Jew, Jack offers rather harsh critiques of religion throughout *Terrorist*, but is cast as something of a realist, though dour in his outlook. Despite this, however, Jack also reacts negatively to the Muslim imam who delivers a benediction at Central High's graduation ceremony. The Jewish teacher studies the imam, physically "slight, impeccable," but "embodying a belief system that not many years ago managed the deaths of, among others, hundreds of commuters from northern New Jersey" (112). Contemplating the continuing battle between Arabs and Jews worldwide, Jack decides, "the man in his white garb sticks like a bone in the throat of the occasion" (112). So the one character in *Terrorist* who is thought to be somewhat levelheaded from a political standpoint cannot get past his own racist sentiments and the aftermath of 9/11.

Neither does Updike forgive the United States for its racist past. He picks up on the vestiges of racism that shine through the nation's newly intensified hatred of the terrorists and those who are suspected of possible terrorist ties. One senses that it is merely a matter of time before suspicions are cast back on the traditional culprits—blacks and Hispanics.

Beth's sister, Hermione Fogel, for instance, is brought into Homeland Security, informally called the "Undersecretary of Women's Purses," the narrator explains, to craft a way for security personnel to rummage through women's purses without offending the owners with "their naked hands" (45). The challenge, according to the unnamed narrator: "The dozing giant of American racism, lulled by decades of official liberal singsong, stirred anew as African-Americans and Hispanics . . . acquired the authority to frisk, to question, to delay, to grant or deny admission and permission to fly" (46). In other words, the majority of airline passengers (white) balked as newly empowered security personnel (black and Hispanic) performed their duties. In addition, a class-based negativity also rose. In the eyes of wealthy (again mostly white) travelers, "it appears that a dusky underclass has been given tyrannical power" (46). Interestingly, these passages are delivered by the narrator as an overview of the post-9/11 United States, not placed in the mind of one of the primary characters, though they do line up closely to the Secretary of Homeland Security's worldview.

An interesting aspect of the novel is that many of its characters realize that in the twenty-first-century United States, they should be open minded about race, perhaps as an outcome of the politically correct language that pervades daily life. As such, upon first meeting Ahmad, Jack's reaction is rather subdued given that the boy has openly spoken out against the American government and wants to learn to drive a truck (and possibly commercial trucks that can carry hazardous materials when he qualifies). Historically, trucks served as a primary delivery weapon for terrorists, so combined with Ahmad's religious and political views, one would assume red flags would go off in Jack's mind. Instead, he questions the boy's commitment to the "technical side of it and all the regulations" (41).

Reviewing *Terrorist* in *The Atlantic,* Christopher Hitchens identifies the preceding scene as a glaring weakness and proof of Updike's failure to fully comprehend the post-9/11 nation. On further examination, though, one wonders whether Updike actually used the truck scenario to present a nuanced exploration of race and political correctness. In fact, many pundits and security experts agreed that any further attacks on U.S. soil would most likely take place via truck or a container carried on a shipping vessel.

Popular Culture

Updike grapples with the twenty-first-century United States, providing a clear view of post-9/11 society, but cannot help also linking to its nostalgic past. The tactic Updike employs is in the thoughts, speech, and actions of Ahmad and Jack, the 63-year-old high school guidance counselor who takes an interest in Ahmad and his future. Ironically, Jack holds two separate (and competing) views in his daily life—a kind of nostalgic yearning for the past and his youth, while being responsible for helping high school students plan for their futures. As such, this inward-looking man, who frames his worldview through the past, must continually confront the potential futures of the students he counsels.

For popular culture scholars, *Terrorist* presents an interesting duality. On one hand, Updike criticizes much of American popular culture, from the pierced and tattooed high school students in fictional New Prospect, New Jersey, to the mind-numbing dialogue of soap operas and drivel offered up in commercials. Familiar popular culture references fill the pages: Google, Disney, *All My Children,* tattoos, and Times Square. Updike is clearly a student of popular culture, capturing the nuances and deeper meanings in the media-centric world comprising modern America.

As he has from the start of his career, Updike remains rooted in popular culture. In *Terrorist,* however, popular culture is used as a kind of anesthesia or poison, depending on the character discussing the topic. For Ahmad, television is nothing more than an instrument "using sex to sell you things you don't need" (38). The teen contrasts his vision of pure Islam with impure popular culture, resulting "in a world that mocks faith" (69). Adding to the criticism of television and movies, he tells Joryleen, "it is all so saturated in despair and unbelief as to repel my interest" (70), even though his religion does not forbid either.

When Ahmad's sexual stirrings for Joryleen mount, he lashes out at her (and his internal doubt) through popular culture, not pausing to look inward for his uncertainty. Instead, Ahmad criticizes her and others like her, labeling them "slaves to drugs, slaves to fads, slaves to television, slaves to sports heroes that don't know they exist, slaves to the unholy, meaningless opinions of others" (73). As a result, he tells Joryleen that she is headed "straight for Hell" (73). Hurt by the verbal assault, Joryleen responds that Ahmad "don't know where he's heading. You're the one don't know which fucking end is up" (73). The sad truth for Ahmad is that for all his devotion and use of popular culture and the shortcomings of others to mask his doubts, Joryleen is correct. He stands away from the rest of society, often judging everyone around him as less than adequate based on his notion of the Straight Path, but this is all to cover the confusion inside him. Ahmad does not know how to align his future with what he has learned, ultimately leaving him careening down a one-way street with his foot on the gas, but neither hand on the steering wheel.

In much of the novel, Updike uses popular culture as a benchmark for what is wrong with the world. Ahmad and Jack each basically view popular culture as overtly evil. For Ahmad, the bare midriffs, belly rings, and low-plunging necklines he sees in school each day represent an attempt to weaken his religious fervor. The older man contrasts today's popular culture influences with those of his youth, seeing in the nostalgia his own losing battle with entropy and aging. In Jack's mind, for example, today's movies shown at the "seedy cineplex" are "too violent or sexy or too blatantly aimed at the mid-teen male demographic" (25). He longs for the "dazzling subversive visions" released when he was first married, from *Midnight Cowboy* to *Dirty Harry* and *American Graffiti*.

When Jack thinks, it is in historical or nostalgic terms. On the brief mention of renaming a local street Reagan Boulevard, which Ahmad does not register, Jack explains it to himself as a lack of political knowledge on the part of high school students, replaced by their focus on "celebrity heaven" (37). As a result, students believe that John F. Kennedy is the second best president ever, behind Abraham Lincoln, based on his "celebrity quality" (38). The idea here is that popular culture, driven by the mass media and its agenda setters, is able to basically rewrite the past, essentially solidifying *facts* based on ideals that have little or nothing to do with reality. Consequently, if history and some version of reality becomes unreal, then people will have nothing left to believe in, no one left to trust. For Updike, it is in this environment that zealotry thrives, as exemplified by the Bush administration and Muslim jihadists.

Even the Tom Ridge-like director of Homeland Security, Haffenreffer gets in on the antipopular culture viewpoint, explaining, "The way things are going, there won't be a thing America makes. Except movies, which are getting crappier each year" (260). For him, old-time actors, such as Kirk Douglas and Judy Garland "gave good honest value, every performance, one hundred ten percent" (260). He concludes his rant, which includes his racist feelings about Arab Americans, by deciding: "If there's anything wrong with this country . . . is we have too many rights and not enough duties" (261). In his mind, the softness of today's "kid movie actors" (260) and society's celebrity obsession are leading the nation to its knees. When he contemplates his own duties, he cites

Jefferson's holding onto his slaves and the iceberg-filled waters that had sunk the *Titanic*. For Updike, the secretary's lack of faith in his position and his country to support his decisions lead him to blame popular culture, rather than look inward.

Updike portrays popular culture as either a way to numb society from its evils—a type of opiate for the masses—or as a mask for individuals to divert their shortcomings outward, rather than undergo the potentially grueling process of internal reflection. In the post-9/11 United States, the author shows popular culture as a central facet of life for individuals across racial, socioeconomic, and cultural divides.

Authority

For an author labeled as resolutely pro-establishment and pro-suburban America, Updike has little use for authority figures or institutions in *Terrorist*. From the teachers that traverse the halls at dreary, cracked New Prospect High School to the police officers patrolling the Lincoln Tunnel, no one that holds a position of power remains unscathed. Even God comes under fire, from Jack's soliloquies against the Jewish religion to Ahmad's temptations and doubts, despite that he proclaims he feels "God standing beside him—so close as to make a single, unique holy identity, *closer to him than his neck-vein*" (144–45). Updike consistently undermines those holding power, showing that the brave facades, whether propped up in public or questioned while in silent contemplation, are illusory. Authority that lacks true belief or faith at its core reveals the absurdity of power in the post-9/11 United States.

The Department of Homeland Security is treated particularly roughly in the novel, with Updike basically undermining every idea and individual that supports the agency. By creating a government body so utterly devoid of power, the author obliges readers to share his viewpoint. For example, Hermione Fogel, the trusted, spinster underling, blabs state secrets and gossips about her boss "The Secretary" to her sister Beth on weekly phone calls. Underneath her air of superiority over her sister, though, is her sexual yearning for her boss, which undercuts what she says.

As the two bureaucrats discuss whether to raise the threat color code in the Northeast, Hermione pines over her position as second fiddle female in her boss's life. "They should be her children," she reasons. "spending twelve, fourteen hours a day in the same room or adjacent rooms, they are just as much one as if legally married . . . This thought gives her so much satisfaction that she must quickly erase an inadvertent smile from her face" (259). By portraying Hermione as little more than an ultra-devoted spinster, Updike tacitly weakens her position. After discussing the loss of "an asset" (Charlie's murder), Hermione, "longs to comfort the Secretary, to press her lean body like a poultice upon his ache of overwhelming responsibility . . . to take his meaty weight . . . upon her bony frame, and cradle him on her pelvis" (260). The public view of her as a powerful government official is trampled by her private weakness, jealousy, and sexual longing.

Updike portrays Secretary Haffenreffer as even worse. As he contemplates his responsibilities, he alternately tells Hermione that "when the Arab League takes over the country, people'll learn what duties are" (261), then internally compares himself with Jefferson, who "People blame . . . now for holding on to his slaves and fathering children by one of them, but they forget the economic context of the times and the fact that Sally Hemings was very pale. *It's a heartless city*" (261). In reality, though, the secretary is not worried about domestic security or lacking the real power to enforce laws that would make the public safer. He declares that if "this thing in New Jersey blows up, there'll be no sitting on fat-cat boards for me. No speaker's fees. No million-dollar advance on my memoirs" (261). Greed is his goal, or viewed from another vantage, the payoff he expects after dedicating his life to government service. The revelation shocks Hermione. The secretary "has fallen in her estimation" (261), but she does her duty, snapping him back to action. The scene ends with the secretary ordering the increased threat level, his masculinity (and faith) momentarily restored.

Haffenreffer puts local officials on alert by raising the threat level, but the incompetent officers guarding the Lincoln Tunnel do nothing to stop Ahmad as he enters the tunnel with a truckload of explosives. Updike exploits the weakness in the link between federal officials in Washington and those charged with carrying out their orders in local settings. These officers are "benign onlookers," more interested in flirting with a female patrol member than actually guarding the tunnel (297). Jack tells Ahmad that he will not get past the tollbooth just before the entrance, but to his surprise, there is no one inside, just an electronic eye that beeps "E-Z PASS PAID" (298). Ahmad, the lone terrorist, once again outwits the forces designed to stop him, just as he had done earlier in the day by eluding federal officers waiting in the Excellency furniture store parking lot to apprehend him.

Updike's caricature of Homeland Security is the ultimate oxymoron. In a nation that enables terrorists to roam free, no one is secure, despite the projected images that support the idea of protection, from color-coded threat levels to the physical presence of armed officers. After witnessing firsthand the devastation of 9/11, perhaps Updike argues through his devastating portrayal of bureaucratic foolishness that the only way to guarantee safety is by restricting the public's constitutional freedoms. However, if this is his aim, why would he subsequently berate the Republican administration criticized by its opponents for moving closer to those objectives?

In Updike's nonfiction piece about 9/11, he views freedom as a cornerstone of American life and makes it "a country worth fighting for" (*Due Considerations* 118). Walking the streets that fateful day, "as ash drifted from the sky," he realized "Freedom . . . felt palpable. It's mankind's elixir, even if a few turn it to poison" (*Due Considerations* 118). In comparison then, the novel celebrates individual freedom in its final pages when Ahmad decides to not carry out the terrorist act. It is as if he finally understands the difference between God's role as a creator and destroyer on his own, without the manipulative efforts of the authority figures in his life. However, by arriving at this conclusion, Ahmad realizes, "*These devils . . . have taken away my God*" (310). What the teen means in this final thought may be that by granting himself the freedom to decide his own course, he chooses to live an ordinary life—God no longer is as close as a vein in his neck. Ahmad is reduced to be like the people he sees after exiting the Lincoln Tunnel: "insects . . . intent in the milky morning sun upon some plan or scheme or hope they are hugging to themselves, their reason for living another day . . . impaled live upon the pin of consciousness, fixed upon self-advancement and self-preservation" (310).

Coming of Age and Sexuality

The uneasy feelings Ahmad contends with extend to his role as a teenager creating his own sexual identity. His religious studies are often at odds with the feelings he harbors for the opposite sex. Once again, he has nowhere to turn to find guidance. For example, Shaikh Rashid boils the relationship down to its most base aspects, telling Ahmad that, "Women are animals easily led" (10). On the other hand, Charlie has a loving wife and family, but wants to hire a prostitute to take Ahmad's virginity. As a result, his burgeoning sexuality and yearning for an authentic male role model influences Ahmad's worldview.

On the first page of the novel, the reader is asked to recognize Ahmad as a teen boy with sexual feelings. Although he chastises the female students at Central High for baring their bellies and sporting "low-down" tattoos, at the same time he asks himself, "*What else is there to see?*" (3, italics in original) The first time the reader views Ahmad interacting with Joryleen Grant, a female student, the narrator reveals that "His long body tingles under his clothes" (8) and "the crease between her breasts bothers him" (10). He wants to be near her, but is repelled by the vague language in the Koran regarding male–female relationships. As a result, he determines, "high school and the world beyond it are full of nuzzling—blind animals in a herd bumping against one another, looking for a scent that will comfort them" (10). Ahmad hardly thinks like a typical teenager charged up with hormones and yearning for an outlet. This is not a kid who is going out drinking on the weekends with his buddies and searching for a girl to lean on. His frustration over his confusion is palpable.

Because of his sexual uncertainty, Ahmad displaces his feelings. Through Shaikh Rashid's connections, Ahmad is hired to drive a furniture delivery truck for Excellency Home Furnishings, run by Lebanese immigrants, The Chehabs. Through the sensation of driving the truck the teen suddenly "feels clean . . . cut off from the base world, its streets full of dog filth and blowing shreds of plastic and paper" (157). He likens the feeling to his boyhood dreams of flying, which caused him to sometimes "awake with an erection, or more shamefully still, a large wet spot on the inside of his pajama fly" (156). After this sexual awakening, with nowhere else to turn, he consulted the Koran, but found no suitable answers.

Some part of Ahmad's casting about regarding his impending manhood can be attributed to his difficult relationship with his mother Teresa. Raised in a single-parent home, since his father left the family when Ahmad was just a boy, Ahmad views his mother negatively because she does not measure up to the standards of Muslim women. He is most critical of her revolving door relationships with various boyfriends over the years and her overtly flirtatious demeanor. Early in the novel, Ahmad thinks that he often sees her less than one hour a day, since she works odd shifts as a nurse's aid at a local hospital. Later, Teresa tells Jack at Ahmad's graduation that the only present he wanted was for her to not look "like a whore" at the ceremony (116). Although he does not admit it to himself or anyone else, Ahmad seems to blame his mother for growing up without a father or siblings for support.

After Ahmad begins working and gets even greater distance from his mother, he begins grouping her with other Americans, whose vices are easy to identify. He thinks to himself that she is a "typical American, lacking strong convictions and the courage and comfort they bring"

(167). Ahmad labels Teresa a "victim of the American religion of freedom," which enables her to do whatever she likes with no real consequences (167). Interestingly, he disparages his mother for lacking the courage and comfort that accompany strong beliefs, yet cannot see his own frailty and doubt as similar weaknesses.

From her perspective, Teresa seems as unsure of the causes for the rift between them as her son, but is more willing to attribute the blame. She sees the turn to Allah as an attempt to find paternal guidance, explaining to Jack, "I guess a boy needs a father, and if he doesn't have one he'll invent one" (117). Probably more damaging, though, are the doubts Teresa holds about Ahmad's sexual orientation. She brazenly questions why he does not have girlfriends like other boys of his age. Ahmad fires back her: "Mom. I'm not gay, if that's what you're implying." Unwilling to let that serve as the final say on the matter, she responds, "How do you know?" Although Ahmad is "shocked," he can merely proclaim, "I know" (144).

Later, when Jack and Teresa launch their affair, Jack also inquires if Ahmad is possibly gay, explaining that "It doesn't seem quite right" that a good-looking kid like her son would not have a girlfriend (166). Teresa is unfazed by the question, since she wonders herself, but chalks up her thoughts on the subject to mother's intuition. She tells Jack, "I could be wrong, but I think I'd know that, too" (166). Next she brings up Shaikh Rashid, labeling him "kind of creepy," basically equating homosexuality with creepiness. Perhaps on an even deeper level, Teresa also implies that the intense religious study conducted over the years between Ahmad and Shaikh Rashid is also disturbing.

Due to Ahmad's lack of experience in relationships with males or females and Charlie Chehab's desire to manipulate the boy, Updike portrays what seems like a growing friendship as something more sinister, perhaps a kind of sexuality between the two. In Ahmad's first test run in the Excellency van—already noted as a feeling he equates with sexuality—Charlie gives directions and rules of the road, using a political analogy comparing Iraq and the United States to announce, essentially that "Bigger [is] better" (157). Although Ahmad thinks the political talk is "slightly out of tune," he realizes "he is in bed with Charlie, and submissively settles himself for the ride" (157).

The friendship between Charlie and Ahmad appears more like older and younger brother at other times. Charlie is obsessed with television commercials and goes into great detail about the roles the actors play in them, particularly ads for erectile dysfunction. After listening to Charlie prattle on about the "sexed-up" actress in a Levitra spot, Ahmad thinks about given entrance to "male talk" (171–72), but lamenting "his father might have provided in measured and less obscene fashion, had Omar Ashmawy waited to play a father's role" (172). Still, Ahmad is hesitant and uncomfortable with the dialogue, admitting that he dislikes the impurity of commercials, which sets Charlie off on a dialogue ranging from Communist brainwashing to Barry Bonds.

In *Terrorist*, however, Updike does not allow the soliloquies to go on without reason. Charlie transitions to a more manipulative stance, using his influence over the boy to his advantage. In response, Ahmad thinks, "Lebanese [Charlie] are not fine-honed and two-edged like Yemenis [Shaikh Rashid] or handsome and vanishing like Egyptians [Omar Ashmawy]" (175). Ahmad clearly identifies Charlie as his replacement father. In turn, Charlie uses the status to further influence the teen, planting ideas that will ultimately convince Ahmad to agree to serve as a suicide bomber. For example, the older man often compares revolutionary (Muslim) forces in the modern world with the American Revolutionary troops led by George Washington. At one point, Charlie explains, "The old revolutionaries . . . have much to teach our jihad" (183). Then, he peppers Ahmad with questions about his own commitment to jihad.

Often, when Charlie probes Ahmad about the teen's commitment to life and death, he ends by calling Ahmad "Good boy," clearly playing a paternalistic role. Later, when Charlie feels that Ahmad has committed to serve, he invokes the nickname he gave the boy when they first met, saying, "Madman, you're a good brave kid" (189). Updike always ends the scene after these phrases of affection, not enabling the reader to know for certain how Ahmad feels. I view this as an unspoken indication that Ahmad, being fatherless, responds well to these verbal pats on the head.

Updike's New America

In a prepublication interview with Charles McGrath in the *New York Times*, Updike discusses some of his reasons for writing *Terrorist*, explaining that he:

> Thought he had something to say from the standpoint of a terrorist . . . I think I felt I could understand the animosity and hatred which an Islamic believer would have for our system. Nobody's trying to see it from that point of view. I guess I have stuck my neck out here in a number of ways, but that's what writers are for, maybe.

He adds that detractors could not have asked for a "more sympathetic and, in a way, more loving portrait of a terrorist" (Updike interview). This belief in himself as an interpreter or interloper inside the mind of a religious zealot, 18-year-old boy, and would-be jihadist speaks to Updike's power as a novelist. The qualified *maybe* in the quote provided earlier not only adds a smidgen of doubt and modesty to the author's words, but also accentuates how he feels about the role of the writer: attempting to understand the inner workings of characters, taking chances that may or may not be popular, and confronting potential critics.

In the pursuit of this character and his world from a broader perspective, though, Updike creates a new America in the process. One finds the seeds of this post-9/11 United States in the nonfiction essay Updike wrote for *The New Yorker* after watching the World Trade Center Twin Towers fall—a steely hope that suffers a dent, but cannot be held down for long. Manifested in *Terrorist* a handful of years later, the combination of faith and hope enables Ahmad to experience an epiphany: "The pattern of the wall tiles . . . explodes outward in Ahmad's mind's eye in the gigantic fiat of Creation, one concentric wave after another, each pushing the other farther and farther out from the initial point of nothingness." He realizes that God wills life and does not want people to "desecrate His creation by willing death" (306). Ahmad's faith is no longer misdirected, because he devises a new worldview based on his own reasoning, not those who put ideas into his mind.

For Updike, perhaps the United States that stands up and gets back on its feet after September 11 is still hyper-focused on popular culture, addicted to consumerism, and growing increasingly fat and apathetic. But the nation is also capable of greatness, particularly when its people hold on to their beliefs. For Ahmad, becoming his own man and thinker transforms his faith from the Straight Path he yearns to travel throughout most of the novel to "the path is straight" when driving the explosive-laden truck into New York City after deciding to not detonate his cargo (309). Yet there is still doubt and uncertainty in the teen. The last line of *Terrorist* echoes the opening, but in the later scene, Ahmad thinks, "These devils . . . have taken away my God" (310). In the anguish of the moment, Ahmad cannot comprehend this step as a victory. The devils took away his angry, misguided God and replaced it with a God who rejoices in creation, not just destruction.

Ahmad and Jack wind slowly through the streets of the Big Apple, with people and automobiles swirling around them in a rush to get somewhere. These New Yorkers have no idea of the danger avoided at the point of Ahmad's revelation in the Lincoln Tunnel or the continuing threat posed by the still-armed truck. The unnamed narrator paints the picture of the scene, pointing out that whether well-dressed or not and attractive or not, the people seem small in the setting, "the size of insects," each acting on "some plan or scheme or hope they are hugging to themselves, their reason for living another day" (310). Each person is "impaled live upon the pin of consciousness, fixed upon self-advancement and self-preservation" (310). Clearly, at that moment, the narrator finds little reason for hope.

Given modern American society's obsession with consumerism, popular culture, and self, one reasons that in Updike's new world, those who do the opposite—focus on societal advancement and preservation—will become the new heroes. Perhaps the larger issue at stake is whether or not Updike thinks it matters. While blips of hope dot the landscape, blind, fat, and stupid America lurches toward the apocalypse, sidetracked by media-generated distractions as the end draws near.

CHAPTER 13

Evolution of a Literary Lion

> It was written, after all, only by Updike; it has nothing to do with me.
> —John Updike, Original ending of *Self-Consciousness*

> I set up shop rather innocently, naively, as a professional writer . . . I don't really do much else but write. And I write every morning and the books, the manuscript pages, do pile up.
> —John Updike, from a 2006 interview

Updike's public persona and self-identity merge in the second epigraph above, which makes it appropriate that he delivered it at a forum sponsored by the New York Public Library in front of a packed house, all turned out to hear the venerable author speak. The first part of the quote puts the reader (listener, too, since it is available on the Web in video and audio format) in familiar Updike territory—the humble idea that such a lauded writer embarked on a career seemingly by accident, as if he stumbled upon the idea one day walking home from the grocery store.

The use of "naively" implies that he knew little about what it meant to be a writer, yet he scoured *The New Yorker* as a youth, reading and rereading his literary heroes, and setting the magazine up as his own Mount Olympus. As a young man, Updike submitted cartoons and literary work to the magazine. Later, he went to Harvard, hardly a college for someone who considered himself naive, even for wide-eyed young students from the central Pennsylvania hinterlands. Furthermore, by the time he "set up shop rather innocently," he had experienced mind-boggling success at *The New Yorker*, serving a two-year stint as a staff writer and had many short stories published in its pages.

The second and third sentences account for Updike's self-image of writer as professional craftsman, in his mind, not much different than anyone else who plies a trade and then realizes the results of the effort. This Updike takes the reader who knows details of the writer's life back to his early career as a freelancer, typing away in a small, cluttered office above the Dolphin Restaurant in Ipswich, Massachusetts. The third sentence addresses Updike's prodigious output by placing it in modest terms, which implies that through consistent hard work, the pages materialize or mystically accumulate.

It is as if Updike means to say that anyone could write as much, if they just dedicated their mornings to the craft. Yet how a single person—even someone as skilled as Updike—could produce so much published fiction and prose is a central question that bedevils those interested in understanding the author. Again, the public persona and the real living author meld here. Surprisingly, for an individual so willing to examine, discuss, and explore his own faith, Updike seems to want to remove the magical aspects of the writing process and leave the reader/listener with the impression that it is merely based on hard work and effort.

What one realizes when attempting to methodically unravel Updike is that finding out who he is at his core is virtually impossible. There is too much intertwined, from his conflicted discussion of celebrity as a mask that eats at the face to the different roles he admits playing in an effort to cope with internal demons and public demands. While these layers confound the scholar attempting to get at the heart of an author, perhaps the inability to do so contains a large part of the magic of literary studies. We can infer, interrogate, analyze, and examine, but in the end, all roads must lead back to what the author has written.

Maybe the closest we can get to a writer is to simply slap the label "storyteller" on him or her and proceed as if that person's entire life consists of creating narratives—in the work itself, as well as all the corollary experiences, such as interviews, marketing copy on dust jackets, archival material, and anything else that emerges from or about the author. Updike would be the first to tell the enterprising investigator that writers are professional liars. In that case, can anything be known about them, other than what they have written?

The challenge is that for writers at the very top of the literary pyramid, there is much more content to interact with, more or less all the trappings that go with modern American celebrity. How should a writer—one engaged in such a deeply solitary pursuit, but with hopes of widespread public readership—handle the parts of the job that by necessity pull one from that lonely act of creating? While some scholars view fame as a negative aspect of popular culture, creating a public identity does not automatically determine that a celebrity is nefarious.

Perhaps, if one believes both Updike's and Norman Mailer's views of celebrity, to counter the negatives of fame, the writer must erect a kind of brick wall around the perceived notion of inner self, which serves as a fountain for all the creative material that the artist might draw on. In this case, then, inventing a public persona might be viewed as a necessity.

Without access to the inner source of lived experience or if the creative fountain runs dry, the writer is left without a narrative. The fear of creativity disappearing or being used up too early haunted Fitzgerald, for example, and it certainly occupied the thinking of many subsequent great writers since his early flameout at the hands of alcohol, stress, and life lived at a sprint provided the example that others did not want to mimic.

In engaging in a discussion of Updike's evolution, one might best examine it in contrast to Mailer, another heavyweight of the era and American literary history. Yet since these icons charted such different courses—with some overlap at various points—their experiences stand at the two opposing sides of stardom. As such, a discussion of Mailer's artistry versus Updike's will provide an interesting dual case study in understanding the literary life from the mid-twentieth century to the end of the 2010s, an incredible 60-year span that incorporates a broad swath of American history.

Updike and Mailer

There are many interesting methods for examining Updike with or against his literary contemporaries. Arguably, Philip Roth and Joyce Carol Oates are the writers most aligned with him in terms of artistry and output. One could also compare him with all-time greats, such as Fitzgerald, Hemingway, or John Steinbeck, but that comparison seems artificial, like trying to determine whether record-setting athletes of the early twentieth century are better or worse than contemporary sports figures.

The two literary giants differed greatly, ranging from physical appearance (the compact, pugnacious Mailer versus the lanky, angular Updike) to public persona (Mailer scrappy, flashy, yet brilliant; Updike modest and erudite). Despite wide-ranging differences that commonly position Mailer and Updike as diametrically opposed, there is a counterbalance to this argument. Drawing a line from one antipodal point to its opposite results in a connection passing through the center of the circle, thus forming a perfect diameter. In this light, the contrasting figures are drawn together, forming opposing poles, but intrinsically connected.

These shared similarities revolve around what mattered most—the writing. Though they acted differently, Mailer and Updike were at their cores writers with profound gifts. Since their careers overlapped, with Mailer already assuming a kind of godfather of the literary world by the time Updike burst onto the scene, it is no wonder that they kept an eye on one another. Their remarks and comments over the decades ranged from sometimes questioning to highly critical, but gradually the two aging authors lapsed into an admiring mode. This kind of progression from foe to friendly rival to friendship takes place in many areas, most notably sports, when onetime bitter enemies gradually develop into comrades in arms, from Magic Johnson and Larry Bird to Arnold Palmer and Jack Nicklaus. Sometimes it takes age and wisdom for these tandems to meld. This evolution is mirrored in the relationship between Updike and Mailer.

As a matter of fact, taken together, the two writers played a critical role in redefining what it meant to be an author/celebrity in their lifetimes simply by not rolling the train off the tracks like many of their most esteemed predecessors, particularly Fitzgerald and Hemingway, another set of friendly rivals: one who sprinted toward self-destruction and the other who faded slower as his writing powers slipped. Instead, Updike and Mailer kept the focus on writing, not allowing fame, celebrity, or wealth to distract them from craft.

Both Mailer and Updike often spoke about reinvention as a key to their success. They took wildly different routes: Mailer went out into the streets, leading demonstrations, and purposely getting in and near the action, while Updike moved among the middle-class people that fascinated him. Mailer marched; Updike joined church councils. Mailer boxed, head-butted, and threw punches. Updike played touch football, engaged in spirited tennis matches on a makeshift court in his backyard, and golfed. Yet while they come to their subjects from different paths—they invented and reinvented themselves over and over to keep the creative spring flowing—Updike and Mailer exist as writers. They closed themselves off from the rest of the world to write.

This shared commitment to language is where Updike and Mailer merged most noticeably, away from the tumult of literary stardom, tucked away behind a desk, crafting words. Scholar Morris Dickstein looks at the private/public nature of the writing life, explaining, "Yet the *process* of writing, though it involves a kind of performance, *is* intensely private—the least worldly, the least social of all callings. Writers are creatures who can live in their heads and tolerate long stretches of solitude" (*Mirror* 194, italics in original). Updike and Mailer were able to carve out time at the desk, despite the demands they faced as members of the literary elite.

While it is difficult to generalize about writers with the range of Mailer and Updike, the fundamental distinction between them is that the former chose to probe culture's edges—its dark, twisting fringes—while the latter focused primarily on its doughy center. This disparity became clearer when they examined American society.

Updike's best-known work (the Rabbit tetralogy) focuses on the tumultuous life of one American patriarch and his family over five decades set in and around the nation's suburban middle class. Mailer, on the other hand, is harder to pin down. Attempts at deducing his best work runs the gamut of numerous novels and nonfiction narratives examining a limitless range of subjects, from World War II and Vietnam to Hitler and Jesus.

The contrast between the two literary lions even seeped into the distinctions between the outlets where their work appeared. Mailer wrote for edgier audiences in *Esquire* and the *Village Voice,* while Updike cozied into the *New Yorker,* essentially becoming its house writer. Even earlier in their lives as Harvard undergraduates, Updike and Mailer took different paths: Mailer writing for *The Advocate,* while Updike rose to president of *The Lampoon.*

The two writers represented the establishment and antiestablishment, a distinction both understood and discussed. In retrospect, though, it seems that Mailer and Updike needed this chip on their shoulders to fuel their work. Yet no one could reach the literary heights they each achieved without being inside or insiders within the system. Both, for example, were influential members of the American Academy of Arts and Letters. They each had best sellers that granted status and a kind of power that does not exist for people outside the ropes looking in on that exclusive club.

Thinking of themselves first as craftsmen and also, to some degree, literary interlopers, however, enabled each to remain relevant well past the age when other writers begin to lose the abilities. For example, included among each writer's final work is Updike's *Terrorist* (2006), centering on a post-9/11 homegrown terrorist, and Mailer's *The Castle in the Forest* (2007), a reexamination of Hitler's childhood. Both novels demonstrate its author's commitment to edgy, difficult subjects at a time when either could have simply taken on less trying topics or stopped producing entirely. These novels embody an obligation to pushing on one's talent despite age and atrophy, the two forces that no human being can ultimately avoid.

The decision to emphasize society's often-blurry radical outskirts versus its everyday middle represents more than just a nod toward artistic temperament. Mailer and Updike hinged their respective worldviews on these choices. Mailer became a post-World War II literary star based on the gritty realism and violence of *The Naked and the Dead* (1948). By contrast, Updike's early career, marked by quick acceptance into the literary elite, took a gentler path with a book of poems, then two well-received novels: *The Poorhouse Fair* and *Rabbit, Run*. The notion of violence and its place in society continued to distinguish the two writers: Mailer placing it at the core, while Updike rarely dealt with physical violence, instead focusing on psychological wounds produced via marriage, adultery, child-rearing, and the attempt at living up to aspirations.

While both started from the dream of producing the Great American Novel, Mailer used his quest as an exploration of self and celebrity, virtually absorbing, then personifying, the popular culture of the age. Updike took a less adventurous route (although audiences considered his early work salacious) by retiring from the limelight of New York City at the tender age of 25. Where Mailer strutted and charged, Updike tiptoed and uncovered. Each man's decision regarding how to deal with early fame appears to have had important ramifications for the subsequent work they produced.

For Mailer, according to Morris Dickstein writing in *The Mailer Review*, fame changed his thinking, because he could no longer take part in "ordinary life," instead leading him to "riskier kinds of fiction that pleased fewer readers, but also to personal reportage fired by the kinds of inwardness and depth that could make fiction so powerful." As a result, "He would move far afield from where he began" (119). This included a variety of creative nonfiction avenues that helped redefine that genre in the late twentieth century.

Mailer's agonizing decision to move away from traditional fiction also set him in stark contrast to Updike, who remained committed to probing the soft underbelly of suburban America, with the occasional wild fling into more global subject matter. In *Advertisements for Myself* (a title one could never imagine Updike employing), Mailer explains, "there was no room for the old literary idea of oneself as a major writer . . . All I felt then was that I was an outlaw, a psychic outlaw, and I liked it, I liked it a good night better than trying to be a gentleman" (quoted in Dickstein 124).

Although Updike sometimes startled readers with graphic language and sexual situations in his fiction, as an individual, *gentleman* might be his most characteristic trait. Using a sports metaphor, which I think both men would appreciate, Mailer embodied boxing (if not a drunken fistfight out in the alley), while Updike golfed—the elegant swing and steely confidence of rolling in a clutch 12-foot putt.

While there is no way to meld boxing and golf into one odd amalgamation, there is a way to strip Mailer and Updike from their subject matter and examine them from the perspective of two of literary history's most productive and successful writers. What sets them apart from their contemporaries (whether Bellow and Malamud or Oates and Roth) is the sheer volume of fine work across genres. Stripping them of fiction, Mailer and Updike still appear in multiple "the best we have produced" categories in other areas. For example, either could have concentrated solely on literary criticism, essays, and forms of creative nonfiction and been considered among the handful of American greats.

As described previously, Mailer and Updike could not be considered allies, though they may have at least been willing to admit that they were (at times) collegial colleagues. They stood too far apart on many issues, from the nation's stake in the world and politics to violence and the topics a writer should tackle, to be genuine friends. Added to this notion is each man's innate competitiveness, which certainly incited much of the bluster they aimed at one another.

Ironically, it took the ego of a fellow writer—Tom Wolfe—and a full-scale literary feud that later ensued to draw Updike and Mailer firmly into the same camp. Both reviewed Wolfe's novel *A Man in Full* (1998). Although the reviews were positive in many sections, both Mailer and Updike felt the novel fell short of the greatness Wolfe had been talking about for nearly a decade that he had been writing it. Mailer, for example, noted points where "Wolfe suddenly becomes startlingly good" (*Time of Our Time* 1290), but also tosses bombs: "Tom may be the hardest-working showoff the literary world has ever owned . . . He lives in the King Kong Kingdome of the mega-best sellers—he is already a Media Immortal. He has married his large talent to real money and very few can do that or allow themselves to do that" (*Time of Our Time* 1299). Basically, Mailer called Wolfe out for whoring himself to the sales charts. Moreover, they did it in high-profile venues for the whole world to see.

Rather than take his licks, Wolfe went on the offensive. In a television interview, he labeled Updike, Mailer, and novelist John Irving "my three stooges," a charge he then elaborated in print in the collection *Hooking*

Up (2000). In it, Wolfe piles on age-related barbs, calling Updike and Mailer "two old piles of bones" and wondering about their "exhausted carcasses" (152). Despite being older than Updike, Wolfe kept up the attack: contrasting his vitality versus their frailty. The feud kept literary wags wagging for about two years. Taking the battle away from the novel and making it personal, Wolfe suddenly went from victim to aggressor, thus facilitating a makeshift alliance between Mailer and Updike.

When old age became a common denominator for Mailer and Updike, an "us vs. them" mentality also drew the two closer. In *The Spooky Art*, Mailer juxtaposes himself, Updike, DeLillo, and several others of that generation against the younger crowd, represented by Jonathan Franzen, David Foster Wallace, and Michael Cunningham. He deduces:

> [T]he younger writers are sick of Roth, Bellow, Updike, and myself the way we were sick of Hemingway and Faulkner . . . we never talked about anyone but them, and that feeling grew into resentment. Since they had no interest in us, we began to think, Yeah, they're great—now get off the stage! We want the lights on us! (294)

A corollary to the battles regarding aging versus younger writers is the larger question regarding literature's role in contemporary society: does it even matter, and how can we measure its consequence? In discussing how a president gets rated as poor, good, or great, renowned historian Sean Wilentz explained that a *good* president needs an event that tests the nation to its core to move into the *great* category. Without this triggering event, a good president, in other words, never gets to prove his mettle under fire (Wilentz). At one time, the same might have been said about literary figures: Hemingway had his wars and Fitzgerald had his decade in the sun. The contemporary world has less time for novelists, though, even when enormous macro events swirl. The immediacy of the Internet, television, and radio trumps the methodical publishing world, which may deliver greater insight and analysis, but cannot compete with the nearness of filmed or recorded events as they unfold.

With *The Naked and the Dead,* Mailer emerged from World War II with a novel that almost immediately made him important. In 1972, scholar and critic Richard Poirier claimed that "most thoughtful and literate young readers prefer Mailer to, say, Updike or Roth or Malamud," because "his timing is synchronized to theirs, while the others move to an older beat" (121). When we view other crises from the same perspective, from Vietnam to terrorism and the Great Recession, writers have a less important role to play in a society numbed by constant chaos driven by mass communications.

As far back as the 1970s and early 1980s, Mailer indicts television for dulling brains and diminishing the ability of writers to impact thinking on the nation. As a result, he lessened his attack on his contemporaries to a degree, blaming their general lack of "greatness" on the era, despite being "highly accomplished and skillful and talented and artful." Even a Hemingway-esque stylist, Mailer explains, "wouldn't move people as profoundly—their senses are too dulled by TV and their higher senses are too diverted by film." He then claims that if he were young in the early 1980s, he would choose writing or directing films over being a novelist (Lennon 295). These kinds of questions plagued Mailer and Updike for decades.

Mailer, in fact, declared his hopelessness, saying, "the things I've stood for have been roundly defeated . . . The profound novel will be a curiosity, a long cry away from what great writing once offered" (*Spooky Art* 62). In battling this wholesale move away from literature, today's scholars, readers, and enthusiasts might adopt a cultist mentality: celebrate one's intense love and devotion to the novel or novelist and search diligently for converts. There is much to learn from the experiences of Mailer and Updike in this quest.

Literature Matters

Let's stick with the thesis of this book—Updike matters. What has followed (and will continue to appear from my sweat-sopped brow for the next couple of decades) is an attempt to prove this declaration. Within the endeavor, though, is also a more encompassing aspiration: to prove that writing and reading still matter in an Age of Technology dominated by Google, television (reality and scripted), and film. As outdated a notion as it may be, I remain committed to the idea that reading is important, even as college students sell back textbooks still in the original shrink wrap, instead choosing to obsess about Facebook status updates and text messaging.

Updike too—looking like an antiquarian fuddy-duddy—fought this battle over the last decade of his life. As a professional writer, he criticized the potential demise of publishing at the hands of Google's desire to create a digital version of every book ever written and he railed against e-book publishing, wondering where the writer-as-creator fit into the picture when a reader no longer needed to purchase the product. In other words, who pays for the content in a world where content is free?

Updike the lover of words found an easy mark in the Internet, blasting it for turning books into "something impalpable and instantaneous." As one who cares about culture, he worried:

> The Web is conjured like the genie of legend wit a few strokes of the fingers, opening, with a phrase or two, a labyrinth littered with trash and pitted with chat rooms, wherein communication is antiseptically cleansed of all the germs and awkwardness of even the most mannerly transaction with another flesh-and-blood human being. (*Due Considerations* 73)

You see, Updike willingly took the highly publicized criticism from journalists and the technology intelligentsia because he believed in the power of books and the central place of the writer and writing life.

Obviously, Updike had a chit in the game, as it were. His livelihood depended on selling books and magazines. Those of us who are proponents of the written word also have a stake in publishing's future. As such, do we furrow our brows at the latest big-name thriller selling 1 million copies on its release day or the publishing empire of J. K. Rowling, now one of the wealthiest women in the world?

My goal is to advocate for literature and settle for reading. As a teacher, that means exploring (great) written words (and worlds) for the lessons they dispense and to continue interrogating authors and texts to reveal what might be learned. As a writer, this effort entails writing books, essays, and articles that stimulate critical thinking on the part of readers, asking them to create new ideas from the material as it interweaves with their own knowledge, lives, and experiences. Part of this task is to explore the work of writers like Updike in hopes that the scrutiny will appeal to future readers and, just maybe, prompt them into reading either more of his work or researching themes, eras, and topics themselves.

Updike's death in January 2009 resulted in renewed interest in his work. Knopf published a posthumous collection of short stories, *My Father's Tears and Other Stories* that received widespread critical appreciation. His passing caused others to re-examine the several books published in the last year of his life, including the nonfiction anthology *Due Considerations* and novel *The Widows of Eastwick*. Even his final posthumous poetry collection, *Endpoint and Other Poems,* gained wider readership and more mainstream reviews than his earlier poetry books. In this regard, Updike carries on the popular culture tradition of a celebrity or artist gaining broader appeal after death. That he left behind enough work to sustain this initial push was most likely a mix of Updike's realization that he faced death, thus producing more at the end, and Knopf's desire to meet the uptick in demand for his work.

The John Updike Society

Most interesting for those hoping to keep Updike's legacy alive, a core group of scholars (spearheaded by James Plath, Marshall Boswell, Lawrence Broer, Jack De Bellis, and James Schiff) launched The John Updike Society (JUS) on May 24, 2009. Included in its mission statement is the goal of "awakening and sustaining reader interest in the literature and life of John Updike, promoting literature written by Updike, and fostering and encouraging critical responses to Updike's literary works" ("History/Mission").

From these beginnings, JUS made tremendous strides as a young organization. Under Plath's leadership as the group's first president and with the support of Alvernia University, the society organized and held the First Biennial John Updike Society Conference in late 2010 at Alvernia, located in Reading, Pennsylvania. Appropriately, the conference theme—Updike in Pennsylvania—drew scholars from across the nation and eight nations around the world. In addition, the group toured many Updike places of note, including his former Pennsylvania homes—his early house at 117 Philadelphia Avenue in Shillington, as well as the family farm in Plowville, some 11 miles south of Shillington.

In 2012, Suffolk University in Boston hosted the Second Biennial John Updike Society Conference. Again the meeting drew scholars, readers, and Updike aficionados from around the world. Tours included the Harvard dormitory rooms, Salem, and the family residences at 26 East Street and 50 Labor-in-Vain Road in Ipswich. At each conference, Updike's children (Elizabeth, David, Michael, and Miranda) and their mother—Mary Weatherall—participated in panel sessions and a great deal of informative discussions with JUS members.

As a scholarly organization, JUS committed early to launching a journal that would examine Updike's life and writing in greater detail. In October 2011, the first issue of *The John Updike Review* came out under the editorship of James A. Schiff, with its academic home at the University of Cincinnati. The inaugural issue featured essays and criticism from a renowned group of writers and scholars, including the keynote speaker at the first JUS conference, Ann Beattie, and academics Donald J. Greiner, William H. Pritchard, and Sylvie Mathé.

Perhaps the most interesting twist in the work of JUS is the purchase of Updike's Philadelphia Avenue home, announced in mid-2012. After receiving a gift from the Robert and Adele Schiff Family Foundation to facilitate the financing, JUS leaders plan to launch a campaign to turn the home (which recently housed an advertising agency) into a museum—The John Updike Childhood Home. Plath outlined the goal, explaining, that the group would, "over time, restore it as it was during Updike's time in the house" ("Letter").

From modest roots, JUS stands in excess of 250 members, a strong beginning for a scholarly organization dedicated to a single writer. In some respects, these enthusiasts, drawn from the academy and dwindling world of serious readers, are responsible for Updike's long-term legacy. His 65 books form a vast cornucopia for further analysis, interrogation, extrapolation, and conjecture.

Updike, American Man of Letters

Of course, the nation changed dramatically over Updike's long career. In contrast to other artists, writers, actors, and musicians who could not adapt across the span, however, Updike remained one of the nation's foremost writers. It is in the guise of America's storyteller that Updike excels. And, one must admit, Updike's own story is part of that effort.

At the end of the day, I argue, readers can still learn much from his work, even as today's Internet-based society seems like it could pass him by. Although it is difficult to quantify the notion that books simply do not matter as much as they used to, one can find evidence supporting this idea by looking at the drop in book sales, particularly in literary fiction, or by talking about reading habits with young people. I think proponents of the publishing industry might point to electronic book sales as a means of proving that books still matter, but personally I am dubious of the claims that more people are *reading* e-books just because they are *downloading* them. Foundational research on people's e-reading habits must be conducted to reveal how these books are changing the landscape.

Perhaps more troubling, when considering Updike's long-term reputation, is that the focus among scholars and critics is onto other topics and new impulses, such as multiculturalism, gender studies, the other, and those privileged and unprivileged by literature. It is this negative, rather narrow view of Updike that raises the hackles of those, such as David Foster Wallace and others, who denounce him and his contemporaries as "phallocrats" or relics of a male-dominated canon. For them,

Updike exists primarily as a stand-in for Rabbit, an American everyman easy to pick apart for his shortcomings.

While the stakes in Updike's historical reputation are only truly important among a relatively small group of literary scholars, one can imagine Updike falling into the second tier of American writers, mimicking, for instance, the declining status of a Sinclair Lewis or William Dean Howells. However, he could also be elevated in the manner of Fitzgerald to stand among the nation's greats.

Factors shaping a literary figure's academic standing run the gamut from how the work seems to compare or contrast with future societal changes to the simple passage of time, which provides commentators with a new subject to research. Updike's long-term standing will no doubt benefit from his archival collection housed at Harvard. Scholars love a paper trail, and once the 170 boxes are cataloged by library archivists—estimated to be completed in 2013—the collection will be opened to the public.

While the mere existence of an Updike archive intrigues readers and the scholarly community, one must at least raise the point regarding its self-serving nature. Obviously, the act of creating an archive by definition means that the person doing so has identified that the items in it are or will be important. And we know that the author himself thought it was necessary. His widow, Martha, told *The New York Times*, "The archive was vitally important to him. He saw it not just as a collection of his working materials, but as also a record of the time he lived in" (Tanenhaus, "John Updike's").

Discussing Updike's legacy, longtime friend and fiction editor at *The New Yorker,* Charles McGrath describes the author as "almost comically modest." But, McGrath adds, "I think he knew how good he was and that his work would last. The Harvard archive is proof of that. The way he so carefully collected and filed away everything suggests that at least part of him was thinking about posterity" ("Updike at Work"). In other words, how does the fact that Updike spent time collecting and donating items to Harvard compare with the public persona of modest artist with a self-deprecating air, who gave off the vibe that he would rather be holed up working?

Analyzing McGrath's comment from a more critical perspective, it is difficult to conclude that only "part of him" thought about his future literary standing. The larger issue is then what to do with this information. Should scholars use the existence of an archive that the author himself meticulously built be used as an indicator toward some greater understanding? Perhaps unwittingly, McGrath points to the dual role of writers in modern America—the contrast between creator and promoter. The often-conflicting realities of these guises, in some respects, enabled Updike to be both modest (even in periods when he was one of the world's most celebrated and recognized authors) and a person that felt the need to collect his ephemera for posterity.

Furthermore, the archive itself promises to reveal certain clues and a deeper understanding of Updike's work, but at the same time also exposes new information about the author himself. Given Updike's distaste for literary biography that digs too deeply into an author's personal life, he must have considered how the archive would open his own life to such speculation. He knew the stakes in an author's standing, having reviewed a great deal of such work. Updike once described poor literary biography, "deflecting our attention from the work itself . . . [which] participates in the curious modern deconstructive neutering of art, which discredits its testimony and belittles its practitioners" (*Due Considerations*, 13). With regard to his own archive, on one hand, he included letters his mother collected and other private correspondence, yet one would guess that some level of self-editing took place in other areas, since Updike made the decisions regarding what to give Harvard and what to keep secret.

Even though there are millions of words Updike crafted and countless more in the archival record, the basic truth is that there is still much more to know about Updike as a writer, critic, editor, celebrity, and man of letters. The way this information is funneled out to the general public and other interested audiences by scholars and writers will help establish and promulgate Updike's long-term reputation. For those of us interested in this struggle, the stakes are immense.

Conclusion

> Be with me, words, a little longer; you . . . formed, of those I loved, more solid ghosts.
>
> —From "Spirit of '76" by
> John Updike (*Endpoint*, 19)

Evaluating or passing judgment on a topic, issue, individual, or organization is a basic tenet of the American mind-set, though this penchant for coming to terms with a writer's work is fraught with challenges. When attempting to analyze a writer's place in the literary world, one stands as a kind of interloper, riding roughshod over bits of the writer's soul.

Moreover, at what point does the interrogation begin or end? Certainly, one must dig deep into the literary past when examining a writer's roots, but is this where the creative fountain begins? How about at the point of first publication or first novel? Also for writers who have died, should we automatically move toward assessing the total output and what the person's lasting contribution might be, as if the comparison is similar to evaluating baseball statistics from those who played in different eras?

Reading from Updike's broad and wide-ranging catalog, one learns much about what it meant to live in the mid-twentieth and early twenty-first-century United States. In this regard, he supersedes any singular title, such as novelist, critic, and so on, to take on a more expansive role, like chronicler or storyteller. William Pritchard simply deemed Updike "America's Man of Letters," a moniker that seems to fit.

Certainly, Updike's breadth sets him apart from the canon of American writers most often used to ascertain his place. Of his contemporaries, only Norman Mailer, Joyce Carol Oates, and Philip Roth produced similar quantities of work. Therefore, it seems almost necessary to put Updike up against other greats, particularly given his amount of work across forms of writing. Even here, though, the competitive attempt to determine a writer's place versus a colleague or legendary figure seems too misleading. Do we simply leave a writer's standing to posterity, as if future audiences will force the cream of the crop to the top? Instead, perhaps scholars and other Updike aficionados should simply continue the work of building the case for his lasting importance.

Lessons Learned

Rather than attempt to just assess Updike's work—whether full of praise or with some stern criticism—I thought it more appropriate to consider what a lifetime of Updike study has taught me about life, writing, and creating a worldview that one might live by.

Style

Of all the lessons one could learn from reading Updike, the most important is that style matters. What Updike readers understand—know deep in their bones—is that regardless of how we examine style or from what fountain it sprouts and even if we call it *voice* or some other *thing*, Updike's style is uniquely his own. Still, Updike's style, according to critic Jack Richardson, fits within the Anglo-American tradition, in which "the writer is esteemed not for his powers to fabricate examples of the outlandish, but rather for his ability to uncover unusual patterns and shadings where an ungifted eye sees only a single, quotidian tone" (Thorburn and Eiland 198). Richardson determines that Updike's technique is about the reader understanding that "a writer is present," which places emphasis on the reader's experience, or "to make certain that the reader attains a certain emotional intensity, that he will see and feel as the author wants him to" (Thorburn and Eiland 198). The connection between literary style and the reader's feeling while absorbing the work is a key to Updike's technique. This notion creates interdependence between Updike's work and life, since the latter infuses the former. The symbiosis may account for why the reader so often feels that Updike is the little angel or devil sitting on the shoulder of his characters, particularly Rabbit Angstrom.

There are many stylists found across literary history, from Nabokov to Hemingway and Fitzgerald to Michael Chabon, but we know Updike's style and can sense it deeply. I agree with writer Ben Yagoda's declaration that "style matters." From his perspective, he explains, "... for writers of the first rank (and many of the rest of us as well) style is unique and irrefutably identifiable, like a fingerprint, or like the sound of close friends' voices, even if they're only saying, 'Hi, it's me' on the telephone" (xvii).

Yagoda's description of style likened to a friend's voice is appropriate. As readers, we often feel a kind of friendship, and maybe even kinship, with our favorite authors. This idea may also account for why we want to know about their private lives and spend time and money collecting their signatures and memorabilia. Their voice dances in our heads when our minds wonder to distant places or empty spaces. For scholars, the pull of critical analysis may follow from the way a writer has yanked at one's worldview. Why else would we invest days, months, and years (even decades) to reading and rereading another's work? For many, that foundational attraction is to style.

In a 1988 interview with Terry Gross, Updike emphasized both the storytelling aspects of writing, calling true "classics" those novels that "tell a pretty solid story." He explained too that style had to go hand in hand with storytelling. He described style quite memorably as the "sentence-to-sentence pleasures" a reader gets from a work so that "any page of a novel could be ripped out and read as kind of a poem" (Plath, *Conversations* 210–11). Style, as Updike related, left a reader with a lasting image that would change the person's worldview. The idea of any single piece of writing being held up as a kind of poem speaks to the power of a master stylist like Updike to transform the reader's world via writing.

Popular Culture

Whether I am more attuned to Updike's use of popular culture as a literary device because of my own interest in contemporary American culture or his employment of the topic becomes more apparent as one reads and rereads his work, it is clear that Updike's use of popular culture changed over time. Like when Don Draper explains the power of nostalgia to Kodak executives in the season one finale of the hit television series *Mad Men*: the transformation is subtle, yet potent.

An interesting link exists between Updike's utilization of popular culture and his lyrical writing style. As noted earlier, Updike used popular culture to create context and nuance, which ranged broadly across decades and mass media channels, from the "Doddisms" of Head Mouseketeer Jimmie Dodd and descriptions of urban decay in

New Jersey and Pennsylvania to an intimate (almost erotic) description of Rabbit Angstrom eating a Payday candy bar at the airport in *Rabbit at Rest*. One reader's nuance, however, is another's flotsam.

In some of Updike's fiction, observers might argue that the long lists of pop songs, films, slang, and other nostalgic items devolve into flabbiness, thus detracting from his lyrical style. Scholar James A. Schiff raises this point, contrasting Updike's short and long fiction, explaining that the latter "tends more easily toward excess (e.g., overextended descriptions, long lists of consumer products and domestic minutiae)" (*Revisited* 113). Whether one enjoys the look back at popular culture ephemera in Updike's work or finds it overkill, there is a fundamental difference in using these items as stage setting and employing it to editorialize or insert himself into the narrative, as we see in *Terrorist*. There seems to be a deliberate stylistic decision to move from popular culture as prop to commentary.

What one finds over time is that Updike gets bolder in using popular culture as a tool to editorialize or render a frank assessment about the United States and its society as it has unfolded. One could certainly speculate that this aspect of Updike's work changed as he grew more comfortable with his powers as a novelist or as he engaged directly with the world around him as a public intellectual. Maybe he even just succumbed to transitioning into a grumpy, aging man and wanted to use his pulpit to settle his score with the way the nation transformed from the days of his youth. Updike's use of popular culture notably changes in the Rabbit tetralogy, and willingness to deliver a verdict on American culture is more direct and forceful in his later work (and certainly drives much of *Terrorist*, as I have outlined in earlier parts of this book).

The evidence for my claim becomes clear when one compares the use of popular culture in *Rabbit, Run* and other early works with his later work. In the former, popular culture is used as a set piece, almost like scenery to demonstrate to the reader that the action is taking place today. As Donald J. Greiner describes, Updike's early critics disliked his decision to not editorialize or offer solutions for Middle America's problems. The critics bashed the writer because, "he prefers posing problems to preaching answers." Greiner notes that over time, "the quest for happiness is today more problematic, more tenuous" ("Updike, Rabbit" 149). My assertion is that by the time he unravels post-9/11 America in *Terrorist*, Updike is downright angry.

One also sees the use of popular culture as a means to criticize the contemporary world in *Toward the End of Time*, as if the nuclear blasts merely hastened the nation's otherwise inevitable downfall at the hands of its popular culture, which debased society from within. In the novel, Ben Turnbull looks around and sees a world already in decay. The only answer is the cycle of death and rebirth that keeps the planet alive:

> Telephone booths are vandalized; graffiti covers stone surface consecrated to beauty and visual harmony. Children acquire guns and shoot each other as casually as images are flicked away on television; adults drown their disquiet and despair in alcohol. The world by itself is not enough; there must be another, to give this one meaning. (300)

There are other examples as well, including the story "Blue Light," reprinted in *My Father's Tears*. The story focuses on Fritz Fleischer, an older man who shows up for a dermatologist appointment and later undergoes a treatment for precancerous cells. As Fritz sits in the hospital waiting for the procedure, he looks around and sees a room full of other older, pale-skinned men and women. He is disgusted, calling them all (himself included), "victims of the same advertisements, the same airbrushed photos of twenty-year-old models, the same absurd American dreams of self-perfection." He recalls his young doctor telling him that he would be younger and scoffs, "A new man, my foot" (246).

While this kind of reproach may seem tame compared with the kind of language used in *Terrorist,* it still represents a shift in Updike's use of popular culture-based criticism. In these later works, Updike's aging male protagonists do not embrace popular culture like his young characters did, surrounding themselves in the songs, hot automobile makes and models, and the latest thrilling headlines. Instead, the older characters stand apart from culture, judging it for its inferiority, futility, and desire to turn us into consumerist robots.

Later, as his face heals from the painful procedure, Fritz hides in the darkness of his apartment, "while the television set in the corner muttered and shuffled its electrons like a demented person playing solitaire" (249). Like his combative colleague Norman Mailer, Updike grew crankier and crankier with television and its numbing effect on viewers' minds. These later characters are not willing to waste any of their remaining time watching television. Moreover, they have no patience for TV's simpleminded philosophies, like the ones Rabbit and Janice take away from the Disney program back in the late 1950s.

Audiences

At the end of the day, being a professional writer means that one engages with audiences by presenting work for their consideration. Exchanges are taking place across multiple platforms. These include the actual purchase that gets the content into the hands of a potential reader via a book or magazine to the value a reader places on reading as an entertainment factor, essentially swapping authorial content in hopes of a return through personal pleasure.

In these examples and the many other possibilities, the writing that at one time seemed a highly personal and private act (i.e., the writer alone in a solitary setting crafting a piece) is transformed into a commodity (i.e., mere digital ones and zeroes and/or actual, physical paper-based products). Moreover, it is not just words and such that are bought and sold. The author too becomes a product in a market-based capitalistic society. Writing for readers and to attract and retain readers is critical within the artistic, creative act.

Obsessed with Death

An aspect of Updike's work that I find both intensely instructive and completely harrowing is his fixation on death. He used death as a central theme in his short fiction, novels, and poetry, as well as in discussing his own life and worldview in interviews and essays. The dreadful part is that death apparently haunted him from a young age, which must have been a burden to carry psychologically. Yet, on the other hand, no writer has written about aging and death's imminence more brilliantly than Updike in the story collection *My Father's Tears* or the poetry in *Endpoint*.

Even a casual Updike reader would recognize the countless times he recalled or fictionalized the deaths of the adults closest to him in his boyhood Pennsylvania home—his mother, father, grandmother, and grandfather—who shared the little, white farmhouse out in rural Plowville. The diligent Updike reader will recall particular instances, such as reimagining and fictionalizing his mother's lonely death in the Plowville sandstone house, where the reenactment includes finding her broken glasses and thinking about how the cut on her head appeared.

Another example is the death of Rebecca June in *Rabbit, Run*, which plagues the family and reappears in each subsequent Rabbit novel and in the novella "Rabbit Remembered." In the latter, both Janice and Nelson frequently use the baby's death as a fulcrum in understanding themselves and their lives, though the drowning occurred four decades in the past. Thinking about Becky at the Angstrom family gravesite, Nelson discloses, "His sister. He has always blamed himself somehow. If he had been more pleasing to Dad he wouldn't have left and Mom wouldn't have gotten drunk and it wouldn't have happened" (*Licks* 271). In passages like this one, Updike's brutal power as a writer is on full display. For readers that have traveled with Rabbit Angstrom across the decades, the notion that Nelson blames himself for the baby's death crushes the soul and reminds us how vile Rabbit could be.

Even in his work that does not center on death, Updike uses the idea as a running undercurrent. For example, in "Separating," the short story from the *Too Far To Go* collection about the Richard and Joan Maples telling their children about their impending divorce, Richard attempts to make up for his physically leaving the family by getting the home he vacates in order—doing the man's work that he will no longer be there to do. Richard contemplates absence, both in the near- and long-term, saying, "The sun poured down, beyond the porch on a world of neglect. The bushes already needed pruning, the windward side of the house was shedding flakes of paint, rain would get in when he was gone, insects, rot, death" (196). This bleak epiphany encompasses decay and death as inevitability, as it also forecasts the physical deterioration that takes place with the body after death.

The poem "Perfection Wasted" begins with the author lamenting death, since it puts an end to one's "own brand of magic," despite the lifetime it took to create it. In a mere 14 lines, the poem touches on many Updikean themes, from intertwining ideas about celebrity and family commitments to the gradual fade away that occurs after death. It is the finality of it all that seems to bother Updike the most. Each person has planned and created a life, which he labels, "The whole act" (*Poems* 231). That creation is important and serves as the glue to one's family and closest friends, but when mortality intervenes, it is the true, unrelenting end.

An observer might read "Perfection Wasted" as a plea for the reader to focus on the magic of family and loved ones; however, I think a closer investigation reveals Updike's deep fear of death. While the living go on living, it is the author who is packed away in their minds, which may or may not fade. Updike asks rhetorically who might rise up to serve in his role, but admits that no one can fill the same shoes, explaining, "That's it: no one." There is real feeling contained in that short phrase. "That's it" serves as an exasperating plea, while "no one" contains a perspective on death as a great void, a gut-wrenching finality of "no one," even those who might try and including family members left behind. Updike ends the poem deflated, "imitators and descendants aren't the same" (*Poems* 231).

In 1993, commenting on the story "Playing with Dynamite," Updike discusses writing about "aging, doddery, nostalgic American men," even though "It is the young we love." In assessing the piece, he explains, "my heroes seem older than I feel to myself, as if, lacking sex appeal to make them dramatic, they are cozying up to death" (*More* 775–76). The idea of "cozying up" to the end of life carries real weight in Updike's work. The linked cycle of aging, nostalgia, and death unquestionably weighed on Updike's mind for much of his career. As a result, death (of those around him and in fictional worlds) played a major role in his writing.

Updike Forever

Some writers *see* their names in print; others develop a *feel* for it. For the latter group, few of life's instances can replace the physical thrill of opening a magazine and quickly skimming through the table of contents or deftly cutting through the packaging tape on a cardboard box that you just know holds your latest book—quickly opening the flaps and finding that sacred "By . . ." on the cover. I have heard some writers liken the rush of publication to an addiction, like yearning for another hit of heroin shot directly in the vein. Some see it as a birthing process, with each publication akin to a child, lovingly brought to life from the artistic loins of its creator.

Returning to this chapter's epigraph, the observer senses that Updike saw publication as a way to turn one's ghosts back into real things, to continue the relationship evermore, not only with people, but also with places, things, eras, and ideas. Through writing, Updike's past is never distant or left simply to be forgotten as age and space intercede.

Bibliography

Altschuler, Glenn C. "Updike's Painfully Human Terrorist; Navigating an America of 'Too Many Paths.' " Rev. of *Terrorist*, by John Updike. *Philadelphia Inquirer* June 4, 2006: C4+. Print.

Appleyard, Bryan. "Our Eye on the Real World." *Sunday Times* [London] July 30, 2006. Web. May 26, 2009. http://www.bryanappleyard.com/article.php?page=4&article_id=49.

Bailey, Peter J. *Rabbit (Un)Redeemed: The Drama of Belief in John Updike's Fiction*. Madison, NJ: Fairleigh Dickinson University Press, 2006. Print.

Baker, Nicholson. *U and I: A True Story*. New York: Vintage, 1991.

Berryman, Charles. "Updike Redux: A Series Retrospective." In *Rabbit Tales: Poetry and Politics in John Updike's Rabbit Novels*. Ed. Lawrence R. Broer. Tuscaloosa, AL: University of Alabama Press, 1998. 17–33. Print.

Bloom, Harold, ed. *John Updike*. New York: Chelsea House, 1987. Print.

Booth, Wayne C. "Resurrection of the Implied Author: Why Bother?" In *A Companion to Narrative Theory*. Ed. James Phelan and Peter J. Rabinowitz. Malden, MA: Blackwell, 2005. 75–88. Print.

Boswell, Marshall. "Updike, Religion, and the Novel of Moral Debate." In *The Cambridge Companion to John Updike*. Ed. Stacey Olster. Cambridge University Press, 2006. 43–57. Print.

Boyers, Robert. "A Fanatical Mind: The Novelist and the Terrorist." Rev. of *Terrorist*, by John Updike. *Harper's Magazine* July 2006: 89–94. Print.

Caldwell, Gail. "Gods and Monsters." Rev. of *Terrorist*, by John Updike. *Boston Globe* June 4, 2006: E4. Print.

Callero, Peter L. "The Sociology of the Self." *Annual Review of Sociology* 29 (2003): 115–33. Print.

Carrigan, Henry L. Jr. Rev. of *Terrorist*, by John Updike. *Library Journal* May 15, 2006: 94. Print.

Chabon, Michael. *Maps and Legends: Reading and Writing along the Borderlands*. New York: Harper Perennial, 2009. Print.

Charon, Joel M. *Symbolic Interactionism: An Introduction, an Interpretation, an Integration*. 8th ed. Upper Saddle River, NJ: Pearson Prentice Hall, 2004. Print.

Curran, Ronald. "*Licks of Love* (Book)." *World Literature Today* 76.1 (2002): 149. Print.
De Bellis, Jack. "The Critical Reception of John Updike." In *John Updike*. Ed. Bernard F. Rodgers Jr. Pasadena, CA: Salem Press, 2012. 85–104. Print.
De Bellis, Jack. *The John Updike Encyclopedia*. Westport, CT: Greenwood, 2000. Print.
Denzin, Norman K. *Symbolic Interactionism and Cultural Studies: The Politics of Interaction*. Cambridge, MA: Blackwell, 1992. Print.
Detweiler, Robert. *John Updike*. Boston: Twayne, 1984. Print.
Dickstein, Morris. "How Mailer Became 'Mailer': The Writer as Private and Public Character." *Mailer Review* 1 (2007): 118–31. Print.
Dickstein, Morris. *A Mirror in the Roadway: Literature and the Real World*. Princeton, NJ: Princeton University Press, 2005. Print.
Dickstein, Morris. "The Rise and Fall of 'Practical' Criticism: From I. A. Richards to Barthes and Derrida." In *Theory's Empire: An Anthology of Dissent*. Ed. Daphne Patai and Will H. Corral. New York: Columbia University Press, 2005. 60–77. Print.
Doctorow, E. L. *Creationists: Selected Essays, 1993–2006*. New York: Random House, 2006. Print.
Duvall, John N. "Conclusion: U(pdike) & P(ostmodernism)." In *The Cambridge Companion to John Updike*. Ed. Stacey Olster. Cambridge: Cambridge University Press, 2006. 162–77. Print.
Epstein, Joseph. "Think You Have a Book in You? Think Again." *New York Times* September 28, 2002. Web. August 10, 2009 http://www.nytimes.com/2002/09/28/opinion/think-you-have-a-book-in-you-think-again.html?pagewanted=print.
Freeman, John. "Updike's Earthly Paradise." Rev. of *Terrorist*, by John Updike. *Age* [Melbourne, Australia] July 8, 2006: A2. Print.
Glass, Loren Daniel. *Authors Inc.: Literary Celebrity in the Modern United States, 1880–1980*. New York: New York University Press, 2004. Print.
Goodheart, Eugene. Rev. of *Terrorist*, by John Updike. *Salmagundi* 153/154 (2007): 184–90. Print.
Greiner, Donald J. *John Updike's Novels*. Athens: Ohio University Press, 1984. Print.
Greiner, Donald J. *The Other John Updike: Poems, Short Stories, Prose, Play*. Athens: Ohio University Press, 1981. Print.
Greiner, Donald J. "Updike, Rabbit, and the Myth of American Exceptionalism." In *The Cambridge Companion to John Updike*. Ed. Stacey Olster. Cambridge: Cambridge University Press, 2006. 149–61. Print.
Grobel, Lawrence, ed. *Endangered Species: Writers Talk about Their Craft, Their Visions, Their Lives*. New York: Da Capo, 2001. Print.
Heddendorf, David. "The Modesty of John Updike." *Sewanee Review* 116.1 (2008): 108–116. Print.
Heddendorf, David. "The Pennsylvanian." *Sewanee Review* 117.3 (2009): 487–490. Print.

Hitchens, Christopher. "No Way." Rev. of *Terrorist,* by John Updike. *Atlantic* June 2006. Web. May 19, 2009 http://www.theatlantic.com/doc/200606/updike.
Irving, John. "Dear John: What I'll Miss about John Updike." *Slate* January 28, 2009. Web. January 28, 2009 http://www.slate.com/id/2209975/.
Johnson, Diane. "Warlock," Rev. of *The Witches of Eastwick,* by John Updike. *New York Review of Books* June 14, 1984. Web. August 18, 2012 http://www.nybooks.com/articles/archives/1984/jun/14/warlock/?pagination=false.
John Updike Society. "History/Mission." The John Updike Society May 28, 2009. Web. May 29, 2009 http://blogs.iwu.edu/johnupdikesociety/.
Just, Daniel. "The Modern Novel from a Sociological Perspective: Towards a Strategic Use of the Notion of Genres." *Journal of Narrative Theory* 38 (2008): 378–97. Print.
Kakutani, Michiko. "A Homegrown Threat to Homeland Security." Rev. of *Terrorist,* by John Updike. *New York Times* June 6, 2006. Web. June 7, 2006 http://www.nytimes.com/2006/06/06/books/06kaku.html.
Kline, Michael F. Personal Interview. June 13, 2012.
Knopf. "In the Beauty of the Lilies: Marketing Plan." Winter 1996. Print.
Lennon, J. Michael, ed. *Conversations with Norman Mailer*. Jackson, MS: University Press of Mississippi, 1988. Print.
Leonard, John. "Rabbit is Radical: John Updike's Terrorist Puts Us in the Head of a Man with 72 Virgins on His Mind." Rev. of *Terrorist,* by John Updike. *New York Magazine* May 28, 2006. Web. September 15, 2007 http://nymag.com/arts/books/reviews/17120/index1.html.
Lodge, David. *Language of Fiction: Essays in Criticism and Verbal Analysis of the English Novel*. London: Routledge & K. Paul, 1966. Print.
Luscher, Robert M. "Marriage, Memory, and Mortality: John Updike's Enduring Legacy in Short Fiction." Rev. of *My Father's Tears and Other Stories* and *The Maples Stories,* by John Updike. *John Updike Review* 1.1 (Fall 2011): 117–29. Print.
Mailer, Norman. *The Spooky Art: Some Thoughts on Writing*. New York: Random House, 2003. Print.
Mailer, Norman. *The Time of Our Time*. New York: Modern Library, 1999. Print.
Maines, David R. "Social Organization and Social Structure in Symbolic Interactionist Thought." In *Symbolic Interactionism*. Schools of Thought in Sociology, 7. Vol. 2. Ed. Kenneth Plummer. Aldershot, Hants, England: E. Elgar, 1991. 235–59. Print.
Maryles, Daisy. "Players Need Platforms." *Publishers Weekly*. March 23, 2007. Web. July 10, 2012. http://www.publishersweekly.com/pw/print/20070326/13260-players-need-platforms.html.
Max, D. T. "Noticers in Chief: John Updike and Rabbit." In *John Updike: The Critical Responses to the "Rabbit" Saga*. Ed. Jack De Bellis. Westport, CT: Praeger, 2005. 243–51. Print.
McCall, Michal M. and Judith Wittner. "The Good News about Life History." *Symbolic Interaction and Cultural Studies*. Ed. Howard S. Becker and Michal M. McCall. Chicago: University of Chicago Press, 1990. 46–89. Print.

McEvoy, Dermot, and Michael Coffey. "Bestselling Books 2009: Hardcover Old and New." *Publishers Weekly*. March 23, 2009. Web. September 15, 2011. http://www.publishersweekly.com/pw/print/20090323/1686-bestselling-books-2009-hardcover-old-and-new.html.

McGurl, Mark. *The Program Era: Postwar Fiction and the Rise of Creative Writing*. Cambridge, MA: Harvard University Press, 2009. Print.

Miller, D. Quentin. *John Updike and the Cold War: Drawing the Iron Curtain*. Columbia: University of Missouri Press, 2001. Print.

Miller, D. Quentin. "Updike, Middles, and the Spell of 'Subjective Geography.'" In *The Cambridge Companion to John Updike*. Ed. Stacey Olster. Cambridge: Cambridge University Press, 2006. 15–28. Print.

Mills, C. Wright. *Power, Politics and People: The Collected Essays of C. Wright Mills*. Ed. Irving Louis Horowitz. New York: Ballantine, 1963. Print.

Moran, Joe. *Star Authors: Literary Celebrity in America*. Sterling, VA: Pluto Press, 2000. Print.

Neumaier, Joe. "X-Raying Emotional Baggage: John Updike Goes inside the Mind of a Would-Be Suicide Bomber." Rev. of *Terrorist*, by John Updike. *New York Daily News* June 4, 2006. Web. August 1, 2009 http://www.nydailynews.com/archives/entertainment/2006/06/04/2006–06–04_x-raying_emotional_baggage__.html.

Oates, Joyce Carol. "Keynote Address." The Second Biennial John Updike Society Conference. Modern Theatre, Boston, June 12, 2012. Keynote speech.

Ong, Walter J. "The Writer's Audience Is Always a Fiction." *PMLA*, 90.1 (1975): 9–21. Print.

Phelan, James. *Narrative as Rhetoric: Technique, Audiences, Ethics, Ideology*. Columbus: Ohio State University Press, 1996. Print.

Plath, James, ed. *Conversations with John Updike*. Jackson, MS: University of Mississippi Press, 1994. Print.

Plath, James. "Letter to John Updike Society Members." July 7, 2012. Email.

Poirier, Richard. *Norman Mailer*. New York: Viking, 1972. Print.

Pritchard, William H. "Into Darkness Undimmed." Rev. of *Endpoint and Other Poems*, by John Updike. *John Updike Review* 1.1 (Fall 2011): 107–15. Print.

Pritchard, William H. *Updike: America's Man of Letters*. South Royalton, VT: Steerforth Press, 2000. Print.

Raban, Johnathan. "The Good Soldier." Rev. of *Terrorist*, by John Updike. *New York Review of Books* July 13, 2006: 8, 10–11. Print.

Radway, Janice. "What's the Matter with Reception Study? Some Thoughts on the Disciplinary Origins, Conceptual Constraints, and Persistent Viability of a Paradigm." In *New Directions in American Reception Study*. Ed. Philip Goldstein and James L. Machor. New York: Oxford University Press, 2008. 327–51. Print.

Rajaratnam J. K., et al. "Neonatal, Postneonatal, Childhood, and Under-5 Mortality for 187 countries, 1970–2010: A Systematic Analysis of Progress towards Millennium Development Goal 4." *Lancet* 375: (2010): 1988–2008. Print.

Reilly, Charlie and John Updike. "An Interview with John Updike." *Contemporary Literature* 43.2 (2002): 217–48. Print.
Samuels, Charles Thomas. "The Art of Fiction XLIII: John Updike." *Paris Review* 45 (Winter 1968): 84–117. Rpt. in *Conversations with John Updike*. Ed. James Plath. Jackson, MS: University of Mississippi, 1994. 22–45. Print.
Schiff, James A. "A Conversation with John Updike." *Southern Review* 38.2 (2002): 420–42. Print.
Schiff, James A. *John Updike Revisited*. Boston: Twayne, 1998. Print.
Schiff, James A. "Updike and Other Writers." The Second Biennial John Updike Society Conference. Suffolk University, Boston, June 14, 2012. Presentation.
Schiff, James A. "Updike, Film, and American Popular Culture." *The Cambridge Companion to John Updike*. Ed. Stacey Olster. Cambridge: Cambridge University Press, 2006. 134–48. Print.
Shainin, Jonathan. "The Plot against America." Rev. of *Terrorist,* by John Updike. *Nation* July 10, 2006: 27–30. Print.
Stone, Robert. "Updike's Other America." Rev. of *Terrorist,* by John Updike. *New York Times Book Review*. June 18, 2006. Web. April 1, 2009 http://www.nytimes.com/2006/06/18/books/review/18stone.html.
Tanenhaus, Sam. "John Updike's Archive: A Great Writer at Work." *New York Times* June 20, 2010. Web. June 20, 2010 http://www.nytimes.com/2010/06/21/books/21updike.html?pagewanted=all&_r=0.
Tanenhaus, Sam. "Mr. Wizard." *New York Times Book Review*. October 24, 2008. Web. March 30, 2009 http://www.nytimes.com/2008/10/26/books/review/Tanenhaus-t.html?_r=1.
Tharoor, Shashi. "The Write Stuff." *Newsweek* (Atlantic Edition) 140.19 (2002): 47. *MasterFILE Premier*. Web. August 10, 2009.
Thorburn, David, and Howard Eiland. *John Updike: A Collection of Critical Essays*. Englewood Cliffs, NJ: Prentice-Hall, 1979. Print.
Trachtenberg, Jeffrey A. "Updike's 'Terrorist' Survives Bad Reviews to Be Best Seller." *Wall Street Journal* June 19, 2006. Web. June 2, 2009 http://online.wsj.com/article/SB115066968346483614.html.
Travis, Molly Abel. *Reading Cultures: The Construction of Readers in the Twentieth Century*. Carbondale, IL: Southern Illinois University Press, 1998. Print.
"A Tribute to John Updike." LIVE from the New York Public Library. March 19, 2009. Web. July 9, 2009. www.nypl.org/live.
"Updike Friends: Charlie Tsoutsouras and Dick Purinton." The Second Biennial John Updike Society Conference. Suffolk University, Boston, June 15, 2012. Presentation.
Updike, John. *Americana and Other Poems*. New York: Knopf, 2001. Print.
Updike, John. *Collected Poems, 1953–1993*. New York: Knopf, 1993. Print.
Updike, John. *The Coup*. New York: Knopf, 1978. Print.
Updike, John. *Due Considerations: Essays and Criticism*. New York: Knopf, 2007. Print.

Updike, John. *Higher Gossip*. New York: Knopf, 2011. Print.
Updike, John. *Hugging the Shore: Essays and Criticism*. New York: Knopf, 1983. Print.
Updike, John. Interview. *BookPage*. June 2006. Web. May 25, 2009 http://bookpage.com/interview/holy-terror.
Updike, John. Interview. Celeste Bartos Forum, Humanities and Social Sciences Library. New York Public Library. June 15, 2006. Web. Jul 9, 2009. http://www.nypl.org/research/chss/pep/pepdesc.cfm?id=1980.
Updike, John. Interview. *New York Times*. May 31, 2006, E1. Print.
Updike, John. Interview with Charlie Rose. *Charlie Rose Show*. October 6, 1997. Web. http://www.youtube.com/watch?v=aZhBomrm-Og.
Updike, John. "Lecture." John W. and Joan Eadie Celebrity Lecture Series. April 27, 1995. Michigan State University, East Lansing, Michigan. Web. August 29, 2009 http://dlv1.matrix.msu.edu:8080/ramgen/livecvt/cache/cls/a0/a0/cls-a0a0u8-a.rm.
Updike, John. *More Matter: Essays and Criticism*. New York: Knopf, 1999. Print.
Updike, John. *My Father's Tears and Other Stories*. New York: Knopf, 2009. Print
Updike, John. *Odd Jobs: Essays and Criticism*. New York: Knopf, 1991. Print.
Updike, John. *Picked-Up Pieces*. New York: Fawcett Crest, 1975. Print.
Updike, John. *Rabbit, Run*. New York: Fawcett Crest, 1960. Print.
Updike, John. *Self-Consciousness: Memoirs*. New York: Knopf, 1989. Print.
Updike, John, and James A. Schiff. *Updike in Cincinnati: A Literary Performance*. Athens: Ohio University Press, 2007. Print.
Wallace, David Foster. "John Updike, Champion Literary Phallocrat, Drops One; Is This Finally the End for Magnificent Narcissists?" *New York Observer* October 12, 1997. Web. August 12, 2009 http://www.observer.com/node/39731.
Wilentz, Sean. "Encore Q&A: Sean Wilentz." *BookTV*. C-SPAN, New York, May 13, 2012. TV.
Wilson, Matthew. "The Rabbit Tetralogy: From Solitude to Society to Solitude Again." *Modern Fiction Studies* 37.1 (1991): 5–24. Print.
Woiwode, Larry. *Words Made Fresh: Essays on Literature and Culture*. Wheaton, IL: Crossway, 2011. Print.
Wolfe, Tom. *Hooking Up*. New York: Farrar, Straus and Giroux, 2000. Print.
Wood, James. *The Broken Estate: Essays on Literature and Belief*. New York: Random House, 1999. Print.
Wood, James. "Jihad and the Novel." Rev. of *Terrorist*, by John Updike. *New Republic* July 3, 2006: 25–30. Print.
The World Bank. "Mortality Rate, Under-5 (per 1,000)." World Development Indicators, n.d. Web. March 31, 2012. http://data.worldbank.org/indicator/SH.DYN.MORT?cid=GPD_15.
Yagoda, Ben. *The Sound on the Page: Style and Voice in Writing*. New York: HarperResource, 2004. Print.
Yurchyshyn, Anya. "How to Make People Buy Books." *Esquire* June 18, 2007. Web. March 30, 2009 http://www.esquire.com/the-side/qa/chipkidd061807.

Index

Alvernia University, 207
America: as an ideal, 17, 107–8; land of extremes, 53–54; and passing judgment, 211–12
Americana and Other Poems (Updike), 57–58
American Dream, 20–22, 24, 30, 73; contemporary belief in, 42, 49–50; and writing, 21–22
Angstrom, Harry "Rabbit" (Rabbit tetralogy), xii, 1, 15, 40, 46; community leader, 96–97; comparison with John F. Kennedy, 70–72; criticized, 65–66, 68; death, 50, 97–102, 216–17; enduring literary character, 94, 104–5; as everyman, 76–77, 209, 214; and Florida, 96, 98; lost, 57; pushed out by younger generation, 131; as Uncle Sam, 97; and Updike's voice, 94–95, 97; and women, 98. *See also* individual characters from Rabbit tetralogy; individual *Rabbit* novel titles
Angstrom, Janice (Rabbit tetralogy, "Rabbit Remembered"), 75, 89, 98; confused, 75; life after Rabbit, 101–2; powerful character, 99–100
Angstrom, Nelson (Rabbit tetralogy, "Rabbit Remembered"), 70, 100, 217
Angstrom, Rebecca June, 73–74; death, 102–3, 104, 178, 216–17
Appleyard, Bryan, 166

Baby Boomers, 128
Baker, Nicholson, 15, 30
Bech, Henry (*Bech* books), 10, 24
"Before the Mirror" (Updike), 58
Bellow, Saul, 23, 204
Big history, 93–94
Bird, Larry, 113
Bloom, Harold, 112, 163
"Blue Light" (Updike): criticism via popular culture, 215
Boswell, Marshall, 207
Broer, Lawrence, 207
Bush, George W., 91, 144, 179; heroic stance after 9/11, 176
Byer, Annabelle (Rabbit tetralogy, "Rabbit Remembered"), 89, 100; reunion with Harry's family, 101–3

226   Index

Capitalism, 19–20. *See also* Celebrity; *Terrorist*; Updike, John
Carver, Raymond, 113–14
Celebrity, 3–4, 7; American obsession, 32; and John F. Kennedy, 64. *See also* Consumer culture; Publishing industry; Updike, John
Centaur, The (Updike), 135; and style, 137
Chabon, Michael: career contrasted with Updike's, 157; style compared to Updike, 125
Cheever, John, 26
Chehab, Charlie (*Terrorist*), 175, 178, 190; critique of consumerism, 182–83; and faith, 179; and sexuality, 192–93
Clinton, William Jefferson "Bill," 72
Complete Henry Bech, The (Updike), 162
Consumer culture, 85, 133–34; criticism, 182–83; and Updike, x–xi. *See also Rabbit, Run*; *Terrorist*
Coup, The (Updike): criticism of, 140; as experimental fiction, 137–40, 145
Couples (Updike), and sexuality, 81–82, 83–85, 87; and Updike's income, 58
Criticism, 15, 135, 138; *Commentary* magazine, 9, 10. *See also* Kakutani, Michiko; Mailer, Norman; Podhoretz, Norman; *Terrorist*; Updike, John

De Bellis, Jack, 207
DeLillo, Don, 19, 163, 178, 204
Due Considerations (Updike), 206

Eccles, Jack (*Rabbit, Run*), 74, 103
Eisenhower, Dwight D., 64, 65, 67, 75

Endpoint and Other Poems (Updike), 56, 58–61, 206; writing about death, 216

Facebook, 205
Faulkner, William, 204
Fitzgerald, F. Scott, 41, 112, 152, 182, 200, 204, 209; comparison to Updike as freelancer, 109–10; and self-destruction, 199; Updike's writing on, 127
Fogel, Hermione (*Terrorist*), 185, 188–89
Freud, Sigmund: theory, 87–88

Golf, xii
Google: Updike criticized, 205–6
Grant, Joryleen (*Terrorist*), 138–39, 140, 186; and sexuality, 191
Greiner, Donald J., 6, 108

Haffenreffer, Director of Homeland Security, 187–88, 189
Harrison, Ronnie (Rabbit tetralogy, "Rabbit Remembered"), 89; life after Rabbit, 101–2
Harvard University, 4, 43, 197, 201; and Updike's archival materials, 209–10
"Hedge, The" (Updike), 58
Hemingway, Ernest, 112, 199, 200, 204; inspiration for Updike's short stories, 126; and self-destruction, 148; subject of Updike essay, 113, 114; Updike's writing on, 127
Hitchens, Christopher: criticism of *Terrorist*, 140, 166, 185
Homeland Security, Department of, 176

"Indian, The" (Updike), 83–84
Infant mortality: in the United States, 102–3

"In the Cemetery High Above Shillington" (Updike), 46; and names, 58
Ipswich (Massachusetts), 5, 41, 67, 82, 155, 198, 207; raising a family, 126, 127; setting for *Couples*, 83–84, 85
Irving, John, 166; feud with Tom Wolfe, 203–4

John Updike Childhood Home museum, The, 208
John Updike Review, The, 59, 207
John Updike Society, 2010 Conference, 45, 46–47, 207; 2012 Conference, 60, 207; cemetery tour, 58; creation of organization, 207–8
Jones, Judith, 154
Jones, Tylenol (*Terrorist*), 184
Jordan, Michael, 136–37

Kakutani, Michiko, 10; criticism of *Terrorist*, 138, 139, 140, 165, 166, 178
Kennedy, John F., 63–64, 68, 84; representing youth and vigor, 65–66. See also Angstrom, Harry; *Time*
Kern, David (character in Updike short stories), 47–49; lost, 57. See also "The Road Home"
Kidd, Chip, 159
Knopf, 149; and Updike's interest in process, 151. See also Marketing; *Terrorist*; Updike, John

Lasch, Christopher, 85
Leonard, Annabelle, 70
Leonard, Ruth (*Rabbit, Run*), 71–72, 77; as oracle, 68–70
Levy, Beth (*Terrorist*), 142, 188
Levy, Jack (*Terrorist*), 87, 89–90, 192; critique of consumerism, 182–83; critique of United States, 174, 177; and popular culture, 186–88; and race, 184
Literacy, 120, 205; in K-12 system, 2
Literature: and biography, 211; importance, 205–7, 208. See also Mailer, Norman; Updike, John
Luscher, Robert M., 120

Mad Men (television), 213
Mailer, Norman, 19, 23, 67, 211; autobiographical writing, 32; and *The Castle in the Forest*, 201; and celebrity, 33–34, 199–205; criticism of television, 205, 215; feud with Tom Wolfe, 203–4
"March Birthday 2002, and After," 59
Marketing, 6–7, 66. See also *Terrorist*; Updike, John
"Me and My Books" (Updike), 151–52
Mickey Mouse Club, The (television), 75, 213
"Midpoint" (Updike), 58–59, 60
Midpoint and Other Poems (Updike), 58
Morrison, Toni, 19, 27
Mulloy, Ahmad (*Terrorist*), 85–88, 89–90, 178; and authority, 190; critique of consumerism, 182–83; and faith, 178–82; and popular culture, 186–88; and race, 183–85
Mulloy, Teresa (*Terrorist*), 85–88; and sexuality, 190–93; and sexual language, 90
My Father's Tears and Other Stories (Updike), 123, 128, 206, 215; writing about death, 216
"My Philadelphia" (Updike), 114

Nabokov, Vladimir, 68
National Book Critics Circle Award (1983), 110
"Near Clifton, Perhaps" (Updike), 57–58
New Yorker, The (magazine), 4–5, 16, 66, 153, 154, 201; providing income, 150, 198; and Updike's 9/11 essay, 173–74, 194; Updike's dream job, 8, 26, 27, 110, 155–56, 197; Updike's ideal reader, 156 and writing short stories, 126–27. *See also* September 11, 2001

Oates, Joyce Carol, 19, 27, 112, 199, 211; and prodigious output, 157
Of the Farm (Updike), 44; and style, 137
Ozick, Cynthia, 112

Pennsylvania, 4, 38; geography, 38–39; location for "Rabbit Remembered," 100; and strangers, 57; work ethic, 36. *See also* Updike, John; "The Road Home"
"Perfection Wasted" (Updike), 217–18
Philadelphia (Pennsylvania), 38–39, 114. *See also* Pennsylvania
Picked-Up Pieces (Updike), 107–8
Plath, James, 207, 208
"Playing with Dynamite" (Updike), 218
Podhoretz, Norman, 9
Popular culture: and life's complexities, 133; and sign systems, 134; Updike's criticism of in his fiction, 142–43. *See also* Angstrom, Harry; September 11, 2001; *Terrorist*; Updike, John
Poorhouse Fair, The (Updike), 134

Pritchard, William H., xiii, 6, 108, 145
Publishing industry, 29, 120; blockbuster mentality, 28, 160; and celebrity, 158; deficit versus film, radio, Internet, and television, 204; difficulty, 148; and electronic books, 208; outdated marketing, 158. *See also* Updike, John
Purinton, Dick, 61

Rabbit Angstrom (Updike), 102, 201
Rabbit at Rest (Updike), 45, 95; and Rebecca June's death, 103
"Rabbit Remembered" (Updike), 41, 70; and Rabbit's ghost, 100–102; and sexual language, 89
Rabbit, Run (Updike), 40, 45, 163, 177–78; contemporary reputation, 65; and culture, 67–68, 75, 214; and faith, 77; reviewed in *Time*, 64–65; and sexuality, 81, 82, 134; and writing, 67, 126, 137. *See also* individual characters
Rashid, Shaikh (*Terrorist*), 177, 192; and faith, 180
Reading (Pennsylvania), 100–101
Reagan, Ronald, 85
Remnick, David, 155
"Road Home, The" (Updike), 44–45; critique of contemporary culture, 129, 131; escaping Pennsylvania, 123, 130; lost, 57, 132
Ross, Harold, 150
Roth, Philip, 19, 199, 204, 211

Salinger, J. D., inspiration for Updike's short stories, 126
Schiff, James A., 6, 108, 207
Seek My Face (Updike), 159
Self-Consciousness (Updike), 5, 162

"Separating" (Updike), 217
September 11, 2001: aftereffects, x, 59; post-9/11 fiction, 8, 122, 163; and popular culture, 176–77; and terrorism, 91, 144; Updike's account, 115–16, 173–74, 194. *See also* Homeland Security, Department of; *New Yorker, The*; *Terrorist*
Sexuality: in America, 79–80, 82; and language, 88–91; and pornography, 80. *See also Couples*; *Terrorist*; Updike, John
Shawn, William, 126
Simpsons, The (television): and Updike as character, 30
Steinbeck, John, 199
Symbolic Interactionism, 34. *See also* Updike, John

Terrorist (Updike), x, 10, 15, 59, 143, 173–74, 201; and authority, 188–90; critical of American culture, 164, 176–77, 182–83, 194–95; and critics, 138, 148, 164–71; as experimental work, 135–36, 164; marketing campaign, 31, 153, 159–64; and popular culture, 186–88, 214, 215; and race, 183–85; reception of, 162–65; and religion, 87; and sexuality, 85–88; and style, 138, 140, 142, 170, 177–93; and symbolic interactionism, 12–13, 174–75. *See also* individual characters; Knopf; September 11, 2001; Updike, John
"03/18/03" (Updike), 59–60
Time (magazine), 36; November 7, 1960, issue, 63–64, 65–66; Updike's appearance on cover (1968), 58, 81–82, 83. *See also Rabbit, Run*
"To a Dead Flame" (Updike), 55–56

Toward the End of Time (Updike), 135, 141; and criticism via popular culture, 214–15
Tsoutsouras, Charlie, 60–61

"Updike and I" (Updike), 45
Updike in Cincinnati (Schiff), 6–7, 30, 123
Updike, John: autobiographical writing, 20, 25–27, 121, 122, 212, 216; background, 4–5; and celebrity, 3, 6, 13, 15, 30–36, 81, 148, 161, 198–210; and craft, 20, 23–24, 35, 43–44, 120–21, 198; as a critic and essayist, 107–17, 171; death, 1, 50–51, 59, 61, 206; and editors, 89, 149–54; experimental writer, x, 6, 134–46; feud with Tom Wolfe, 203–4; and fixation on death, 59, 216–18; as a freelance writer, 27–28, 60, 67, 150, 152, 206; and ideal readers, 156–57; and marketing, 6–7, 20, 160–61; and Middle America, 134, 136, 145–46, 182, 201; and nonfiction, 14–15, 33; and Pennsylvania, 38–51, 122, 216; personality traits, 6, 11, 31, 152, 165, 209–10; poetry, 54–61; and popular culture, 2–3, 19, 80, 99, 125, 186–88, 213–15; and psoriasis, 33, 153; as a public intellectual, 155, 214; representative of America, ix, 208; and reputation, 1–3, 6, 17, 33, 208–9, 210, 211; and sexuality, 80–92, 203; and short stories, 119–32; as a social historian, 95–96, 113; and spirituality, xii, 16–17, 54, 81, 84; studied by scholars, 109, 123, 152, 162, 198, 209; and stuttering, 14, 33, 153; and style, 17, 25, 74, 86, 88, 111–14, 124–28, 136–40, 142, 177–93, 212–13; and symbolic

interaction, 10–17, 140–42, 150, 153; and truth in writing, 55–56, 123–24; and Vietnam War, 9, 58, 144–45; and writing, 197–98, 200–210, 218
Updike, Martha, 57, 209

Villages (Updike), 159

"Walk with Elizanne, The" (Updike), 47–49
Wallace, David Foster, 9, 23, 204, 208
Washington, George, 175
Widows of Eastwick, The (Updike), 206; magical realism and Middle America, 143–46
Witches of Eastwick, The (Updike), 28, 163
Wolfe, Tom, 9; feud with John Irving, Norman Mailer, and John Updike, 203–4
Woods, Tiger, 136
World War II, 60

About the Author

BOB BATCHELOR is an assistant professor in the School of Journalism and Mass Communication at Kent State University and academic coordinator of its online MA program in public relations. He received his undergraduate degrees at the University of Pittsburgh, master's degree at Kent State University, and doctorate in English at the University of South Florida.

Bob is the author or editor of 21 books, including three volumes in Greenwood's "Popular Culture through History" series: *The 1900s, The 1980s, and The 2000s*. In addition, he edited the four-volume *American Pop: Popular Culture Decade by Decade* (Greenwood), the three-volume *Cult Pop Culture: How the Fringe Became Mainstream* (Praeger), and the three-volume *American History through American Sports* (Praeger).

Bob has published articles in *Radical History Review*, *The Journal of American Culture*, *The Mailer Review*, *The American Prospect Online*, and *Public Relations Review*, as well as some 30 book chapters. Bob also serves as the series editor for the "Contemporary American Literature" book series from Scarecrow Press. He is a member of the editorial advisory boards of *The Journal of Popular Culture* and the *International Journal for the Scholarship of Teaching & Learning*. An active member of the John Updike Society, Bob was recently named Director of Marketing & Media for The John Updike Childhood Home Museum in Reading, PA.